London Irish Fictions

Narrative, Diaspora and Identity

London Irish Fictions
Narrative, Diaspora and Identity

TONY MURRAY

Liverpool University Press

First published 2012 by
Liverpool University Press
4 Cambridge Street
Liverpool L69 7ZU

This paperback version published 2014

British Library Cataloguing-in-Publication data
A British Library CIP record is available

ISBN 978-1-84631-831-3 cased
978-1-78138-015-4 paperback

Typeset in Bembo by XL Publishing Services Ltd, Exmouth
Printed and bound by CPI Group (UK) Ltd, Croydon CR0 4YY

To my mother and the memory of my father

Contents

Acknowledgements

First and foremost, I would like to express my deep gratitude to Shaun Richards and Aidan Arrowsmith for their invaluable scholarly guidance in completing the thesis upon which this book is based. I am also indebted to Doug Field, Declan Kiberd, James Moran and Clair Wills for their expert advice in bringing the book to fruition. I would particularly like to thank Joanne O'Brien and John Simms for their astute and insightful comments on the final manuscript. I am also grateful to Anthony Cond and Helen Tookey at Liverpool University Press for their professional guidance.

I would like to express my appreciation to the following writers for being interviewed or for talking about their work at the Irish Writers in London Summer School: John Bird, Maude Casey, Áine Collins, Shane Connaughton, Emma Donoghue, John Healy, Gretta Mulrooney, Edna O'Brien, Timothy O'Grady and John Walsh. My thanks, also, to the Garnett Foundation for supporting the summer school and to all of the writers and students over the last seventeen years who have helped provide the forum within which the subject matter for this book has been nurtured. I am also grateful to the following organisations which have helped support my research in different ways: Institute for the Study of European Transformations (London Metropolitan University); British Association for Irish Studies; International Association for the Study of Irish Literature.

I am indebted to the numerous people who supported or advised me in different ways over the years, including: Laura Agustin, Marie Arndt, Lucy Bland, Avtar Brah, Sean Campbell, Derek Collins, Shirley Cully, Anna Davin, Polly Devlin, Sieglinde Dlabal, Ricardo Domizio, Steve Donelan, Mary Doran, Eibhlín Evans, Martina Evans, Seamus Finnegan, Aidan Flood, Alan Foulkes, Geoffrey Frosh, Lisa Frost, Irene Gedalof, John Goodby, Breda Gray, Jackie Harnett, Liam Harte, Mary Hickman, Eamonn Hughes, Sean Hutton, Lisa Hyde, Laura Izarra, David Kelly,

Helen Kelly, Michael Kenneally, Madeleine Kingston, Jessica March, Ann Marshall, Zacarias Marco Pastor, Margaret McCurtain, Tony McDonnell, Nicole McLennan, Ellen McWilliams, Frank Molloy, Jonathan Moore, Sarah Morgan, Maureen Murphy, Máirín Nic Eoin, Mary Nelis, Jerry Nolan, Miriam Nyhan, Bernard O'Donoghue, John O'Donoghue, Sean O'Donovan, Kathy O'Regan, Brian O'Shea, Michael Parker, Crispin Partridge, Martine Pelletier, Lance Pettitt, Susannah Radstone, Megan Redmond, Ann Rossiter, Damhnait Rumney, Louise Ryan, Deirdre Shanahan, Gerry Smyth, Barbara Taylor, Lyn Thomas, Richard Trevan, Corinne Turner, Stanley van der Ziel, Francie van Hout, Cecily and Didier Villain, Hazel Walker, Bronwen Walter, Inge Weber-Newth, Wendy Wheeler, Bridget Whelan, Alan Williams, Briar Wood, Brian Wright.

I have benefitted enormously from the inspirational teaching of a number of people, in particular Eric Smith (St Aloysius College, London), Barry Baker (Manchester Polytechnic), Noel O'Connell (Irish Literary Society), Mary Hickman, Sabina Sharkey and Paul Sheehan (Polytechnic of North London). I would particularly like to thank Bernard Canavan for agreeing to let me use his marvellous painting for the cover and Seán Ó Domhnallain who, perhaps unwittingly, set me forth upon this course many years ago. Finally, I am eternally grateful to my family and friends and, in particular, Joanne, for her unwavering support and encouragement and without whom this would not have been possible.

1

Introduction

> So for what seems a long time London remained partly a not quite convincing fiction, partly a symbol of ambiguity, partly an overcast physical fact.[1]

For centuries, London has occupied a powerful place in the imagination of artists of all kinds. Writers, in particular, have profoundly influenced popular perceptions of the city. This has especially been the case for people who have visited or migrated to London from elsewhere. New arrivals, whether from the provinces, continental Europe or further afield, have all formed relationships with the city in the light of work by writers such as Samuel Pepys, Charles Dickens, Virginia Woolf and Zadie Smith. For arrivals from other parts of the former British Empire or the Commonwealth, coming to London has often been a wholly recognizable yet profoundly unsettling experience. This is nowhere better illustrated than by the case of the Irish. The long entangled history of Britain and Ireland has resulted in a mutually familiar but deeply ambivalent relationship between its peoples. The often passionate yet sometimes conflicted attitudes to questions of cultural identity that this has provoked are at the heart of the literature I examine in this book.

Writing has been one of the traditional ways in which the Irish have negotiated such matters. Obliged, as a consequence of colonization, to communicate through a foreign tongue, the Irish made a virtue of necessity and produced some of the greatest literature in the English language. This facility with words has been commonly attributed to a Gaelic oral tradition which held the skills of good storytelling in high regard. Certainly, for the Irish in London, a facility with words was a quality which helped smooth the process of adjustment to a new environment and society. Writing about this in 1801, one commentator observed: 'In almost every tavern or coffee-house you may meet with one or more of these orators, whose wit and fluency are exerted for the amusement of the company.'[2] For a long time, London provided an important platform for Irish politicians and journalists, and it was no different for writers who saw the city as their primary means of professional advancement. Despite this long-established relationship with the city, the experience of the London Irish is not as immediately evident in contemporary literature as, for instance, that of the Afro-Caribbean and South Asian communities.[3] However, the exploration that I have conducted over many years into novels, short stories and autobiography about the Irish in London has revealed a substantial body of work worthy of serious attention.

The vast majority of individuals claiming an Irish identity live beyond the island of Ireland, and it is notable how migration and diaspora have become especially prominent features of contemporary Irish literature. In recent years, novels about the Irish abroad by Edna O'Brien, Colm Tóibín and Sebastian Barry have all been best-sellers.[4] By meshing memory and imagination into narrative, prose literature enables us to see human experience from new perspectives and in so doing rework our perceptions of the world around us. The texts I examine in this book are a case in point. They allow us to travel and migrate, vicariously, through migrants' hopes and disappointments, through complex emotional landscapes of belonging and cultural allegiance brought into high relief by the specificities of personal perspective on a profoundly Irish experience.

Some years ago, Maude Casey stated that 'coming to terms with Irish identity in Britain can feel like psychic gymnastics',[5] a sentiment that any of the subjects of the texts I discuss in this book might have expressed about the topic. For most of them, nationality and ethnicity are to the fore, but this may not always be the most significant aspect of a migrant's experience. Other registers of cultural identification such as class, gender or sexuality often produce deeper resonances, something explored, respectively, in the work of critics such as Bernard Canavan, Bronwen Walter and Livia Popoviciu et al.[6] Migration is sometimes perceived as a form of traditional narrative itself. It appears to have a beginning, a middle and an end. When migrants recount their experiences, however, they rarely opt for linear forms of storytelling. Furthermore, no journey of migration takes place in a social or historical vacuum. All such journeys are defined, to some extent, not just by equivalent experiences from the past, but the particular ways in which those experiences have been recorded, represented and disseminated. Migration does not end at the point of arrival. Instead, it continues to impact upon individual lives and identities for some time thereafter. If we accept that migration is not simply the journey itself, therefore, but the subsequent process of arrival, settlement and adjustment, the diasporic dimension of the experience becomes apparent. As well as encountering members of the host community, Irish migrants in London come into contact and dialogue with migrants from other countries. The notion of diaspora also incorporates those left behind as well as those who choose to leave. 'The forms and conditions of movement', to quote the editors of a key study on the subject, 'are not only highly divergent [...] but also necessarily exist in relation to similarly divergent configurations of placement, or being "at home"'.[7] Communities of origin, communities of destination and other communities encountered along the way, therefore, all affect (and are affected by) the phenomenon of migration.

In the analysis that follows, I demonstrate how the intertextual and intergeneric features of London Irish literature contribute to our understanding of the role of narrative in this process. Narrative both underpins and disrupts diasporic identities across a number of binary oppositions, such as exile and escape; leaving and arriving; staying and going; past and present; and, perhaps most significant of all, memory and imagination. In order to examine how this happens in the literature of the post-war Irish in London, I utilize the concepts of 'diaspora space' and 'narrative identity', elaborated below: the former as a paradigm within which to contextualize my analysis of the texts and the latter as a means of interrogating how migrant subjects configure a sense of self. I look at established writers such as John McGahern, Edna O'Brien, Joseph O'Connor and Emma Donoghue and, by reading their work through the lens of diaspora, bring new light to bear on familiar texts such as *The Country Girls Trilogy* (1960–64), *Amongst Women* (1990) and *Cowboys and Indians* (1991). I also devote space to the (auto)biographies of Brendan Behan and Patrick Kavanagh, along with work by their friend Anthony Cronin and contemporary John B. Keane. No less important in terms of the unique perspective they bring to bear on questions of migrant identity are, amongst others, Donall Mac Amhlaigh's autobiographical writings of the immediate post-war period, Robert McLiam Wilson and Margaret Mulvihill's work from the 1980s, and fiction and memoir by second-generation authors as diverse as Gretta Mulrooney, John Healy and John Lydon (a.k.a. Johnny Rotten). By being as inclusive as possible, my aim is to provide a broad introduction to London Irish literature for those new to the subject. For those already familiar with the writers included, I aim to provide radically new readings of their work.

Emigration, Exile and Escape

In 1990, Liam Ryan wrote:

> Emigration is at the centre of the Irish experience of being modern. It is the safety valve that enabled Ireland to cope successfully with the problems of transition from a traditional rural society to a modern industrial one [...] [T]here is scarcely a single political, social, economic, intellectual or religious problem which has not been influenced directly or indirectly by emigration. Emigration is a mirror in which the Irish nation can always see its true face.[8]

As young people once again leave Ireland due to economic recession, Ryan's metaphor of the mirror seems as apposite as ever.[9] However, such a mirror by no means provides a complete or coherent picture. It has cracks, abrasions and missing pieces which distort our understanding of what is really happening with regard to migration at any given moment. This is nowhere more true than in its literary reflections. Nevertheless, the texts dealt with in this book tell us a great deal about not only the lives, but also the thoughts, feelings, hopes and fears of Irish Londoners since the Second World War. Oral histories, ballads, visual texts and various forms of socio-political discourse (e.g. journalism; legal and governmental documentation) are all examples of ways in which the experience of Irish migration to London has been mediated and represented. But literature, and narrative in particular, is uniquely placed to provide insights into collective, as well as individual, consciousness. As Luke Gibbons points out, 'understanding a community or a culture does not consist solely in establishing "neutral" facts and "objective" details: it means taking seriously their ways of structuring experience, their popular narratives, the distinctive manner in which they frame the social and political realities which affect their lives'.[10]

Historical accounts of migration do not always equate with people's personal experiences and the degree to which, for instance, a migrant feels welcomed or not by the host community varies considerably according to personal circumstance and perspective. Sociological studies have provided valuable ways of quantifying and qualifying the phenomenon of migration, but it is the warp and weft of personal narrative that arguably best illuminates the complex circumstances, expectations and reactions of individual migrants and their descendants. As J. J. Lee declared in his history of modern Ireland: 'It is to the writers the historian must turn, as usual, for the larger truth.'[11] Most writers, of course, do not begin writing primarily for political or sociological reasons. It is only in retrospect that we as readers and critics identify social and political characteristics in the preoccupations and content of their work. Regardless of how representative a literary text is of a particular community, it relies (in the first instance at least) on an individual for its realization. Authors create for themselves and their readers a form of reality within and through narrative, so that rather than simply reflecting the experience of migration, literature can also be understood to constitute a mode of migrant consciousness in itself. As Russell King observed some years ago: 'For those who come from elsewhere, and cannot go back, perhaps writing becomes a place to live.'[12]

Such 'a place to live' has traditionally been conceived of in Irish culture, as in many others, as exile. Exile has a long and established presence (oral as well as written) in Irish historical and cultural discourse, so it is not surprising that it features strongly in post-war London Irish literature. In both its external and its internal manifestation, it was a prominent characteristic of Irish life and culture throughout the eighteenth and nineteenth centuries when the effects of colonization and famine in Ireland informed much of the literature of the period.[13] After Irish independence in 1922, the political and social measures undertaken by the fledgling government to establish and consolidate the Irish Free State (while arguably a political necessity for an isolated and vulnerable new nation) resulted in the suppression of alternative and dissenting voices, particularly among artists and intellectuals. The consequence of this was a generation of Irish writers (of whom Joyce was only the most prominent) who not only chose to leave Ireland in order to pursue their ambitions, but whose work, in part, became an exploration of exile itself.[14] Some authors argue that writing and exile are natural bedfellows. At the Irish Writers in London Summer School in June 2005, for instance, Edna O'Brien said:

> Writers are by nature exiles. Sometimes it's voluntary exile. Sometimes you have to leave your own country. But in order to write about something, whatever it be, there has to be that rupture, that terrible separation, because it is in that separation that the depth and profoundness and everything else returns to one.[15]

That rupture, or what Edward Said terms the 'unhealable rift', is a familiar theme in postcolonial societies.[16] The proliferation of popular ballads on the theme is, perhaps, the most familiar example in an Irish context, and Patrick Ward has traced the etymological and psychological history of the trope of exile in Irish writing back to the monastic tradition, when it was conceived of as a form of martyrdom.[17] Other critics have pointed out that, because the trope remained in the ascendant in Irish migrant literature up until the 1960s, it resulted in an over-emphasis on depictions of leaving compared to those of arrival. Patrick Duffy, for instance, argues that, rather than exploring their subsequent lives in the diaspora, most Irish fiction writers 'abandoned their emigrant characters at the boat'.[18] This appears to be borne out by the paucity of fictional or autobiographical accounts of the post-war London Irish prior to this time. But by implication, those that do exist provide a rare and valuable record of such experience. In a key essay on the subject, George O'Brien stated that 'there are undoubted difficulties in finding ways of not only acknowledging the reality of exile, but of discovering how its reality may be imaginatively recuperated'.[19] Despite such difficulties, however, many of the texts I examine in this book demonstrate how the trope of exile has continued to be exploited by Irish writers – and often in a decidedly self-conscious and sometimes mythologized way. Rather than fading away, therefore, exile has continued to provide a potent ingredient in the configuration of identities in London Irish literature up to the present day.

Compared to 'exile', 'escape' is not a term one hears used a great deal in Irish history and culture. But, in the context of migration, it is equally important. Narratives of escape can tell us just as much about the conditions that lead an individual to take that momentous step onto the boat or the plane in the first place. This is something which is often forgotten or unconsciously repressed in more traditional narratives of Irish migration such as, for instance, Percy French's 'The Mountains of Mourne' (1896). Furthermore, if one did not know otherwise, the impression one might get from this particular ballad is that it was only Irish men who migrated to London. In fact, by the twentieth century, more women than men were leaving Ireland for Britain and, in contrast to the sense of exile suggested by the ballad, a sense of escape was the case for many of them. Economic factors have, generally, been cited as the primary reason for Irish migration, but pioneering research in the 1980s found that leaving the country provided a means by which Irish women migrants were able to free themselves from the onerous expectations of traditional Irish family life.[20] In work carried out by Gerard Leavey and others, female interviewees, for instance, 'spoke about the desire to escape a claustrophobic and depressing existence in a rural environment that provided little chance for social intercourse and individual growth'.[21] Louise Ryan has stressed how important it is to go beyond traditional images of 'exile' to examine the active agency of women migrants and the ways in which they have sustained and negotiated family loyalty and obligation across the Irish Sea, a phenomenon which is particularly apparent in some of the texts I examine in this book.[22] For others, however, maintaining links with home is much more problematical and escape proves to be a response to a deeper psychological rupture. The following extract from Edna O'Brien's memoir, *Mother Ireland* (1976), provides a useful preface to this theme:

> I had got away. This was my victory. The real quarrel with Ireland began to burgeon in me then; I had thought of how it had warped me, and those around me, and their parents before them, all stooped by a variety of fears [...] Pity arose too, pity for a land so often denuded, pity for a people reluctant to admit there is anything wrong. That is why we leave. Because we beg to differ. Because we dread the psychological choke. But leaving is only conditional. The person you are, is anathema to the person you would like to be.[23]

The final line of this quotation suggests that the migrant is escaping not only his or her home country but also himself or herself. The identity a migrant prefigures for himself or herself prior to leaving, therefore, is often very different to the one which the same migrant must refigure in the light of events and circumstances once abroad. This is a process which is intrinsically diasporic, and narrative is at the heart of how it takes place.

London Irish Narratives: A Framework

One of the most visible and defining contemporary characteristics of human existence is the large-scale movement and displacement of peoples across the globe. A wide variety of different forms of migration and trans-nationalism have created ever more complex diasporic communities, particularly in the major metropolitan centres of the West, of which London is a prime example. This book is an attempt to understand the experiences of one particular migrant group in the city since the end of the Second World War. It is motivated by two strategic declarations. The first is Robin Cohen's statement at the launch of the Arts and Humanities Research Council programme on 'Diasporas, Migration and Identities' in April 2005, when he proposed that the future of such research 'lies in the examination of diasporic consciousness, subjectivity and representation, the narratives, beliefs and performances of migrant populations, and in the cultures of cosmopolitanism'.[24] The second comes in the introduction to Colin Graham and Richard Kirkland's book *Ireland and Cultural Theory: The Mechanics of Authenticity* (1999), where the authors state, 'The bringing together of postcolonial theories with emigration and diaspora studies is [...] crucial to furthering the widest possible theoretical perspective on the construction of Irishness.'[25] Studies of minority ethnic groups within British society (including the Irish) have made an important contribution to our understanding of the often hidden histories of migrant communities in recent times. The 'hidden literature' of such communities can provide complementary insights into the cultural and psychological aspects of such histories. It is notable that a recent book-length history of Irish migration to Britain draws on autobiographical and oral accounts to illustrate what its author describes as 'the fragmented sphere of the migrant *mentalité*, the ways in which people conceptualized their world and their understanding of their place within it'.[26] Common to all of the texts I examine in this book is a concern with such matters: in essence, the relationship between migration and identity.

In a landmark speech in 1995, the President of Ireland, Mary Robinson, made the following statement:

> The men and women of our diaspora represent not simply a series of departures and losses. They remain, even while absent, a precious reflection of our own growth and change, a precious reminder of the many strands of identity which compose our story.[27]

Tracing these 'many strands of identity' in the literature of the post-war Irish in London, as in all writing, entails a close examination of the often uneasy dialogue that takes place between personal memory and imagination. For this reason, I look at both fictional and autobiographical work, but more importantly at how fictional and factual components operate in all of the texts, regardless of how they might be categorized. The differing ways in which the same or similar source material is crafted into the respective genres of fiction and autobiography is instructive of how memory and imagination are mutually dependent. This is also apparent in the differing forms of narration each writer chooses to mediate events and experiences and how, within individual texts, shifts take place in both directions along the fact/fiction spectrum. In the same way that history might be viewed as a narrative interpretation of the collective past from the perspective of the present, autobiography and memoir serve the same function in respect to a personal past. One of the reasons I have included autobiographical texts in this study is because they often employ the aesthetic markers of fiction, both in terms of their narrative drive and with regard to the ways in which the identities of their subjects are revealed. I am also conscious of the fact that autobiography and memoir often tell us as much about the preoccupations of their authors at the time of writing as they do about the historical period they are attempting to recreate. As Eugene Goodheart points out, 'autobiography is not simply the representation of facts, it is the relentless shaping of them in the light of the writer's present understanding of what he [sic] has become'.[28] There would appear to be a somewhat equivocal relationship, therefore, between the way facts are recovered from the past and the way they are reshaped with the benefit of hindsight in the present. However, this essentially fictionalising tendency need not necessarily be duplicitous. It may simply be the result of a legitimate impulse on the part of the autobiographer, like the historian, to provide an interpretive narrative of past events with a view to better understanding them.

By providing an insight into the way the post-war London Irish have represented themselves and their experiences in their own cultural vernacular, this book aims to address a deficit in research on post-war London literature, from which Irish authors and characters are almost entirely absent.[29] It is particularly notable, for instance, that even where the Irish are mentioned in studies of postcolonial London fiction they only appear (usually, in a negative light) in reference to novels by non-Irish writers.[30] The texts I examine here also constitute an important counter-discourse to the proliferation of often negative media portrayals of the Irish in Britain since the war. In this respect, I hope this research may be not only of literary and historical value, but also of contemporary relevance to debates about migration and social cohesion in Britain, Ireland and further afield.

While the diversity of the texts I cover is self-evident, this book is by no means an exhaustive study of the literature of the post-war Irish in London. I have not been able to include drama or poetry, for instance, and even the number of qualifying prose texts is far more than I could accommodate here. Nevertheless, I examine fourteen novels, five short stories and nine auto/biographical texts written over a period of almost fifty years, making the research broad in both its generic and its chronological scope. The scope of the study extends, approximately, from the end of the Second World War to the turn of the millennium and focuses specifically on the two waves of post-war Irish migration to London, which roughly equate to the dates 1945–62 and 1984–95. The allocation of texts to the respective periods is dictated by the era in which they are set rather than by the era in which they were written. So, Part I focuses on texts primarily set in the earlier period, Part II with texts primarily set in the latter period and, finally, Part III looks at how the earlier period is revisited by second-generation authors writing from the perspective of some decades later. The relationship in all the texts between the date of setting and the date of writing is important because it reveals how the configuration of identities is an ongoing and mutating process rather than a fixed one. The years between the two phases of migration (i.e. from 1962 to 1984) saw a downturn in overall numbers of Irish migrants coming to London. Nevertheless, a substantial Irish population still existed in the city, something reflected in the work of writers as diverse as J. M. O'Neill, Desmond Hogan and William Trevor.[31] Due to the chronological parameters of the research, I have not been able to include such work here but have covered some of it elsewhere.[32] During the second half of the twentieth century, considerable (perhaps even revolutionary) social and cultural change took place both in Ireland and in London and I begin each of the three parts of the book with a brief historical overview before dealing with the texts in separate chapters. Given that this is the first book on the topic, I have also provided (in the following chapter) a short history of the Irish in London up to the Second World War, along with a brief review of how the Irish in London have been historically represented in literature and the media.

Diaspora and 'Diaspora Space'

According to the editors of a key collection of essays on the topic almost a decade ago, diaspora theory 'marks not a postmodern turn from history, but a nomadic turn in which the very parameters of specific historical moments are embodied and – as diaspora itself suggests – are scattered and regrouped into new points of becoming'.[33] Postcolonial literary critics anticipated the emergence of this trend, identifying the work of diasporic writers as one of their primary concerns.[34] Diaspora, it could be argued, was sewn into the very definition of postcolonial studies from the outset. Stuart Hall saw poststructuralist analyses of the persistently shifting and deferred nature of cultural identity as especially pertinent to the diasporic condition and construction of selfhood. 'Diaspora identities,' he states, 'are those that are constantly producing and reproducing themselves anew through transformation and difference.' They are defined, Hall argues, 'by the recognition of a necessary hetero-geneity and diversity' and by a notion of identity that 'lives in and through, not despite, difference',[35] a view which is borne out by some of the texts I examine in this study. Paul Gilroy argued that diaspora 'disrupts the fundamental power of territory to determine identity by breaking the simple sequence of explanatory links between place, loca-tion and consciousness'.[36] He advocated a multi-locational sense of postcolonial identity predicated on 'routes' or 'where you're at' as much as 'roots' and 'where you're from'.[37] In his book, *The Black Atlantic* (1993), he used Du Bois's theory of 'double consciousness'[38] to interro-gate the relationship between, on the one hand, black people's awareness of their identities as constructed from within the discourses of their own culture and, on the other, those identities constructed by discourses of white racial superiority.[39] The literature of the Irish in London can be read in a similar way with regard to the way migrant identities are constructed by the hegemonic discourses of both Irish and British culture. This is particularly apparent in the case of second-generation subjects who appear to live within and between two cultures at the same time. However, while literatures of migration often highlight the national, ethnic and postcolonial dimensions of their subjects' experi-ences, they also reveal a diversity of intersectional identity formations too complex to be bound solely by such parameters.[40] So, while nation-ality/ethnicity provides the primary orientation of this study, it is by no means the only lens through which the texts will be analysed.

With such concerns in mind, recent studies of diasporic literatures have looked for new ways in which to frame their objects of enquiry. Critics of Black British and British Asian literature such as Mark Stein and Susheila Nasta, for instance, have questioned the extent to which postcolonial theory is adequate for approaching the diversity of subject positions invoked by migrant literatures.[41] Shaun Richards, an early advocate of postcolonial theory in Irish Studies, has pointed out that, because it is predicated on an essential binary opposition between colonizer and colonized, it is 'tested at best, irrelevant at worst within the time/space compression of globalization'.[42] So, while it is useful for analysing representations of the colonial subject in the former colonies and, to some extent, has proved helpful for exploring such representations in exile, postcolonial theory becomes more problematic when applied to the multi-axial relationships of a diasporic metropolis such as London.

The work of Avtar Brah and, in particular, her concept of 'diaspora space' offers a way of working through such difficulties.[43] It provides a framework for appreciating 'the confluence of economic, political, cultural and psychic processes' of migration, historically as well as geographically.[44] On the geographical plane, diaspora space incorporates the global and the local: the former through its traditional definition as dispersal; the latter through its acknowledgement of the relationship between point of departure and point of destination. On the historical plane, diaspora space incorporates the study of how migrations are differentiated in a socio-political and generational way by events and contexts over time. As a result, identities are subject to collision and contestation at certain times and to reassembly and reconfiguration at others. So, where 'traumas of dislocation' may predominate in one era, 'hope and new beginnings' may predominate in another (193). A key aspect of diaspora space is how it is inhabited both by migrant and host communities and how it involves, in Brah's words, the 'entanglement of genealogies of dispersion with those of "staying put"' (16). By those who 'stay put', she is referring to the host or receiving community, who, she argues, are part of the diasporic experience as much as those who migrate. The literature of the Irish in London demonstrates that the term 'staying put' can equally apply to the sending community (i.e. those left behind in the country of origin). In other words, migrants move between two sets of subjects who 'stay put', those in their place of origin and those in their place of destination, and must negotiate the often contested cultural allegiances of diaspora space that this entails. So, in this study, as well as discussing how Irish migrant identities are configured in relation to the host community, I look at how they are configured in relation to the sending community and how complex forms of diasporic Irishness emerge as a result.

Central to the concept of diaspora space is how both individual and collective identities are produced in and through cultural/imaginative discourses as well as historical/political discourses. For the purposes of this research, I intend to treat the prose literature of the post-war Irish in London as a form of *narrative diaspora space* within which various forms of identity are temporally and spatially mediated. My motivation for this approach can be found in the following passage from Brah's book, *Cartographies of Diaspora: Contesting Identities* (1996):

> multiple journeys may configure into one journey via a *confluence of narratives* as it is lived and re-lived, produced, reproduced and transformed through individual as well as collective memory and re-memory. It is within this confluence of narrativity that 'diasporic community' is differently imagined under different historical circumstances. By this I mean that the identity of the diasporic imagined community is far from fixed or pre-given. It is constituted within the crucible of the materiality of everyday life; in the everyday stories we tell ourselves individually and collectively. (183)

Narrative, therefore, is central to Brah's understanding of diasporic identity. She notes, for instance, that 'the autobiographical mode is useful [...] as a disruptive device' within which 'the "individual" narrator does not unfold but is produced in the process of narration' (10). Narrative, in other words, is an intrinsic part of how an identity is constituted, rather than simply a vehicle for its expression. Brah's notion of a 'confluence of narratives' emerges at the point where various stories of migration and identity intersect. It is here that the concept of diaspora space is best appreciated as a 'site of immanence' where multiple subject positions are 'juxtaposed' and 'proclaimed or disavowed' according to historical circumstances (208). This 'subject-in-process', as she terms it, 'consciously and unconsciously replays and resignifies positions in which it is located and invested' (125). In other words, by configuring migrant identities individually and collectively, narrative is central to understandings of diaspora, providing its process of 'through and how' as well as its axis of 'to and from'.

Narrative and 'Narrative Identity'

H. Porter Abbott reminds us of an important distinction: 'The difference between events and their representation is the difference between *story* (the event or sequence of events) and *narrative discourse* (how the story is conveyed).'[45] The essence of narrative, he contends, is that it leaves its mark on the stories it tells by virtue of all the conscious or unconscious devices employed by writers (e.g. framing, point-of-view, rhetoric). What then is the relationship between narrative and identity? Peter Brooks describes it in the following way:

> Our lives are ceaselessly intertwined with narrative, with the stories that we tell and hear told, those we dream or imagine or would like to tell, all of which are reworked in that story of our own lives that we narrate to ourselves in an episodic, sometimes semi-conscious, but virtually uninterrupted monologue. We live immersed in narrative, recounting and reassessing the meaning of our past actions, anticipating the outcome of our future projects, situating ourselves at the intersection of several stories not yet completed.[46]

Narrative, therefore, is well equipped to mediate the mutability of personal identity as revealed by a life in process over time. According to Paul John Eakin, 'our sense of continuous identity is a fiction, the primary fiction of all self-narration', but it is also 'an existential fact, necessary for our psychological survival amid the flux of experience'.[47] Questions of fact and fiction, therefore, are continually present in the relationship between narrative and identity, but it is the desire for their resolution which drives many of the texts I consider in this study.

Paul Ricoeur saw narrative as crucial to the understanding of our lives and identities. He argued that reading, writing and the interpretation of texts are all mutually dependent and are a constituent part of what gives life meaning. Contrary to trends in some late twentieth-century continental philosophy, Ricoeur asserted a faith in language or discourse to reveal, rather than elude or elide, meaning. Although he acknowledged that authors often conceal their intentions, they do not, he maintained, necessarily set out to deceive. In his penultimate book, he elaborated on his notion of 'narrative identity' in the following way:

> The person, understood as a character in a story, is not an entity distinct from his or her 'experiences'. Quite the opposite: the person shares the condition of dynamic identity peculiar to the story recounted. The narrative constructs the identity of the character, what can be called his or her narrative identity, in constructing that of the story told. It is the identity of the story that makes the identity of the character. [...] In this sense, literature proves to consist of a vast laboratory for thought experiments in which the resources of variation encompassed by narrative identity are put to the test of narration.[48]

Elsewhere, Ricoeur argues that human life is 'an activity and a passion in search of a narrative',[49] but that we only reach a satisfactory understanding of our identities courtesy of interpretive detours through the 'significations of history and culture, which reside outside our immediate consciousness'.[50] Echoing Brah's comments about 'diaspora space', Ricoeur describes 'narrative identity' as the product not only of the factual and reflective aspects of historical discourse, but also of the imaginative and aspirational components of fictional discourse. 'The story of a life,' he declares, 'continues to be reconfigured by all the truthful or fictive stories a subject tells about himself or herself. This reconfiguration makes this life itself a cloth woven of stories told'.[51] So, by demonstrating how factual and fictional practices constitute the twin components of all narrative discourse, Ricoeur highlights how self-knowledge is derived from a combination of aspiration (prefiguration) and interpretation (refiguration). David Kaplan helpfully summarizes his position:

> Both individuals and communities form their identities by telling stories about themselves that become their history. Like any story, a narrative identity has a historical component and a fictional component, the former being bounded by argument, verification and fidelity to what happened; the latter utilizing imaginative variations of what happened to create new interpretations and new ways of seeing.[52]

Ricoeur argues that the continual re-reading, reinterpretation and reinscribing of our lives (whether consigned to paper or not), in itself, creates meaning. 'Narrative,' as Toni Morrison said, 'is radical, creating us at the very moment it is being created.'[53] Life can only really be understood, therefore, as a form of narrative continually in process or, as Richard Kearney states, as '*always already* an implicit story [...] always *on the way* to narrative'.[54] Reading, writing and living, therefore, continually feed off each other for meaning and by the same token continually nurture each other. Ricoeur sees metaphor and narrative as the two most important elements of any text in terms of both how they reveal a writer's intentions towards meaning and how they reveal in us, as readers, a predisposition towards interpretation. He argues that just as we 'willingly suspend our disbelief' as readers in order to pursue new meanings through metaphor, we do something similar by responding to the allure of narrative and its ability to assimilate (primarily, but not solely, by the mechanism of plot) multiple scattered events into a coherent story.[55] Life, in other words, demands to be narrativized in order to be understood and texts replicate what we as individuals do mentally day to day. As Ricoeur points out: 'It is precisely because of the elusive character of real life that we need the help of fiction to organize life retrospectively.'[56] In our early years we learn to make sense of the world through stories and we continue to rely on them, albeit in more complex and sophisticated forms, for the rest of our lives. We re-read and rewrite our selves over time and somewhere on the spectrum between fact and fiction our identities take on their often ambiguous narrative shape.

Narrative, of course, is not the only means by which identities can be defined. Non-narrative cultural and artistic forms of expression, more apparent in music and the visual arts perhaps, offer other ways of mediating and understanding a personal and collective sense of who we are. But narrative provides a richly textured means of tracking and interrogating this process. Ricoeur's theory of narrative identity offers a means of examining how identities are constructed not only in the changing relationship between society and the individual, but also in the shifts between fact and fiction that take place in the accounts of everyday life. As noted above, this is something to which Brah also alludes in her reference to the imaginative prerogatives of storytelling in diasporic communities. The point of synthesis between the work of Brah and Ricoeur is apparent, therefore, where the 'confluence of narratives' in diaspora space, introduced by the former, meets the notion of narrative identity advanced by the latter. By applying these twin concepts to my analysis, I reveal how individual and collective migrant identities are prefigured, configured and refigured through the narrative diaspora space of London Irish literature.

Notes

1 Elizabeth Bowen, 'Coming to London', in Hermione Lee (ed.), *The Mulberry Tree: Writings of Elizabeth Bowen* (London: Vintage, 1999), p.86. This essay was originally published in *The London Magazine* 3.3 (March 1956).

2 John Corry, *A Satirical View of London* (London: Robert Dutton, 1809), p. 23.

3 For post-war representations of the Afro-Caribbean community in London, see George Lamming, *The Emigrants* (London: Michael Joseph, 1954) and Samuel Selvon, *The Lonely Londoners* (London: Allan Wingate, 1956). For a portrayal of the South Asian community in London, see V. S. Naipaul, *The Mimic Men* (London: Andre Deutsch, 1967).

4   Edna O'Brien, *The Light of Evening* (London: Weidenfeld & Nicolson, 2006); Colm Tóibín, *Brooklyn* (London: Viking, 2009); Sebastian Barry, *On Canaan's Side* (London: Viking, 2011).

5   Interview conducted by the author with Maude Casey, 16 May 1991. Casey published a novel about how a London Irish teenage girl is reconciled to her Irish identity after a family holiday in Ireland. It does not qualify for examination here, however, because it does not explore the protagonist's London background. See Maude Casey, *Over the Water* (London: The Women's Press, 1987). For a critique of the novel, see Aidan Arrowsmith, 'Plastic Paddy: Negotiating Identity in Second Generation "Irish-English" Writing', *Irish Studies Review* 8.1 (2000), pp. 35–43.

6   See Bernard Canavan, 'Story-tellers and Writers: Irish Identity in Emigrant Labourers' Autobiographies, 1870–1970', in Patrick O'Sullivan (ed.), *The Irish Worldwide: History, Heritage, Identity: The Creative Migrant* (Leicester: Leicester University Press, 1994); Bronwen Walter, *Outsiders Inside: Whiteness, Place and Irish Women* (London: Routledge, 2001); Livia Popoviciu, Chris Haywood & Máirtín Mac an Ghaill, 'Migrating Masculinities: The Irish Diaspora in Britain', *Irish Studies Review* 14.2 (2006), pp. 169–87.

7   Sara Ahmed et al. (eds.), *Uprootings Regroundings: Questions of Home and Migration* (Oxford: Berg, 2003), p. 1.

8   Liam Ryan, 'Irish Emigration to Britain since World War II', in Richard Kearney (ed.), *Migration: The Irish at Home and Abroad* (Dublin: Wolfhound, 1990), pp. 45–46.

9   The metaphor seemed equally appropriate during the years of the 'Celtic Tiger' when it reflected reactions in some parts of Irish society to unprecedented levels of inward migration.

10 Luke Gibbons, *Transformations in Irish Culture* (Cork: Cork University Press, 1996), p. 17.

11 J. J. Lee, *Ireland 1912–1985: Politics and Society* (Cambridge: Cambridge University Press, 1989), p. 384.

12 Russell King, 'Preface', in Russell King, John Connell and Paul White (eds.), *Writing across Worlds: Literature and Migration* (London: Routledge, 1995), p. xv.

13 See, for instance, Eiblín Dubh Ní Chonaill, *Caoineadh Airt Uí Laoghaire* (c. 1783); Charles Maturin, *Melmoth the Wanderer* (1820); Charles Kickham, *Knocknagow or the Homes of Tipperary* (1879).

14 See, for instance, Samuel Beckett, *Murphy* (London: Picador, 1973); Kate O'Brien, *Pray for the Wanderer* (London: Heinemann, 1938); Sean O'Faoláin, *Come Back to Erin* (London: Joanathan Cape, 1938).

15 Edna O'Brien at Irish Writers in London Summer School, London Metropolitan University, 15 June 2005.

16 Edward Said, 'The Mind of Winter': Reflections on Life in Exile', *Harper's & Queen* 269 (September 1984), p. 51.

17 Patrick Ward, *Exile, Emigration and Irish Writing* (Dublin: Irish Academic Press, 2002), p. 27.

18 Patrick Duffy, 'Literary Reflections on Irish Migration in the Nineteenth and Twentieth Centuries', in Russell King, John Connell and Paul White (eds.), *Writing across Worlds: Literature and Migration* (London: Routledge, 1995), p. 33.

19 George O'Brien, 'The Aesthetics of Exile', in Liam Harte and Michael Parker (eds.),

Contemporary Irish Fiction: Themes, Tropes, Theories (Basingstoke: Macmillan, 2000), p. 53.

20 See, for instance, Mary Lennon, Marie McAdam and Joanne O'Brien, *Across the Water: Irish Women's Lives in Britain* (London: Virago, 1988) and Ide O'Carrol, *Models for Movers: Irish Women's Emigration to America* (Dublin: Attic Press, 1990).

21 Gerard Leavey, Sati Sembhi and Gill Livingston, 'Older Irish Migrants Living in London: Identity, Loss and Return', *Journal of Ethnic and Migration Studies* 30.4 (July 2004), p. 768.

22 Louise Ryan, 'Family Matters: (E)migration, Familial Networks and Irish Women in Britain', *Sociological Review* 52.3 (2004), p. 357.

23 Edna O'Brien, *Mother Ireland* (London: Weidenfeld & Nicolson, 1976), p. 143.

24 As quoted in Kim Knott, 'Towards a History and Politics of Diasporas and Migrations: A Grounded Spatial Approach', paper presented at 'Flows and Spaces', Annual Conference of the Royal Geographical Society/Institute of British Geographers, London (30 August–2 September 2005), http://www.diasporas.ac.uk, accessed 17 September 2008.

25 Colin Graham and Richard Kirkland (eds.), *Ireland and Cultural Theory: The Mechanics of Authenticity* (Basingstoke: Macmillan, 1999), p. 3.

26 Enda Delaney, *The Irish in Post-War Britain* (Oxford: Oxford University Press, 2007), p. 7.

27 Mary Robinson, 'Cherishing the Irish Diaspora: Address by Uachtarán na hÉireann Mary Robinson to Joint Sitting of the Houses of the Oireachtas', 2 February 1995, http://www.oireachtas.ie/viewdoc.asp?fn=/documents/addresses/2Feb1995.htm, accessed 7 December 2010.

28 Eugene Goodheart, *Novel Practices: Classic Modern Fiction* (London: Transaction Publishers, 2004), p. 168.

29 See, for instance, Julian Wolfreys, *Writing London, Volume 2: Materiality, Memory, Spectrality* (Basingstoke: Palgrave Macmillan, 2004); Lawrence Philips (ed.), *The Swarming Streets: Twentieth-Century Literary Representations of London* (Amsterdam: Rodopi, 2004); Lawrence Philips, *London Narratives: Post-war Fiction and the City* (London: Continuum, 2006).

30 John Clement Ball, *Imagining London: Postcolonial Fiction and the Transnational Metropolis* (Toronto: University of Toronto Press, 2004), p. 85; John McLeod, *Postcolonial London: Rewriting the Metropolis* (Abingdon: Routledge, 2004), pp. 83–84; pp. 99–100.

31 J. M. O'Neill wrote three novels set in the London Irish underworld of the late 1970s and early 1980s. See J. M. O'Neill, *Open Cut* (London: Heinemann, 1986); *Duffy is Dead* (London: Heinemann, 1987); *Canon Bang Bang* (London: Hodder & Stoughton, 1989). Many of Desmond Hogan's short stories are set in London in the late 1960s and 1970s. See, for instance, 'Soho Square Gardens' and 'Memories of Swinging London' in *The Children of Lir: Stories from Ireland* (London: Hamish Hamilton, 1981). William Trevor was one of the few writers who dealt with the experiences of the Irish in London during the Troubles. See, for instance, 'Another Christmas' in *The Stories of William Trevor* (Harmondsworth: Penguin, 1983).

32 See, for instance, Tony Murray, 'Curious Streets: Diaspora, Displacement and Transgression in Desmond Hogan's London Irish Narratives', *Irish Studies Review* 14.2 (2006), pp. 239–53.

33 Jana Evans Braziel and Anita Mannur (eds.), *Theorizing Diaspora: A Reader* (Oxford: Blackwell, 2003), p. 3.

34 See, for instance, Bill Ashcroft, Gareth Griffiths and Helen Tiffin, *The Empire Writes Back: Theory and Practice in Post-Colonial Literatures* (London: Routledge, 1989), pp. 217–19.

35 Stuart Hall, 'Cultural Identity and Diaspora', in Jonathan Rutherford (ed.), *Identity: Community, Culture, Difference* (London: Lawrence & Wishart, 1990), p. 235.

36 Paul Gilroy, 'Diaspora and the Detours of Identity', in Kay Woodward (ed.), *Identity and Difference* (London: Sage, 1997), p. 328.

37 See Paul Gilroy, 'It Ain't Where You're From, It's Where You're At', *Third Text* 13 (1991), pp. 3–16.

38 W. E. B. Du Bois, *The Souls of Black Folk* (Oxford: Oxford University Press, 2007), p. 8.

39 Paul Gilroy, *The Black Atlantic: Modernity and Double Consciousness* (London: Verso, 1993).

40 Floya Anthias argues that 'the intersections of ethnicity, gender and class may construct multiple, uneven and *contradictory* social patterns of domination and subordination; human subjects may be positioned differentially within these social divisions'. See Floya Anthias, 'Evaluating "Diaspora": Beyond Ethnicity?', *Sociology* 32.3 (August 1998), p. 574.

41 Susheila Nasta, *Home Truths: Fictions of the South Asian Diaspora in Britain* (Basingstoke: Palgrave, 2002); Mark Stein, *Black British Literature: Novels of Transformation* (Columbus: Ohio State University Press, 2004). See also Sukhdev Sandhu, *London Calling: How Black and Asian Writers Imagined a City* (London: Harper Perennial, 2004).

42 Shaun Richards, '"To Me, Here Is More Like There"', *Irish Studies Review* 15.1 (2007), p. 4.

43 The term 'diaspora space' has been widely applied since the mid-1990s, especially within the social sciences. However, this sometimes happens in a rather reductive manner to refer to a specific geographical location. While the concept does not preclude such usage, it has a much more sophisticated and challenging meaning than this. At the conclusion of the AHRC programme 'Diasporas, Migrations and Identities' (2005–10), its director advocated the revisiting of 'diaspora space' as a concept which, she argued, has 'yet to be fully examined'. Kim Knott, 'Space and Movement', in Kim Knott and Seán McLoughlin (eds.), *Diasporas: Concepts, Intersections, Identities* (London: Zed Books, 2010), p. 83.

44 Avtar Brah, *Cartographies of Diaspora: Contesting Identities* (London: Routledge, 1996), p. 181. Subsequent references to this text are cited in parentheses.

45 H. Porter Abbott, *The Cambridge Introduction to Narrative* (Cambridge: Cambridge University Press, 2002), p. 13.

46 Peter Brooks, *Reading for the Plot: Design and Intention in Narrative* (Oxford: Clarendon Press, 1984), p. 3.

47 Paul John Eakin, *How Our Lives Become Stories* (Ithaca: Cornell University Press, 1999), pp. 93–94.

48 Paul Ricoeur, *Oneself as Another*, trans. Kathleen Blamey (Chicago: University of Chicago Press, 1992), pp. 147–48.

49 Paul Ricoeur, 'Life in Quest of Narrative', in David C. Wood (ed.), *On Paul Ricoeur:*

Narrative and Interpretation (London: Routledge, 1991), p. 29.

50 As explained in an introduction to Ricoeur's work. See Richard Kearney, *Modern Movements in European Philosophy* (Manchester: Manchester University Press, 1986), p. 92.

51 Paul Ricoeur, *Time and Narrative, Vol. 3*, trans. Kathleen McLaughlin and David Pellauer (Chicago: University of Chicago Press, 1984), p. 246.

52 David Kaplan, *Ricoeur's Critical Theory* (New York: SUNY Press, 2003), p. 10.

53 Toni Morrison, 'Nobel Lecture', 7 December 1993, http://nobelprize.org/nobel_prizes/literature/laureates/1993/morrison-lecture.html, accessed 15 December 2007.

54 Richard Kearney, *On Stories* (London: Routledge, 2002), p. 129; p. 133.

55 Ricoeur, *Time and Narrative, Vol 3*, p. x.

56 Ricoeur, *Oneself as Another*, p. 162.

2

The Irish in London

A Brief History up to the Second World War

Irish people have been deeply woven into the fabric of London life for centuries. The first records of Irish migrant workers originate from the twelfth century, when the majority were employed as labourers and street-vendors, although some had to resort to other means of survival, as evidenced by a statute in 1243 to expel Irish beggars.[1] By Tudor times, the Irish were no strangers to a city which had, in John Denvir's lurid description, 'seen many an Irish chief and noble brought in chains to perish miserably in the gloomy dungeons of the Tower'.[2] Lesser mortals were excluded from work by the regulations of the trade guilds and settled outside the walls of the City of London,[3] but Irish enclaves were discernible in other parts of London from as early as the sixteenth century.[4] Even in these early years, Irish writers had already started to have an impact in London. The first play staged by an Irish writer in the capital was *Ram Alley* by Lordinge Barry, a contemporary of Shakespeare, whose bawdy comedy appeared in 1608. It was titled after the notoriously crime-ridden quarter of the city in Whitefriars, near Fleet Street, where it was set, and proved so popular that it continued to run almost uninterrupted for the next twenty years.[5]

Overt public displays of national identity by Irish people were rare due to widespread anti-Irish prejudice, which was endemic in English culture at this time. This was not only directed at Catholics, however, as the Protestant playwright George Farquhar discovered. Despite having immortalized William III's victory at the Battle of the Boyne in verse, he found that he was as subject to racial stereotyping as any other Irish person once he arrived in London. His experience of this is reflected in his first play, *Love and a Bottle* (1698), through the character of Roebuck. Refusing to be bound by the rules of honour in London society, he is an early example of what Roy Foster has described as 'a Mick on the make',[6] something revealed in a notable exchange with a young Englishwoman called Lucinda. Rather than taking exception to her preposterous notions of the Irish as semi-wild beasts, Roebuck mischievously indulges her fantasies for the purpose of personal advancement.

Religion was as decisive a factor in determining how Irish people were received by Londoners as nationality. In his history of the Irish in Britain, John Archer Jackson states that 'more potent than the fact that the immigrant lived in a strange and simple way was the fact that he belonged to a foreign church'.[7] Despite their illegality, there is evidence of illicit Catholic Mass houses in the city, such as that found in Black Lion Court and closed down by the authorities in 1767.[8] A particularly vivid example of Irish visibility is apparent in a letter which Jonathan Swift sent to his friend Esther Johnson in 1713, where he records seeing the Mall on St Patrick's Day 'so full of crosses, that I thought all the world was Irish'.[9] By the end of the century, other examples of Irish culture had begun to make a mark. Writing in 1801, Joseph Strutt recalls seeing hurling played 'in fields at the back of the British Museum' and was 'greatly amused to see with what facility those who were skilful in the pastime would catch up the ball upon the bat, and often run with it for a considerable time'.[10] Sporadic outbreaks of anti-Catholic rioting took place across the city from the seventeenth to the nineteenth century, but the most serious were the Gordon Riots of June 1780. Huge numbers of protesters, led by the president of the Protestant Association, Lord George Gordon, gathered in the centre of London after Parliament passed the Papists Act lifting some restrictions on Catholic priests and schools. In the ensuing disturbances many chapels were destroyed, as well as houses, shops, public houses and business premises owned or occupied by Catholics. The military only succeeded in suppressing the disturbances at the cost of several hundred lives. The following extract from Dickens' novel *Barnaby Rudge* (1840–41) captures the intensity of the riot in Moorfields:

> Beginning with the private houses so occupied, they broke open the doors and windows; and while they destroyed the furniture and left but the bare walls, made a sharp search for tools and engines of destruction [...] From the chapels, they tore down and took away the very altars, benches, pulpits, pews and flooring; from the dwelling-houses, the very wainscoting and stairs.[11]

Edmund Burke expressed his surprise at the order Catholic priests managed to keep over their parishioners during the riots and, despite widespread hostility, a visible Irish Catholic presence was maintained in the very heart of the city.[12] After the passing of the Catholic Relief Act of 1791, St Patrick's in Soho became the first Catholic church in Britain to be established since the Reformation. It was a symbolic moment and indicated that the Irish had finally become an accepted part of London life.

Throughout the eighteenth and nineteenth centuries, the majority of the London Irish were concentrated in the unskilled and lowest paid sectors of the economy. As a result, they were too poor to live anywhere other than the overcrowded courts and alleys of ethnic enclaves in Wapping, Marylebone or Bermondsey. As Harrington Benjamin puts it, 'the wheels of the Industrial Revolution may have been able to turn more easily because of the constant supply of Irish labor, but these same wheels crushed and mangled many'.[13] Such were the high concentrations of Irish households in the parish of St Giles (immediately east of present-day Oxford Street) that the area became known as 'Little Dublin'.[14] This was one of the earliest Irish settlements in the city, dating back as far as the mid-sixteenth century. A government investigation into conditions there in 1816 found approximately six thousand Irish men, women and children living in what John Timbs later described as 'one great maze, as if the houses had originally been one block of stone eaten by slugs into numberless small chambers and connecting passages'.[15] The observations of writers and correspondents, however, were often superficial. Beyond the squalor and apparent disorder, there is evidence of a complex migrant community with sophisticated ethnic support mechanisms. As Lynn Hollen Lees points out in her seminal study of the Irish in Victorian London, the Irish were congregated not so much in a large ghetto as in 'a string of settlements tucked into the tumbledown corners' of the city, 'where they lived close to the English, but [...] remained apart'.[16] 'What outsiders saw as an undifferentiated slum,' she stresses, 'were in fact a series of communities organized on social rather than spatial lines [...] a multitude of Irish networks that crisscrossed the working-class territory that they inhabited.'[17] The Census of 1841 found some 74,000 Irish-born immigrants resident in London (approximately 3.9 per cent of the population) and, according to Jackson, there were by this time 26 Catholic chapels, 106 priests and four convents in the city.[18] In the 1840s, branches of Irish nationalist organizations such as the Repeal Association and the Young Ireland movement were established in areas such as Southwark, Hammersmith and Soho.[19] There is also evidence of some Unionist organization in London, with the first Orange Lodges established in the city as early as the first decade of the eighteenth century.[20] While sectarianism did not become a problem on the same scale as it did in Liverpool and Glasgow, Benjamin indicates that there were sizeable numbers of Orangemen in the newly formed London police force and some evidence of the persecution of Irish Catholics.[21]

The Great Famine of the 1840s resulted in an unprecedented wave of Irish migration to Britain, when whole families were forced to flee the land and start new lives abroad. Between the years 1846 and 1854, roughly one and three quarter million people left Ireland. Most went to America, while those who chose Britain settled mainly in the industrial heartlands of north-west England and central Scotland. However, many also continued (often on foot) to London to supplement an existing Irish population which, by 1851, had swollen to 108,548 (4.6 per cent of the total population).[22] In the middle decades of the nineteenth century, the majority of Irish migrants in London were rural labourers and small farmers originating from the south-west of Ireland, especially County Cork. By this time, the Irish had become closely associated with certain sectors of the London economy. They dominated the fruit-selling business, for instance, and, according to Jerry White, by 1850 nine out of ten ticketed porters in the Covent Garden market were Irish.[23] The following extract from Charles Mayhew's celebrated study of mid-nineteenth-century London life vividly captures the scene:

> Groups of apple-women, with straw pads on their crushed bonnets, and coarse shawls crossing their bosoms, sit on their porter's knots, chatting in Irish, and smoking short pipes; every passer-by is hailed with the cry of, 'Want a baskit, yer honor?' The porter, trembling under the piled-up hamper, trots along the street, with his teeth clenched and shirt wet with the weight, and staggering at every step he takes.[24]

Although the majority of Irish migrants at this time (as at most other times) were unskilled or semi-skilled, many professionals and artisans also made the journey. Artists as well as writers were attracted by the opportunities that the city offered. Painters such as Daniel Maclise, John Lavery and Augustus Nicholas Burke made their careers in London in the latter half of the nineteenth century, and Irish women models who became fashionable at this time featured prominently in the work of painters such as Ford Madox Brown and James McNeill Whistler.[25]

During the latter half of the nineteenth century the numbers of Irish-born in London declined significantly as migration tailed off from its mid-century peak. From a recorded figure of 106,879 in 1861, the figure dropped to 91,171 by the following census in 1871 and to just 60,211 in 1901. By this time, the Roman Catholic Church had established a network of parish churches and schools along with associated devotional and educational activities. This provided an important cultural, as well as religious, foundation for the London Irish and provided newly arrived migrants with 'an essential resource in their struggle to adapt to urban life'.[26] The 1860s saw the first appearance of newspapers specifically aimed at the Irish in London,[27] and the involvement in ethnic cultural activities of both the Irish-born and the descendants of the original Famine migrants.[28] Radical political organization around Irish issues also began to emerge, with the founding of a London branch of the militant Irish Republican Brotherhood (IRB). The most audacious example of the IRB's activities in the city took place in November 1867 during an attempt to spring a member of the organization from the House of Detention in Clerkenwell. When a barrel of gunpowder was ignited at the perimeter walls, it resulted in the deaths of twelve people and injury to forty more, an event which led to widespread fear of the Irish, the establishment of the Special Branch and the fitting of bullet-proof glass in Scotland Yard.[29]

While further Fenian bombings took place in the 1880s, including a series of explosions on the Underground, such tactics did not garner the support of most Irish people across the capital. By the turn of the century, a report on the Irish in London in *Blackwood's* magazine could confidently, if somewhat condescendingly, conclude that

> the London Irish dearly love playing at revolutionaries, but they are careful not to overdo the jest [...] The London Irish element among the working classes will not, so far as sane prediction goes, become actively anti-British, or be persuaded, indeed, to take more than a languid interest in politics. They will live apart, believing their country to be deeply wronged, but perceiving that schemes of vengeance had best remain unrealised.[30]

It is certainly true that in the last quarter of the century Irish political activism had taken a clear constitutional turn. The Irish Home Rule Confederation of Great Britain had over forty branches across the city by 1883.[31] Irish involvement in the British labour and trade union move-

ment, which dated back as far as Chartism in the 1840s, was also prominent at two key moments of late nineteenth-century labour history. The
register for the matchgirls' strike of 1888 showed many Irish names,
twenty-three of whom lived in a notorious group of streets in Lime-
house known as 'the Fenian Barracks'.[32] The following year, about a
mile further up the road, the dockers' strike was led and supported by
Irish trade unionists such as James Toomey and Tom McCarthy. Most
Protestant Irish in London were supporters of the Union and some, like
the members of the Ulster Club (founded in the city in 1896), were stri-
dently loyalist.[33] Other Protestants, such as the novelist Annie Smithson,
supported the nationalist cause and recalled how, while training to be a
nurse in Chelsea in 1897, she provoked the ire of the matron for wearing
a spray of shamrock in her uniform on St Patrick's Day.[34] London offered
much in terms of career advancement, but for some city life proved to
be an alienating experience. In an autobiographical novel from the time
by Shan Bullock, a young Protestant finds the experience of working as
a clerk in London so mind-numbing that he longs to return to his native
Fermanagh.[35]

By the late nineteenth century, the Irish had firmly established themselves within the print media. A number of major British newspapers
and periodicals were owned and/or edited by Irishmen, some of them
by nationalists such as T. P. O'Connor, who was elected to Parliament
in 1885. This gave a certain stratum of the London Irish community
considerable access to power and influence. The role London played in
personal literary ambition is evident in Gerald O'Donovan's novel *Father
Ralph* (1913), in which a disillusioned priest leaves his parish in the west
of Ireland to pursue a writing career in the city. It is also apparent in
James Joyce's short story 'A Little Cloud' (1914). When Little Chan-
dler meets an old acquaintance who tells him about his success as a
journalist in London, it prompts the would-be poet to contemplate a
move there himself in the hope of reinventing himself as one of 'the
Celtic school'.[36] Instrumental in reviving such notions was the Gaelic
League, which along with a number of other Irish societies and organizations had established offices in the heart of the city at 55 Chancery
Lane to further the cause of Irish self-determination. Among such bodies
were the Gaelic Athletic Association (GAA), established in 1895, the
Irish Republican Brotherhood, the Irish Folk Song Society and the
Young Ireland Society. Rather than being simply satellites of a head-
quarters back in Dublin, some Irish organizations had agendas and
constitutions which reflected the specific needs of the migrant commu-

nity. The Southwark Irish Literary Club, founded in January 1883 by Francis Fahy, is a good example of this. While it later evolved into the Irish Literary Society under the influence of Yeats and his broader vision of a literary revival, Fahy's original purpose was a distinctly diasporic one, providing Gaelic language and literature classes for the children of Irish migrants in that part of London. John Hutchinson points out how important newly arrived young Irish migrants were to the leaders of cultural nationalism in the diaspora:

> These revivalists found a constituency in the growing numbers of Irish-born minor civil servants in the post office and excise, and schoolteachers who flocked to London in search of employment. Ambitious, shocked by the squalor of the urban Irish and gripped by a nostalgia for Ireland, they were drawn to revivalist themes of individual and collective moral regeneration and by those of communal self-help, which provided an outlet for their energies.[37]

While the number of Irish-born in London had dropped to 51,685 by 1911 (1.1 per cent of the overall population), the female to male ratio was 1340:1000, and the highest concentrations were now in the west of the city.[38] The Post Office employed large numbers of Irish workers, mainly women, many of whom were committed nationalists.[39] In 1902, a columnist with the *Catholic Herald* newspaper observed that 'Irish women working in the Post Office were practically all enthusiastic supporters of the Gaelic League'.[40]

The War of Independence in Ireland had direct repercussions for the Irish in London. In 1919, the Irish Self-Determination League was formed under the chairmanship of Art O'Brien. Its meetings were regularly banned and 'on a number of occasions its offices were raided and its papers and publications seized'.[41] In October of the following year, Terence MacSwiney died in Brixton Jail after 74 days on hunger strike. MacSwiney, who was elected Lord Mayor of Cork as the Sinn Féin candidate, had been imprisoned for sedition. Thousands of Irish people lined the streets and escorted his body to Euston station from St George's Cathedral in Southwark. According to the 1921 Census, the Irish-born population of the city had increased marginally for the first time since the 1850s, and it continued to rise gradually over the next two decades. By the mid-1920s, 43 per cent of Irish-born people were living abroad and during the next decade, in a trend evident for most of the twentieth century, substantially more women than men left the country.

The inter-war years are one of the most under-researched periods in the twentieth-century history of the Irish in London. Literature, however, provides impressions, at least, of what life was like for Irish Londoners at the time. The lack of work and the economic hardship that migrants faced in the years before the creation of the welfare state are captured in Rearden Connor's memoir, *A Plain Tale from the Bogs* (1937). He describes a fruitless search for clerical work, a growing disillusionment with the economic conditions of the time and even an attempted suicide.[42] When Samuel Beckett first came to the city in the summer of 1932, he was not much happier. He lived near King's Cross, a locality which features in his novel, *Murphy* (1938). The main protagonist is a semi-itinerant intellectual who has fled a motley group of creditors and female admirers in Dublin. Dressed in rust-coloured suit and lemon-coloured bow tie, he spends much of his time traipsing the streets immersed in existentialist ennui. In the following extract, he has time to reflect on such matters before meeting his lover, an Irish-born prostitute called Celia:

> By far the best part of the way was the toil from King's Cross up Caledonian Road, reminding him of the toil from St. Lazare up Rue d'Amsterdam. And while Brewery Road was no Boulevard de Clichy nor even des Batingnolles, still it was better at the top of the hill than either of those, as asylum (after a point) is better than exile.[43]

Unlike Celia, most Irish women went into service or nursing, occupations which promised secure accommodation as part of their conditions. As Catherine Ridgeway, a Dubliner who first came to London in 1928 to work as a chambermaid, pointed out, 'we all took jobs where you were assured of your bed and board'.[44] Others went into secretarial work, like the young female protagonist from Belfast in George Buchanan's novel *Rose Forbes* (1937).

Representations of the Irish in London

The high visibility of Afro-Caribbeans and south Asians in London since the Second World War has understandably resulted in their being a prime focus of political and media attention concerning immigration. This has been especially so given the highly charged debates surrounding questions of race and colour over this period. However, it is important to recognise that this did not automatically mean that the Irish were no longer subject to racialization and discrimination during the post-war era. By migrating to London in these years, the Irish came into direct contact with a people for whom they had been historically portrayed as indolent, dishonest and prone to violence and alcohol abuse.[45] Notions of an assumed 'ethnic fade' or naturalized assimilation of the Irish into the host community are problematic, as the proliferation of signs such as 'No Irish, No Blacks, No Dogs' in boarding-house windows throughout the 1950s and into the 1960s clearly shows.[46] Theories of racism in Britain, predicated on differences of colour, have tended to obscure the incidence of discrimination directed against white minority ethnic groups such as the Irish and the Jews. For the Irish, this consisted of a mixture of long-standing colonial antipathy and a deeply embedded anti-Catholicism.[47] During the Second World War and into the immediate post-war years, this was exacerbated by resentment at the Irish state's policy of neutrality.[48] Later again, during the height of the Troubles in the 1970s and 1980s, it was once more apparent. Press reaction to the IRA's bombing campaign in the city in the early 1980s is a case in point, when the Irish were depicted as monsters in one particular London newspaper.[49] More recently, research conducted in the 1990s established that the Irish continued to be routinely discriminated against with regard to employment, housing, healthcare and criminal justice.[50]

At other times, while anti-Irish sentiments never disappeared completely, the attitude of the host community to the Irish has been more benign. In the late nineteenth century, when there was a shift away from the revolutionary activities of organizations like the Fenians to the more constitutional campaign for Home Rule, the Irish in London were regarded as less of a political and social threat. A century later, during the late 1990s and the first decade of this century, the combination of the burgeoning Northern Ireland Peace Process, the emergence of the 'Celtic Tiger' economy in the Republic of Ireland and the worldwide success of Irish cultural enterprises such as *Riverdance* had a generally positive influence on British attitudes to the Irish.[51] This has been reflected in the greater presence of Irish people and Irish accents on British TV and radio, although this particular phenomenon needs to be seen in the historical context of the media's role as social and cultural arbiters in British society. While celebrities such as Eamonn Andrews, Terry Wogan and Graham Norton have all constituted popular and politically non-threatening representations of the Irish in Britain over the years, more negative representations on British television screens have continued alongside this. Significantly, research into this topic has found that a key way in which prejudice manifested itself was through derogatory portrayals of Irish characters in British television drama.[52] A 1997 thesis on media representations of the Irish in Britain found that, although such representations were not as overtly racist as Victorian depictions of the Irish in magazines such as *Punch*, 'the stereotypes of "Irishness", symbolic and trait-laden, are hidden as part of everyday, normative discourse; they are not recognised as racialized constructions of the Irish because these stereotypes are firmly positioned within the commonsense ideologies present in the mass media in Britain'.[53]

Like most migrant communities, the Irish have been under-represented in the formal institutions and transmission of British culture.[54] As one of the earliest groups in a long history of 'white' European movement to London (which also included Huguenots, Poles, Italians, Jews and Cypriots), the Irish have been rendered invisible due to their skin colour. As a result, it is often assumed in government and media circles that they have unproblematically assimilated into British society. This is a phenomenon referred to by Mary Hickman as 'the myth of homogeneity', which 'assumed that all people who were white smoothly assimilated into the "British way of life" and that the problems all resided with those who migrated and had a different skin colour […] The myth of homogeneity therefore had to entail the denial of difference among the white population.'[55] This may also be why, despite the continuing size and significance of the Irish population in London, there is surprisingly little historical documentation of their lives and activities in the official records. Some attempts have been made to address this issue through research and oral history initiatives over the years, but accounts by the migrants themselves are still rare.[56] As the character of P. J. says in one of the novels I examine later, '"We dig the tunnels, lay the rails and build the roads and buildings. But we leave no other sign behind us. We are unknown and unrecorded."'[57]

The majority of literary representations of the Irish in London, prior to the twentieth century, are to be found in the work of dramatists. The phenomenon of the 'stage Irishman' has long and sinuous roots and is central to any discussion of the topic.[58] The plays in which the 'stage Irishman' appeared, on the whole, were crafted to appeal to the tastes of the theatre-going public in London, but a counter-discourse can be traced back to subversions of the trope already clearly evident by the mid-nineteenth century in the work of Dion Boucicault.[59] At the turn of the twentieth century, London Irish characters began to appear in fiction as well as drama, notably in work by writers such as Yeats, George Moore and Pádraic Ó Conaire.[60] However, for most of the first half of the twentieth century, the favoured medium for portraying the personal experiences of the Irish in London was autobiography.[61]

In one of the first studies of the subject in 1995, Eamonn Hughes argued that there was an inherent 'semantic difficulty' in studying the literature of the Irish in Britain.[62] While hyphenated labels such as 'Black-British' or 'British-Asian' writing had been widely used and accepted for some time, Hughes pointed out that the term 'Irish-British' still appeared inappropriate for two reasons. In one respect, he argued, the term seemed insubstantial, given how integral and long-standing the Irish involvement in British life had been. On the other hand, the term appeared presumptuous given the history of irreconcilable political and cultural differences that had existed between the two countries. Much has happened in Irish–British relations in the interim to suggest that the second of these two assertions may no longer be the case, although the term 'Irish-British' has still not found general currency. Despite living in the city for many years, many writers saw no reason to describe themselves as anything but Irish. Others adopted Anglicized identities in order to maximize opportunities for professional success. The term 'Anglo-Irish' was regularly applied by writers and critics alike up to Irish independence in 1922. Many prominent Irish writers in London prior to this, such as Yeats, Shaw and Wilde, fitted the description very well, but it had historical connotations (particularly in relation to religion and class) and the term became increasingly inappropriate for most writers after independence. For some writers from Protestant backgrounds, such as O'Casey, Beckett and Bowen, the term still carried some relevance, but for writers from a Catholic or nationalist background, such as Ó Conaire, O'Faolain and Kavanagh, the term was effectively moribund. Since the Second World War, it has become even more archaic, although it is not altogether extinct, as attested by its continuing application to certain Irish writers in Britain, such as Iris Murdoch and William Trevor.[63]

Prior to the First World War, the term 'London Irish' was quite widely used in cultural, military and sporting circles.[64] It was not, however, a label which many migrants who came after Irish independence would have recognized or subscribed to. This was because the term carried inappropriate colonial connotations from which a new generation of Irish people preferred to distance themselves. However, in the latter part of the twentieth century, the term became increasingly common once again among both first- and second-generation Irish people living in the city. It attained widespread use in the 1980s, when it began to be applied by Irish migrants who formed the backbone of the cultural and political renaissance of the Irish community in London at that time.[65] When John Broderick chose the title *London Irish* for a novel in 1979, for instance, the term was relatively unusual, but by the time Zane Radcliffe adopted the same title for his novel in 2002, the term had entered general usage.[66] Today, some people describe themselves as 'London Irish' because it reflects their dual sense of identity, others see the term as a means of circumnavigating the 'semantic difficulty' referred to above, and still others see it as a means of expressing an indentification with the explicitly multicultural nature of London. Not all of the authors nor indeed the protagonists I examine in this book necessarily choose the label 'London Irish' to describe themselves. However, it provides a succinct means of reflecting not just the more obvious geographical and political dimensions of the literature but its intrinsically diasporic and cosmopolitan characteristics.

Regardless of the labels we choose to apply to such writing, however, there remains the question why, until relatively recently, members of such a long-established community have been so reluctant to express their experiences of life in Britain through literature. Why the 'aphonic emptiness', to quote Patrick Ward?[67] Eamonn Hughes offers three possible explanations: firstly, the Irish in Britain have not been 'coherent or stable enough' to generate their own literature; secondly, 'the business of living' in a foreign country obviates 'cultural activity reflecting on one's status'; thirdly, 'emigration was perceived as a servile failure' with which writers were reluctant to engage.[68] The first two of these explanations are questionable: the former because the Irish are one of the oldest ethnic groups in Britain with a well-established history of cultural enterprise, as illustrated above; the latter because the same argument applies to Jewish and Asian communities, yet they do not appear to have experienced this problem to the same extent. The third reason, however, does bear closer scrutiny and has also been cited by other commentators as a possible reason for the apparent silence. In 1993, Joseph O'Connor noted that 'at the heart of the Irish emigrant experience there is a caution, a refusal to speak, a fear of the word'.[69] Donall Mac Amhlaigh noted that, during the immediate post-war years, there was very little reflection in literature of the internal 'constraints, taboos and hang-ups' that he witnessed within the Irish community at that time.[70] James Ryan has also referred to a sense of collective denial and/or guilt about migration, which has impacted on twentieth-century Irish writers.[71] In the introduction to his anthology of Irish autobiography in Britain, Liam Harte takes issue with such views, arguing that 'such over-easy generalisations' are not borne out by his research.[72] Such research has been invaluable in unearthing hitherto obscure or undervalued texts, but the fact remains that, given the sheer numbers of Irish migrants who came to Britain over the centuries, there are still disproportionately few accounts of their experiences prior to the Second World War. Where Harte's argument is valid, however, is in relation to London in the post-war period, and this is corroborated by the preliminary work for this book, in which I identified well over a hundred potential texts worthy of investigation.

The Irish navvy provides an interesting case-study for identifying when and how Irish migrant writers began to record their experiences in their own words. An essay by Bernard Canavan on autobiographical accounts of Irish labourers in Britain emphasized that what had been a predominantly oral tradition for centuries within both the British and Irish working class (i.e. the spoken exchange of experiences about migration) only began substantially to enter the written and literary domain towards the end of the nineteenth century.[73] This shift, he argues, inaugurated a transition from an essentially unselfconscious and communal tradition to a more explicitly personalized and self-reflexive form of literary practice. It is a phenomenon which becomes increasingly evident over the period I cover and is particularly noticeable in the texts I examine by second-generation Irish writers in Part III of the book. By examining this closely, I trace over time how texts differentially portray the relationship between interior and exterior facets of the migration experience – that is, its subjective psychological impact on the individual and the objective historical and social context within which this takes place.

The prominence of such issues in the work of second-generation Irish writers in Britain may be one of the reasons why some of the most searching critiques of Irish migrant literature in recent years have been focused on this genre. Two critics in particular, Aidan Arrowsmith and Liam Harte, have written extensively in this field. Work by writers such as Moy McCrory, Maude Casey and Martin McDonagh alerts us, according to Arrowsmith, to the 'indeterminacy and confusion' of being inside and outside 'Englishness' and 'Irishness' at the same time.[74] Meanwhile, Harte sees recent examples of second-generation autobiography by writers such as John Walsh, Blake Morrison and Terry Eagleton as the key to understanding the 'transgenerational ramifications of dias-poric identities'.[75] These are helpful insights. However, some of the autobiographical texts I examine in the final part of this book also reveal a stubborn desire to regenerate the more essentialized tropes of exile and masculinity that were prevalent during the London Irish upbringings of their subjects. This demonstrates how, in second-generation texts, older configurations of migrant identity continue to co-exist alongside the new.

Notes

1   Kevin O'Connor, *The Irish in Britain* (London: Sidgwick & Jackson, 1972), p. 2.
2   John Denvir, *The Irish in Britain from the Earliest Times to the Fall of and Death of Parnell* (London: Kegan Paul, Trench, Trübner & Co., 1894), p. 34.
3   Throughout this book, the term 'City' is used to refer to the historical heart of London (east of Westminster), while the term 'city' is used to refer to London as a whole.
4   John Gage, 'The Rise and Fall of the St.Giles Rookery', *Camden History Review* 12 (1984), p. 20.
5   Whitefriars was the district at the junction of Fleet Street and Fetter Lane, named after the medieval priory which stood on this site. Number 4 Ram Alley (known today as Hare Place) was home in 1787–88 to Theobald Wolfe Tone, who lived here while studying law nearby at the Middle Temple. The latter was home to numerous Irish men of letters, including Richard Sheridan, Oliver Goldsmith and Thomas Moore.
6   R.F. Foster, *Paddy and Mr. Punch: Connections in English and Irish History* (London: Allen Lane, 1993), p. 281.
7   John Archer Jackson, *The Irish in Britain* (London: Routledge & Kegan Paul, 1963), p. 154.
8   Jackson, *The Irish in Britain*, p. 138.
9   Jonathan Swift, 'Journal to Stella', in *The Works of Jonathan Swift, D.D.* (London: A. Constable, 1814), p. 186. It was traditional for Irish people at this time to wear crosses in their hats instead of shamrock on St Patrick's Day.
10 Joseph Strutt, *The Sports and Pastimes of the People of England* (London: William Reeves, 1830), p. 99.
11 Charles Dickens, *Barnaby Rudge* (Oxford: Oxford University Press, 2003), p. 419.
12 Jackson, *The Irish in Britain,* p. 135.
13 Harrington W. Benjamin, 'The London Irish: A Study in Political Activism 1870–1910' (unpublished MA thesis, Princeton University, 1976), p. 36.
14 David R. Green, 'Historical Perspective on the St. Giles Rookery', in Sian Anthony, *Medieval Settlement to 18th-/19th-Century Rookery* (London: Museum of London Archaeology, 2011), p. 56.
15 John Timbs, *Curiosities of London* (London: David Bogue, 1855), p. 330.
16 Lynn Hollen Lees, *Exiles of Erin: Irish Migrants in Victorian London* (Manchester:

Manchester University Press, 1979), p. 56, p. 63.

17 Lees, *Exiles of Erin*, p. 87.

18 Jackson, *The Irish in Britain*, p. 138.

19 Lees, *Exiles of Erin*, pp. 226–27.

20 Hereward Senior, *Orangeism in Ireland and Britain, 1795–1836* (London: Routledge & Kegan Paul, 1966), p. 153.

21 Benjamin, 'The London Irish', pp. 85–86.

22 Jackson, *The Irish in Britain*, p. 9.

23 Jerry White, *London in the Nineteenth Century: A Human Awful Wonder of God* (London: Vintage, 2008), p. 132.

24 Henry Mayhew, *Mayhew's London: Being Selections from 'London Labour and the London Poor'* (London: Spring Books, 1951), p. 109.

25 See, for instance, Ford Madox Browm, *The Irish Girl* (1860) and James McNeill Whistler, *Weary* (1863).

26 Lees, *Exiles of Erin*, p. 186.

27 For instance *The Universal News* (1860–69); *The Irish Liberator* (1863–64); *The Irish News* (1867). For a detailed study of these publications, see Anthony McNicholas, *Politics, Religion and the Press: Irish Journalism in Mid-Victorian Britain* (Oxford: Peter Lang, 2007).

28 Lees, *Exiles of Erin*, p. 235.

29 John Newsinger, *Fenianism in Mid-Victorian Britain* (London: Pluto Press, 1994), pp. 64–65.

30 Anon., 'The London Irish', *Blackwood's Edinburgh Magazine* 170 (July 1901), pp. 133–34.

31 Lees, *Exiles of Erin*, p. 236.

32 David Feldman, '"There was an Englishman, an Irishman and a Jew…": Immigrants and Minorities in Britain', *Historical Journal* 26.1 (1983), p. 188.

33 Jackson, *The Irish in Britain*, p. 131.

34 Annie M. P. Smithson, *Myself – and Others: An Autobiography* (Dublin: Talbot Press, 1944), pp. 120–21. I am grateful to Liam Harte for drawing my attention to this book. See Liam Harte, *The Literature of the Irish in Britain: Autobiography and Memoir, 1725–2001* (Basingstoke: Palgrave Macmillan, 2009), pp. 121–24.

35 Shan Bullock, *Robert Thorne: The Story of a London Clerk* (London: T. Werner Laurie, 1907).

36 James Joyce, 'A Little Cloud', in *Dubliners* (London: Penguin, 1992), p. 68.

37 John Hutchinson, 'Diaspora Dilemmas and Shifting Allegiances: The Irish in London between Nationalism, Catholicism and Labourism (1900–22)', *Studies in Ethnicity and Nationalism* 10.1 (2010), p. 110.

38 John Archer Jackson, 'The Irish in London: A Study of Migration and Settlement in the Last Hundred Years' (unpublished MA thesis, University of London, 1958), p. 98. The figures Jackson provides are as follows: Westminster (4343); Kensington (4136); Wandsworth (3434); Lambeth (3114); Islington, Woolwich, St Pancras, St Marylebone, Paddington (all over 2000).

39 Peter Hart, *Mick: The Real Michael Collins* (London: Macmillan, 2005), pp. 26–28.

40 As quoted in John Hutchinson and Alan O'Day, 'The Gaelic Revival in London, 1900–22: Limits of Ethnic Identity', in Roger Swift and Sheridan Gilley (eds.), *The Irish in Victorian Britain: The Local Dimension* (Dublin: Four Courts Press, 1999), p.

266.

41 Jackson, *The Irish in Britain*, p. 124.

42 Rearden Connor, *A Plain Tale from the Bogs* (London: John Miles, 1937).

43 Beckett, *Murphy*, p. 45.

44 Lennon et al., *Across the Water*, p. 49.

45 See L. P. Curtis, *Apes and Angels: The Irishman in Victorian Caricature* (Newton Abbot: David & Charles, 1971), pp. 29–31; Liz Curtis, *Nothing but the Same Old Story: The Roots of Anti-Irish Racism* (London: Information on Ireland, 1984), pp. 6–11.

46 For personal accounts of such practices, see the film *I Only Came Over for a Couple of Years…: Interviews with London Irish Elders* (London: David Kelly Productions, 2005). For an account of institutionalized Irish discrimination in a labour exchange in south London in 1961, see Jackson, *The Irish in Britain*, p. 177. Prejudice of this kind was evident also in the legal profession. A newspaper report in 1957 quotes the Chairman of the London Sessions as follows: 'This court is infested with Irishmen who come here to commit offences and the more that can be persuaded to go back the better.' See *The Manchester Guardian*, 4 May 1957.

47 Mary J. Hickman, *Religion, Class and Identity: The State, the Catholic Church and the Education of the Irish in Britain* (Aldershot: Avebury, 1995), p. 5.

48 Clair Wills, *That Neutral Island: A History of Ireland during the Second World War* (London: Faber and Faber, 2007), p. 126. The IRA bombing campaign which took place in London in 1939 also resulted in subsequent anti-Irish hostility in the city.

49 A cartoon by JAK depicting a poster for an imaginary film, entitled 'The Irish: The Ultimate in Psychopathic Horror', resulted in the Greater London Council withdrawing its advertising from the offending newspaper. See *The Standard*, 29 October 1982.

50 See, respectively, Mary J. Hickman and Bronwen Walter, *Discrimination and the Irish Community in Britain: A Report of Research Undertaken for the Commission for Racial Equality* (London: Commission for Racial Equality, 1997); Christopher Bennett, *The Housing of the Irish in London: A Literature Review* (London: Polytechnic of North London Press, 1991); Rory Williams and Russell Ecob, 'Regional Mortality and the Irish in Britain: Findings of the ONS Longitudinal Study', *Sociology of Health and Illness* 21.3 (May 1999), pp. 344–67; Paddy Hillyard, *Suspect Community: People's Experience of the Prevention of Terrorism Act in Britain* (London: Pluto Press/Liberty, 1993).

51 Caution needs to be exercised in respect of the place of the latter two examples within the broader historical context of representations of the Irish in Britain. One critic has argued that the St Patrick's Day Festival in London is 'fraught with ambivalence, lying uneasily as it does in between an important politics of recognition and a dangerous reification of culture and ethnicity and the reduction of identities to a fetishized surplus value'. See John Nagle, '"Everybody is Irish on St. Paddy's": Ambivalence and Alterity at London's St. Patrick's Day 2002', *Identities: Global Studies in Culture and Power* 12.4 (October–December 2005), p. 563.

52 A notorious example of this was an episode of the British television soap opera *Eastenders* in 1997, which resulted in a formal letter of complaint being sent to the BBC by the Irish Ambassador to Britain. See Martin Doyle, 'Is this really the face of the Irish?', *Irish Post* (11 April 1998), pp. 20, 33.

53 Sarah Morgan, 'The Contemporary Racialization of the Irish in Britain: An Inves-

tigation into Media Representations and the Everyday Experience of Being Irish in
Britain' (unpublished PhD thesis, University of North London, 1997), p. 210.

54 An exhibition on the Irish in London at the National Portrait Gallery in 2005, for
instance, was the first of its kind to be staged outside the Irish community. See Fintan
Cullen and R. F. Foster, *Conquering England: Ireland in Victorian London* (London:
National Portrait Gallery, 2005).

55 Hickman goes on to argue that the exclusion of the Irish from the 1962 Commonwealth Immigrants Act 'directly contributed to the subsequent invisibility of the
Irish as both migrants and as members of an ethnic minority in Britain'. Mary J.
Hickman, 'Reconstructing Deconstructing "Race": British Political Discourses
about the Irish in Britain', *Ethnic and Racial Studies* 21.2 (March 1998), p. 305.

56 See the Archive of the Irish in Britain for an indication of the kinds of records available, at www.londonmet.ac.uk/irishstudiescentre/archive. See also work
conducted by the Irish Oral History Archive at www.ioha.co.uk.

57 Timothy O'Grady and Steve Pyke, *I Could Read the Sky* (London: Harvill Press,
1997), p. 69.

58 The subject has been well researched by scholars. See, for instance, Owen Dudley
Edwards, 'The Stage Irish', in Patrick O'Sullivan (ed.), *The Irish Worldwide: History,
Heritage, Identity: The Creative Migrant* (Leicester: Leicester University Press, 1994);
George Duggan, *The Stage Irishman* (London: Longmans, Green & Co., 1937);
Declan Kiberd, 'The Fall of the Stage Irishman', in Declan Kiberd, *The Irish Writer
and the World* (Cambridge: Cambridge University Press, 2005); Maureen Waters,
The Comic Irishman (Albany: State University of New York Press, 1984). The
London-based version of this phenomenon, however, is something which still
awaits a study. Examples of London-based stage Irishmen include Roebuck in
George Farquhar's *Love and a Bottle* (1698), Lucius O'Trigger in Richard Sheridan's
The Rivals (1774), and Michael O'Dowd in Dion Boucicault's *The O'Dowd* (1880).

59 See, for instance, Dion Boucicault, *The Shaughraun* (1874).

60 See W. B. Yeats, 'John Sherman', in *John Sherman and Dhoya* (London: Fisher
Unwin, 1891); George Moore, *The Lake* (London: William Heinemann, 1905);
Pádraic Ó Conaire, *Deoraíocht* (Baile Átha Cliath: Conradh na Gaeilge, 1910). For
lesser known examples of such writings (perhaps because they were written by
women), see Elizabeth Owens Blackburne, *Molly Carew* (London: Tinsley Bros,
1879); Charlotte Riddel, 'The Banshee's Warning', in *The Banshee's Warning and
Other Tales* (London: MacQueen, 1903); Ella D'Arcy, *Monochromes* (London: John
Lane, 1895).

61 See, for instance, Bonar Thompson, *Hyde Park Orator* (London: Jarrolds, 1935);
Connor, *A Plain Tale from the Bogs*; J. S. Collis, *An Irishman's England* (London:
Cassell & Co., 1937); Nesca A. Robb, *An Ulsterwoman in England 1924–1941*
(Cambridge: Cambridge University Press, 1942).

62 Eamonn Hughes, '"Lancelot's Position": The Fiction of Irish-Britain', in A. Robert
Lee (ed.), *Other Britain, Other British: Contemporary Multicultural Fiction* (London:
Pluto Press, 1995), p. 142.

63 While religion has tended to dominate the ways in which people of Irish descent
configure their identities in Scotland, some literature indicates that the issues and
concerns of the second-generation Irish north of the border are often similar to
those highlighted by their peers in England. See, for instance, John Boyle, *Galloway*

Street: Growing Up Irish in Scotland (London: Doubleday, 2001).

64 Articles about the Irish community in London in periodicals from the late nine-teenth and early twentieth century, such as *The Weekly Freeman*, *The Irish Packet* and *New Ireland*, regularly referred to 'the London Irish'. London Irish Rugby Football Club was founded in 1898 and a regiment of the British Army called the London Irish Rifles was founded in 1859. An example of literary usage is evident in the introduction to a novel published in 1915, where the author signs off under the term 'London Irish'. See Patrick MacGill, *The Rat Pit* (London: Herbert Jenkins, 1915).

65 This renaissance was funded in large part by the Greater London Council and was evident in the creation of numerous new welfare organizations, festivals and other projects across the capital. One such venture was the Green Ink Writers Group, founded in 1979, which produced six anthologies of short stories and poetry between 1982 and 1995. See, for example, Green Ink Writers, *Anthology of Short Stories* (London: Green Ink Writers Group, 1982).

66 John Broderick, *London Irish* (London: Barrie & Jenkins, 1979); Zane Radcliffe, *London Irish* (London: Black Swan, 2002). Neither of these texts is analysed here because they are set outside the chronological parameters of my study, the former in the 1970s, the latter at the turn of the millennium.

67 Ward, *Exile, Emigration and Irish Writing*, p. 241.

68 Hughes, '"Lancelot's Position"', p. 150.

69 Joseph O'Connor, 'Introduction', in Dermot Bolger (ed.), *Ireland in Exile: Irish Writers Abroad* (Dublin: New Island, 1993), p. 16.

70 Donall Mac Amhlaigh, 'Documenting the Fifties', *Irish Studies in Britain* 14 (Spring/Summer 1989), p. 10.

71 James Ryan, 'Inadmissible Departures: Why Did the Emigrant Experience Feature So Infrequently in the Fiction of the Mid-Twentieth Century?', in Dermot Keogh, Finbarr O'Shea and Carmel Quinn (eds.), *The Lost Decade: Ireland in the 1950s* (Cork: Mercier Press, 2004), pp. 221–32.

72 Harte, *The Literature of the Irish in Britain*, p. viii.

73 Canavan, 'Story-tellers and Writers', pp. 154–55.

74 Arrowsmith, 'Plastic Paddy', p. 37. See Moy McCrory, *The Water's Edge and Other Stories* (London: Sheba, 1985); Casey, *Over the Water*; Martin McDonagh, *The Beauty Queen of Leenane* (London: Methuen,1996).

75 Liam Harte, '"Somewhere beyond England and Ireland": Narratives of "Home" in Second Generation Irish Autobiography', *Irish Studies Review* 11.3 (2003), p. 293. See John Walsh, *The Falling Angels: An Irish Romance* (London: Harper Collins, 1999); Blake Morrison, *Things My Mother Never Told Me* (London: Chatto & Windus, 2002); Terry Eagleton, *The Gatekeeper: A Memoir* (London: Allen Lane, 2001).

Part I

THE MAIL-BOAT GENERATION

By the mid-1930s Britain had overtaken the United States as the primary destination for Irish migrants.[1] By the end of the Second World War, when Ireland experienced the largest wave of emigration since the Great Famine of the 1840s, this had become overwhelmingly the case.[2] Whereas in the nineteenth and early twentieth centuries Scotland and the north of England had been the favoured destinations for Irish migrants, London and the south-east of England now emerged in this position.[3] According to Jackson, the Irish-born population of London rose by more than half between 1951 and 1961 to reach 172,493.[4] After the Second World War, London became much more socially and culturally diverse. The 1948 Nationality Act conferred UK citizenship on all members of Britain's colonies and in the period up to 1962 (when immigration regulations were tightened by the Commonwealth Immigrants Act) migrants from the Caribbean, the Indian subcontinent and Africa joined European migrants such as Poles and Greek Cypriots to create a increasingly multicultural metropolis.

In Ireland in the late 1950s, major reforms heralded the end of de Valera's policy of economic isolationism. Their effects in terms of job creation, however, took time to come to fruition and unemployment levels remained high.[5] This coincided with the economic reconstruction of London after the Second World War. Recruitment campaigns by employers such as the National Health Service and London Transport were designed to address severe labour shortages. Some of these campaigns were directed specifically at Ireland, where the standard of living was generally lower than in Britain. Improved transport links with the ferry ports of Holyhead and Fishguard also made London more accessible for Irish migrants than before the war.[6] As well as providing young Irish people with better employment prospects, London also offered them the opportunity to widen their social circle.

While remnants of the older London Irish slum enclaves still survived, such as the one studied by the educational psychologist B.M. Spinley in the late 1940s and early 1950s, the capital city became an increasingly attractive option for the Irish.[7] Finbarr Whooley summed up the situation in the immediate post-war years in the following way: 'London represented an economic bolt-hole from poverty in Ireland. It was near and relatively cheap to get to. There was work for those who had no difficulty with hard physical labour and there were plenty of other Irish people in London to welcome the emigrant upon arrival.'[8]

Most Irish migrants in Britain during this period came predominantly from Catholic, rural and nationalist backgrounds, sharing a common value-system and, in the main, preferring to socialize within their own community. Catholic Church societies, the growing network of Gaelic Athletic Association (GAA) clubs, Irish county associations and other cultural organizations became hubs of social life for the post-war generation.[9] In London, Irish centres (such as that founded in Camden Town in 1955) provided welfare support as well as places to meet and socialize.[10] So did the numerous Masses taking place across the city every Sunday. A network of Irish dancehalls, which included the Bamba in Kilburn, the Round Tower in Holloway and the Shamrock in Elephant & Castle, attracted hundreds of young Irish people every night of the week.[11] Irish traditional music sessions began in pubs in Camden Town in the late 1940s and due to their popularity quickly spread to other areas of Irish London, providing another social network for migrants to connect with on first arrival.[12]

Pubs and dancehalls provided not only entertainment but also an opportunity to exchange information about potential employment and accommodation and 'catch up on the news from home'.[13] In one of the few autobiographical accounts written at the time, Donall Mac Amhlaigh captured the sense of a self-confident and self-sufficient community: 'The Irish in London,' he recorded, 'have a great life, plenty of their own people all around them, galore Irish dances and somewhere to go every night of the week.'[14] The fact that the Irish tended to socialize mainly with each other was partly due to the considerable, if often overlooked, cultural differences between the migrant and host communities. Such 'Irish-dominated spaces' were, Enda Delaney argues, part of 'an inevitable stage in the process of adjustment [...] after the displacement of migration'.[15] While more women than men migrated to London for most of the twentieth century, the dominant image of the Irish migrant during this time was masculine, typified by that of the 'Irish navvy'. This is reflected in the literature I discuss in Chapter 3, which depicts the lives of Irish construction workers in

London, and in Chapter 5, which focuses on the predominantly male world of the Irish literati in London. In Chapters 4 and 6, on the other hand, I look at novels which depict a predominantly female experience of migration by two of Ireland's most important post-war writers, Edna O'Brien and John McGahern.

Notes

1 Enda Delaney, *Demography, State and Society: Irish Migration to Britain, 1921–1971* (Liverpool: Liverpool University Press, 2000), p. 96, pp. 160–64.
2 According to Jackson, approximately three out of five Irish people growing up in the 1950s were destined to leave their native land and most of these left out of necessity rather than by choice. See John Archer Jackson, 'The Irish', in Ruth Glass et al. (eds.), *London: Aspects of Change* (London: McGibbon and Kee, 1964), p. 305.
3 According to Enda Delaney, 'roughly a third of the Irish-born population of England and Wales in the mid-twentieth century lived in Greater London'. Delaney, *The Irish in Post-War Britain*, p. 89.
4 Jackson, *The Irish in Britain*, p. 15.
5 In 1958, Ireland's Minister of Finance, T. K. Whitaker, laid the foundations for the national recovery that was to take place over the next two decades. One of the key measures was the removal of tariff barriers to free trade and the encouragement of foreign investment. As a consequence, average net migration from Ireland fell from 43,000 per annum between 1956 and 1961 to 16,000 between 1961 and 1966 and to 11,000 between 1966 and 1971. See Lee, *Ireland 1912–1985*, pp. 359–60.
6 The development of overnight mail-boat services made it possible to travel between the west of Ireland and London in a day. The term 'Mail-Boat Generation' was first used in David McWilliams' article 'Life's a Beach for Ireland's Latest "Generation Exodus"', *Irish Independent* (30 December 2009), p. 11.
7 B. M. Spinley, *The Deprived and the Privileged* (London: Routledge & Kegan Paul, 1953), p. 40. The precise location of the enclave is not identified by Spinley, but was close to one of the city's main railway stations.
8 Finbarr Whooley, *Irish Londoners: Photographs from the Paddy Fahey Collection* (Stroud: Grange Museum/Sutton Publishing, 1997), p. 5.
9 See Paddy Fahey, *The Irish in London: Photographs and Memories* (London: Centerprise, 1991).
10 See Gerry Harrison, *The Scattering: A History of the London Irish Centre 1954–2004* (London: London Irish Centre, 2004).
11 Catherine Dunne, *An Unconsidered People: The Irish in London* (Dublin: New Island, 2003), pp. 1–2.
12 Reginald Richard Hall, 'Irish Music and Dance in London 1890–1970: A Sociocultural History' (unpublished PhD thesis, University of Sussex, 1994), pp. 312–22.
13 Delaney, *The Irish in Post-War Britain*, p. 171.
14 Donall Mac Amhlaigh, *An Irish Navvy: The Diary of an Exile*, trans. Valentin Iremonger (London: Routledge & Kegan Paul, 1964), p. 28.
15 Delaney, *The Irish in Post-War Britain*, p. 175.

3

Navvy Narratives

In the closing days of 2003, heated debates took place in the Irish parliament over the plight of elderly Irish men in Britain in the wake of a documentary shown on national television.[1] Many of the interviewees in the programme had spent the best part of their working lives on the building sites of England, but due to major changes in the construction industry over the previous twenty years and the financially insecure nature of their employment, such men were now living out their final days in extremely impoverished conditions in the very towns and cities they helped rebuild after the Second World War. At a moment when the economic boom in Ireland had reached its peak, these disturbing images of destitute men exiled in the diaspora were an uncomfortable reminder of the potential consequences of a phenomenon which had, until the birth of the 'Celtic Tiger', appeared to be a permanent feature of Irish society, namely emigration. The images were all the more shocking because of their stark contrast with the popular impression of the navvy as a heroic representation of national strength and masculinity abroad. In this chapter, I analyse how literature has played a role in mediating and qualifying such heroic images in relation to the post-war Irish in London.

Historical studies into the experience of the Irish navvy in Britain have existed for some time, along with a growing body of criticism on autobiographical accounts, but very little research (excepting that on Patrick MacGill) has been conducted into fictional representations of this remarkably homogeneous group of migrants.[2] In this chapter, I look at two novels about Irish construction workers in London, *The Contractors* (1994) by John B. Keane and *I Could Read the Sky* (1997) by Timothy O'Grady and Steve Pyke. In addition, I discuss extracts from Keane's autobiography, *Self Portrait* (1964), in order to demonstrate how an interaction takes place over a span of many years between autobiographical and fictional aspects of Keane's writing. I also show how both novels draw on powerful discourses of exile and mythology to render differing experiences of the diasporic condition. These texts provide a rare insight into the lives and mindsets of a generation of men who, although a familiar sight on the streets and building sites of London, remained a hidden and somewhat mysterious sub-sector of the city's population in the post-war years. Their protagonists are typical of a generation of Irish migrants who took advantage of the post-war reconstruction programme to find work in London. But while for some navvies this led to wealth and status, for others it eventually resulted in social isolation and destitution. Almost all of the action of the novels takes place in the recognizably Irish migrant context of the building site, dancehall or 'digs'. As arenas for the performance and mythologization of Irish exile, these locations denote a marginal yet finely delineated milieu where unspoken social codes and practices of masculinity, imported from rural Ireland, are refigured in an urban ethnic context.

Masculinized discourses of Irish nationalism and their translation into migrant narratives are particularly marked in the workplace. A recent ethnographic study demonstrates that such accounts are not simply an archaic product of the immediate post-war years. Interviews conducted with Irish migrant men in the English workplace in the 1990s revealed how Irish nationalism was still seen as 'a potentially powerful political mobilising force in imagining an heroic (male) subject position within a nation for whom a normal mode of citizenship is that of emigrant status, social exclusion and subordinated/dislocated masculinity'.[3] The publication of Keane's and O'Grady's texts in the final decade of the twentieth century suggests that these narratives continued to have a resonance in Irish culture some time after the generation with whom they were most associated had retired. While both novels focus on Irish navvies' lives in London in the post-war period, neither was published until the mid-1990s. As a result the identities of the protagonists are retrospectively configured from the perspective of some forty to fifty years later. In 1991, Paul Ricoeur wrote: 'In place of an *ego* enamoured of itself arises a *self* instructed by cultural symbols, the first among which are these narratives handed down in our literary tradition.'[4] With this in mind, I show how the 'navvy narratives' of London Irish literature migrate intertextually and intergenerically between myth, folklore, ballads, dreams and reminiscence to reveal how personal and collective identities are forged in relation to ethnicity, regional allegiance and masculinity.[5]

The influence of Celtic mythology on modern Irish literature, particularly on Yeats and the writers of the Literary Revival, is well documented.[6] Declan Kiberd, for instance, points out that the tales of the Celtic hero Cuchulain (resurrected by Standish O'Grady in the late 1870s) held a magnetic attraction for both cultural nationalists and the political leaders of the 1916 Rising. He states that Cuchulain provided 'a symbol of masculinity for Celts, who had been written off as feminine by their masters',[7] a view which is particularly relevant to the texts I discuss in this chapter. More generally, anthropologists have noted how their subjects often unconsciously narrate their life-stories in mythical genres appropriate to the nature of the events they comprise.[8] In light of this, it is perhaps not surprising that the figure of Cuchulain repeatedly crops up in these texts to serve as an inspiration for Irish men on foreign soil. Storytelling provides the means for individuals to narrativize their personal identities in a number of new ways according to different contexts, and this is demonstrated by characters in both *The Contractors* and *I Could Read the Sky*. While Cuchulain provides the template for personal identities expressed by individual navvies, the inter-clan rivalry of the Celtic sagas serves a similar function with regard to inter-county rivalry and questions of collective allegiance. The county structure of Ireland is a historical relic of the Norman conquest, but the continuing persistence of county rivalries (reflected most vividly today in the GAA) is an indication of how forms of tribal allegiance dating back to the Celts survive alongside national identity. The texts examined here demonstrate how such allegiances migrated intact to London and continued to be expressed and refigured in the diasporic imagination.[9] They are, in effect, latter-day mythologies of a recent yet almost already forgotten era of London Irish life. The principal focus of my analysis is the way their authors navigate the border between the facts and fictions of this specific migrant milieu and how this, in turn, influences the identities of their subjects.

The Contractors (1994) and *Self Portrait* (1964) by John B. Keane

Best known as a playwright, John B. Keane's work was not critically well received in Ireland until relatively recently.[10] His novels have attracted even less attention from scholars. *The Contractors*, however, which is set in the early 1950s, portrays an experience familiar to any Irishman connected with the building industry in Britain at that time.

The action of the novel takes place in the fiercely competitive world of Irish building contractors, who vie with each other to turn economic exile into commercial success.[11] The central protagonist, Dan Murray, and his gang are mainly from County Kerry, while their competitors, Reicey's Rangers, are mainly from County Mayo. The rivalry between them mirrors that between the real-life Irish building firms run by John Murphy and the McNicholas brothers, who were associated, respectively, with these two counties. A revealing example of such rivalry occurs when Dan hears how a member of Reicey Rangers has incited a friend and fellow Kerryman to work harder by unfavourably comparing his aptitude for digging to that of a Mayoman. As the narrator explains, the navvy in question

> took this to heart and was determined that the honour of Kerry should not be besmirched a second time. The following day he dug like a man demented. He did more work in ten hours than a normal man would do in three days. He did not last long but what did it matter? There were others to take his place. Ireland was a brimming labour pool.[12]

One of the reasons Reicey Rangers are so despised by Dan is that, in his view, when 'a man's county mattered not at all' (29) he was a less than legitimate representative of Ireland. It appears, therefore, that what Avtar Brah refers to as a 'confluence of narrativity' is taking place here in the narrative diaspora space of the novel as one form of collective identity (i.e. national identity) is brought into question by navvies not adhering closely enough to another (i.e. county allegiance).[13] Dan also believes that county allegiance is being cynically exploited by the brothers who run Reicey's Rangers in order to secure higher productivity, a practice which oral history interviews with former navvies have since corroborated.[14]

Keane did not work 'on the buildings' himself but his knowledge of navvy life in England was considerable. This is evident from his autobiography *Self Portrait*, in which he refers to an unpublished novel he wrote 'in the Patrick McGill [sic] style' while living in Northampton in the early 1950s.[15] *The Contractors*, therefore, would seem to have had a long gestation. When the book finally appeared some forty years later, it topped the best-seller lists in Ireland and sold well in Britain too, indicating that the author had tapped into a collective nostalgia for many migrants, returned or otherwise. Keane's predilection for nostalgia is also evident in *Self Portrait*, particularly when he refers to his childhood in

County Kerry in the 1930s: 'Wet nights were spent around the fire and there were stories about great men and great deeds.' 'Men were remembered,' he recalls, 'for their prowess with a slean, or a spade or a shovel' (13).[16] It appears, therefore, that a form of storytelling first encountered as a youth informed Keane's diasporic fiction years later. This indicates that such experiences and the discourses within which they were mediated left a powerful impression on the writer and contributed directly to the narrative approach of *The Contractors*.

References to the fighting spirit of Irish navvies in Britain have a long pedigree. In his book *In Camden Town* (1983), David Thomson recounts a major riot which took place at the Roundhouse construction site in August 1846. Three local police forces took most of the day to quell fighting between English and Irish navvies and, according to a contemporary report in *The Times*, seven constables were required to transport one of the Irishmen to a nearby police station.[17] Where fact slips into fiction in such a story is a moot point. Historians are wise to warn about the provenance of such accounts, yet their epic nature has a certain appeal. Keane draws upon this kind of discourse to describe a central scene of his novel, where 'a confluence of narrativity' takes place between discourses of masculinity and inter-clan rivalry from Celtic mythology. A pre-planned fight between the two gangs of navvies takes place outside an Irish dancehall in Hammersmith on St Patrick's Night. The confrontation is engineered by Dan Murray to ensure that he and his band of loyal workers have the opportunity to overthrow the dominance of Reicey Rangers in the most public way possible. As a result, the location in question is no longer just a source of entertainment for these men, but becomes an arena for a county/tribal contest upon which collective and personal reputations will rest for some time to come. Indeed, it acquires the mythical significance of a Celtic battleground, and the nicknames and deeds of particular individuals there allude to the heroes and anti-heroes from the sagas.

This is particularly the case for the character of Dick Daly, who has infamously 'fought [his] way from one end of Kilburn to the other' (170). Crazy Horse (as he is better known) is chief bouncer at the dancehall and, like Cuchulain, whose name translates as 'the hound of Culann', he guards his master's property with a fierce dedication. He plays a critical role in the victory of Dan's gang and during the set-piece battle in question faces down Reicey's henchmen, the Morrican brothers. Their name is a clear reference to the shape-shifting figure of the Morrígan from the Celtic saga *Táin Bó Cúailnge*, with whom Cuchulain clashes on his way to the eponymous battle.[18] Crazy Horse's role in the ensuing encounter is described in the following way:

> It was Crazy Horse's greatest hour. He accepted everything that was offered. He never winced nor sacrificed a single fraction of an inch as the blows rained in on him from all sides. [...] A reputation to last a lifetime would be the reward of the man who struck the blow to bring him down. Here indeed was a chieftain worth deposing. (174)

By referring to Crazy Horse as 'a chieftain worth deposing', Keane deliberately alludes to the way in which performance on the battlefield in Celtic society was inextricably linked to tribal honour. By appropriating such a trope for his novel, he lends epic status to what in comparison might seem a prosaic dispute between two competing firms of Irish contractors in west London.[19]

In the early 1950s, the period which he describes as the most important for his development as a writer, Keane worked as a publican in Northampton. In *Self Portrait*, he recalls listening to the conversations of Irish navvies from the vantage point of the bar. 'They liked to work,' he writes. 'They couldn't do without it and they boasted about great feats of tunnel-digging, block-laying and masonry. They were clean men with sunburned faces and mighty brown hands' (64). Describing how one such individual intervened on his behalf when he was accosted by a group of drunks in the backyard of his pub, he states, 'I got the back gate opened for him and he stormed in. He is a farmer's son, weighs about fifteen stone and stands about six feet two inches in his socks. It reminded me of Cuchullain breaking his bonds' (82). Well before *The Contractors* appeared, therefore, the trope of the Celtic hero was already firmly implanted in Keane's imagination and would germinate there until the opportunity arose to refigure it in fictional terms, long after he had returned to live in Ireland.

In an interview with the *Irish Times* in July 2001, Keane describes his hospitalization after a fight in a dancehall in England as a turning point in his life.[20] However, despite regularly depicting himself as a 'fish out of water' in such places, Keane cannot resist the opportunity, in *Self Portrait*, of employing the purple prose that re-emerges years later in his fiction. He recalls how, during an altercation at his local Irish club in Northampton, a fiery young compatriot snatched his teacup and threw it against the back wall. During the fight that followed, Keane claims that he 'hit the cup-smasher with a straight left on that most sensitive of organs, the nose' (60). He then proceeds to give detailed advice to his readers about how to employ 'the straight left' to maximum effect, demonstrating his willingness to glorify the proficiency of a good street-fighter and how such predilections fed directly into *The Contractors*.

However, another side to Keane is reflected in the novel through the character of Sylvester O'Doherty, who is a surrogate father-figure to the younger Dan. During a train journey to London at the beginning of *The Contractors*, Sylvester gives his charge some advice about the dangers of frequenting a particular Irish dancehall. 'If you'll take my advice,' he warns, 'you'll give the Green Shillelagh a wide berth' (10). This warning is delivered in much the same paternalistic tone that Keane employs in his memoir when addressing prospective young emigrants among his readership. 'The best advice that can be offered to the young Irish emigrant is this,' he writes. 'Avoid Irish pubs and notorious Irish dancehalls as you would the plague' (46). Keane is concerned, therefore, to temper the volatile alchemy at the heart of Irish diasporic masculinity when he sees fit. Another example of this is when Crazy Horse rescues, in archly chivalrous fashion, one of the key female protagonists of the novel from the brutalizing clutches of a malevolent suitor. The scene is described in the following way: 'Paddy Joe was well used to taking care of himself but the size and the dogged lumbering gait of the oncoming giant sent him scurrying out of danger. Crazy Horse lifted the girl in his arms and brought her back to the Molly Malone [dancehall]' (295). Similar acts of gallantry appear in earlier novels about Irish construction workers in Britain, suggesting that, consciously or unconsciously, Keane was drawing upon a migrant narrative tradition as well as on wider heroic discourses.[21] Overall, his attitude to violence is ambivalent. Regardless of the genre in which he is writing, however, a clear masculinist nationalism informs the author's work. *The Contractors* is the result of a long discursive relationship between facts and fictions, central to which are Celtic mythology and the trope of the Irish navvy in exile. The inter-relationship of the autobiographical and the fictional across the narrative diaspora space of Keane's work can be read as configuring not just the identities of his characters but also his persona as a chronicler of Irish migrant experience.

I Could Read the Sky (1997) by Timothy O'Grady
and Steve Pyke

Four years after Keane's book was published, another novel about Irish navvies appeared, written by Timothy O'Grady with photographs by Steve Pyke.[22] It is narrated by a retired construction worker living in north London. Identity is configured through a complex form of narrative diaspora space consisting of Celtic myth, traditional ballads and oral testimony, which weave in and out of each other to create what Ricoeur terms 'a cloth woven of stories told'.[23] The narrator's isolation in London provides space for myths of exile to prosper as the narrative travels between his memories, his dreams and his moments of lucid observation of the 'here and now'. Earlier, I referred to the way in which naming in *The Contractors* has a direct link with Celtic mythology. On building sites, first names were interchangeable, and their substitution with a moniker such as 'Horse' or 'Mule' (to reflect an individual's prodigious strength) helped create a powerful mythology. This practice became part of a discrete oral tradition within the close-knit community of Irish navvies in Britain and mirrors *dinnseanchas*, the Celtic lore of naming, where names ascribed to individuals and places often referred to a key event in a community's past.[24] However, there were also much more prosaic reasons for such name-shifting. During the post-war period, many Irish navvies in Britain gave false names as a means of evading taxes and national insurance contributions, on the assumption (wrongly in most cases) that their stay in Britain would only be temporary.[25] While a man might be known as Mick Duffy on one building site, on the next he might be Mick Breslin or Mick Maguire, and so on.[26] This practice is depicted in *I Could Read the Sky*; as the narrator says, 'You could be on a site those days and half of them would be calling themselves Michael Collins for the crack' (91). It was a code of honour among workers to respect their colleagues' anonymity, and to reveal a man's true name was considered a serious breach of trust.[27]

Like Keane, O'Grady had no direct experience of working as a navvy himself. Instead, his text is based on material gathered from interviews with elderly Irish men in London Irish community centres over previous years.[28] Unlike *The Contractors*, much of the novel takes place in the narrator's mind as he reflects on his past life. The borders between fact and fiction appear to be repeatedly transgressed as the story unfolds as a series of dramatic tableaux, some of which relate to the narrator's childhood in County Clare and others to his time 'on the buildings' in

London in the post-war years. As Aidan Arrowsmith observes, the 'deliberate blurring of fantasy and reality is central both to the text's form and its content'.[29] The novel criss-crosses back and forth between the narrator's past life in Ireland and his present life in London to produce a richly textured form of narrative diaspora space. In the following passage, these images take on a hauntingly detached immediacy, as if he is methodically describing the stage-set for a play about an Irish migrant in London:[30]

> I open my eyes in Kentish Town. Always this neutral air. There is some grey light coming in but it hasn't that cold steely look of the winter sea I could see from the rock. A chair beside the bed. Tablets. A shirt with little blue squares, the collar shot. A bottle of Guinness here and another on the ledge. Maggie's rosary, crystal beads. The paper from home. The black box with the accordion. A bowl, spoonful of soup in it. A wardrobe made by people I've never met. (15–16)

The passage conjures up an archetypal image of Irish migrant accommodation in post-war London. Complete with its iconic trappings of national, religious and cultural identity, it is an entirely familiar yet surreal *mise en scène* on the cusp between memory and imagination. This quintessentially urban environment sits in stark opposition to the narrator's memories of the rural landscape in the west of Ireland whence he originates. References to highly specific locations in that landscape – 'a high rock above the house in Labasheeda' and 'the Rathangan road taking a turn in under the oaks' (15) – periodically punctuate the text like valedictory incantations. This intensely personalized yet mythologized recitation of place-names is very reminiscent of *dinnseanchas*. In the context of migration, it becomes the means by which a navvy, at the end of his working life in London, pays tribute to his rural inheritance, but by so doing, poignantly underscores his exile, cultural displacement and sense of mortality.[31]

As was the case in *The Contractors*, a Cuchulain-like figure emerges from the novel in the shape of 'the King', based on the infamous ganger 'Elephant John', who worked for the building contractors Murphy.[32] The King is responsible for reinforcing one of the abiding myths of Irish navvy folklore (i.e. the feat of lifting a bag of cement with his teeth). He responds in the following way to the sight of two struggling trainee bricklayers:

'Will you look at them?' says the King. He leaves the cigarette on the ledge of the window and walks over. He tells the lads to stand aside. He leans over from the waist, grips the bag with his teeth and lifts it over the wall. He walks back to me then and takes up the cigarette. (125)

Overt exhibitions of masculinity are commonplace on building sites, but what is striking is how accounts of such events become mythologized through repetition in other contexts.[33] In his memoir, *With Breast Expanded* (1964), Brian Behan wrote about his experiences of working as a navvy on the Festival of Britain site on the south bank of the Thames in 1950. He refers to a fellow-worker, Reilly, who, observing two bricklayers struggling to lift a heavy girder onto two pillars, 'just put his back under it and straightened up, lifting it clean up onto the wall'.[34] In his memoir of the Irish in London in the early years of the twentieth century, Harry O'Brien refers to an Irishman known simply as Sean Óg who helped lay tramlines in Dalston. One day, bemused by a group of Italian workers who were attempting to lift a large cornerstone onto the back of a cart, he went over and lifted the stone single-handedly. Afterwards, Sean Óg looked at the Italians with great disdain, and said, '"and to think they make Popes out of the likes of ye!"'[35] The account strongly resembles the climactic scene from the Ossian Cycle in Celtic mythology. On returning to Ireland from the legendary Tir na nÓg ('The Land of the Forever Young'), Finn Mac Cool's son, Oisín, is stopped by a group of men who ask him to help them lift a huge stone onto a wagon. Oisín consents to their request, but as he stoops from his horse, the reins snap and he falls to the ground. The foretold consequence of his touching Irish soil is that he ages, instantly, by three hundred years.[36] We do not know whether Sean Óg had any knowledge of this particular legend. One is tempted to suggest that, if he had, he might not have risked exhibiting his prodigious strength in this particular way given Oisín's eventual fate. This digression into folklore, however, has serious purposes. Anecdotes employed by O'Grady in *I Could Read the Sky*, such as the bag of cement story, are drawn from this wider narrative diaspora space and arrive on the pages of his novel, embellished and modified as they are, with strong traces of their roots in an ancient discourse.

In Celtic mythology the boundaries between humans and the rest of the natural world were said to become unstable during sleep. The horse, which carried sacred significance in Celtic society,[37] plays an important role in this regard in *I Could Read the Sky*. While recollection and daydreaming provide the means by which the narrator reconnects with his past, dream narrative provides the means by which his past, as 'the return of the repressed', enters into his present. An example of this is the narrator's recollection of the following extract from one of his dreams:

> To bury a horse you need a grave twice the length and twice the width of a man's. I hear then the sound of crying, a gagged and pitiful sound. I can't find it but I know it is coming from the ground. [...] A hoof breaks through, pawing at the air, a kind of caress [...] and then with a great heave the horse is finally up, wet and stained, the mud falling away, blood still seeping from the wound in the side of the head where Da shot her. (104–108)

Here, the horse possibly represents the narrator's ambitions to acquire strength, power or the social status he lacked as a youth. This, in turn, may have contributed to his decision to emigrate to England. The horse's fate at the hands of his father, however, and its subsequent resurrection, suggests an unresolved paternal conflict. Such an interpretation is supported by the subsequent account of an incident on a building site in London. Here, the narrator recalls how he helped manoeuvre a pallet of bricks being lifted by a crane-driver across the site:

> The Horse McGurk is driving the crane. You'd think he was throwing the hammer the way he swings the load of bricks. [...] I see it might move towards the side wall and I try to guide it there with my weight. The powder of the bricks and blood and bone and darkness. The wall gets closer. I can see the holes in the bricks. I wait. The touch of the Horse is sure. He lets me gently down to the ground. (111–12)

The Horse McGurk was a semi-legendary figure on the building sites of London and was immortalized in Dominic Behan's ballad 'Building Up and Tearing England Down' (1965). While the reference to 'blood and bone' indicates a premonition of the narrator's death, the Horse McGurk (in the 'gentle giant' mode reminiscent of his namesake in *The Contractors*) ensures his safety. For the narrator, therefore, McGurk represents a protective and surrogate father-figure in an otherwise merciless environment. Because this father-figure is symbolized by the image of a horse, however, the memory also carries overtones of the paternal conflict from his earlier dream.

I Could Read the Sky is an unusual and intriguing contribution to the genre of 'navvy narratives'. It draws upon factual accounts of Irish migration to London collected by its author in interviews over a number of years. By orchestrating and transforming these accounts through multiple registers into the fictionalized past of his migrant protagonist, O'Grady creates a powerful and sometimes mesmerizing form of narrative diaspora space. It is in the interactions of various recollections and imaginings within this meditation on exiled masculinity where the novel has its maximum purchase and where the uncertain identity of its troubled protagonist is configured.

The texts that I have analysed in this chapter suggest that the sense of nationhood envisaged by de Valera in the middle decades of the twentieth century as 'joyous with the sounds of industry'[38] rather than being realized in the fields and mountains of Ireland had, as a result of emigration, to be reimagined and re-mythologized on the building sites of London. In their differing ways, Keane's and O'Grady's texts immortalize a specific generation of economic exiles who were forced to make their lives abroad due to lack of opportunities in Ireland. On first impression, some of the characterizations in the novels appear to reinforce negative stereotypes of Irish navvies as 'all brawn and no brain'. The propensity to violence, particularly the fight scenes in *The Contractors*, might be read as a masculinist attempt to reassert a virility undermined by the 'failure' of migration and could be interpreted as a perpetuation of rather than a challenge to dominant media representations of the Irish in Britain. However, there is a complex set of significations and discourses at play below this stage-Irish surface. In *The Contractors*, tales of physical prowess that Keane heard as a child in Kerry in 1930s combine with recollections of the author's migration to England in 1950s to provide the generic and narrative foundations for a novel which did not finally appear until the 1990s. While it took decades to reach fruition, it is the product, in part, of a migrant and migrating oral tradition whose roots stretch back centuries to Celtic mythology. *I Could Read the Sky*, on the other hand, is the product of accounts appropriated from oral history interviews and reimagined through the narrative diaspora space of an innovative late twentieth-century novel. The identity of its protagonist is more subliminal than those of the characters depicted in *The Contractors*, but the influence of Celtic mythology is just as apparent. This is revealed through the narrator's inner thought processes, memories and dreams, where the practice of name-changing and feats of physical prowess are related to ancient forms of Irish storytelling as well as to an inter-generic chain of twentieth-century migrant discourse.

While the migrants of these novels are subordinated to a neo-colonial economic equation of British demand and Irish supply, their identities are celebrated, nevertheless, through the narrative mechanics of a long-established oral tradition of Irish exile and masculinity. The novels also reveal how the relationships of competing cultural allegiances between nation, county and gender intersect to create a rich tapestry of belongings in a distinct migrant milieu. They offer a rare insight into this somewhat closed corner of London Irish experience, and demonstrate that, while migrant identities are configured according to individual circumstances, they are also narrativized within wider discourses of Irish history and mythology.

Notes

1 *Prime Time: Ireland's Forgotten Generation* (RTÉ 1, 22 December 2003).
2 For historical accounts, see Terry Coleman, *The Railway Navvies* (London: Hutchinson, 1965); James Handley, *The Navvy in Scotland* (Cork: Cork University Press, 1970); Ultan Cowley, *The Men That Built Britain: A History of the Irish Navvy* (Dublin: Wolfhound Press, 2001). For critiques of autobiographical accounts, see Canavan, 'Story-tellers and Writers', and Duffy, 'Literary Reflections on Irish Migration'. Like most studies of MacGill's navvy fiction, Patrick O'Sullivan's essay 'Patrick MacGill: The Making of a Writer', in Sean Hutton and Paul Stewart (eds.), *Ireland's Histories: Aspects of State, Society and Ideology* (London: Routledge, 1991), approaches the work as *de facto* autobiography.
3 Popoviciu et al., 'Migrating Masculinities', p. 175.
4 Ricoeur, 'Life in Quest of Narrative', p. 33.
5 Other novels about the experience of Irish construction workers in Britain rely on more realist traditions for their impact. See, for instance, O'Neill, *Open Cut*, a *noir* treatment of the semi-criminal underbelly of the London construction industry, and Philip Casey, *The Water Star* (London: Picador, 1999), which traces the lives of four north London characters in the early to mid-1950s, two of whom are Irish navvies.
6 See, for instance, John Wilson Foster, *Fictions of the Irish Literary Revival: A Changeling Art* (Syracuse: Syracuse University Press, 1987).
7 Declan Kiberd, *Inventing Ireland: The Literature of the Modern Nation* (London: Vintage, 1996), p. 25.
8 Luisa Passarini, *Fascism in Popular Memory* (Cambridge: Cambridge University Press, 1987), p. 60.
9 The proliferation of Irish county associations across London and the rest of Britain in the post-war years is graphic evidence of this migration, with an umbrella body, the Council of Irish County Associations, founded in the early 1950s. See Whooley, *Irish Londoners*, pp. 7–16.
10 For a reappraisal of Keane's work, see Anthony Roche, 'John B. Keane: Respectability at Last!', *Theatre Ireland* 18 (April–June 1989), pp. 29–32.

11 For a novel with a similar plotline, set in pre-war London, see Walter Macken, *I Am Alone* (London: Macmillan, 1949).

12 John B. Keane, *The Contractors* (Cork: Mercier Press, 1993), p. 32. Subsequent references to this text are cited in parentheses.

13 This is somewhat ironic given the aforementioned colonial legacy of the county system.

14 See, for example, the following accounts: Anon., 'Sonny from Galway', in Jim McCool (ed.), *The Bhoys from the Big House*, http://www.aisling.org.uk/pages/frame2.htm, accessed 16 April 2008; Anon., 'Geaney', in *Face the Facts: Migrant Workers* (BBC Radio 4, 28 July 2006).

15 John B. Keane, *Self Portrait* (Cork: Mercier Press, 1964), p. 49. Subsequent references to this text are cited in parentheses.

16 A slean is a spade designed for cutting peat.

17 David Thomson, *In Camden Town* (London: Hutchinson, 1983), pp. 168–74. See also Jackson, *The Irish in Britain*, p. 178.

18 See a translation of the relevant passage in Thomas Kinsella, *The Táin* (Oxford: Oxford University Press, 1970), pp. 136–37.

19 It could be argued that this incident is indebted to J. M. Synge's *The Playboy of the Western World* (1907), where a localized case of patricide is mythologized into a tale of heroic proportions for the sake of enhancing masculine and regional reputation for its hero, Christy Mahon.

20 Kathy Sheridan, 'Interview with John B. Keane on his 73rd Birthday', *Irish Times* ('Weekend' magazine, 21 July 2001). For an account of a similar experience, see Richard Power, *Apple on a Treetop*, trans. Victor Power (Dublin: Poolbeg, 1980), p. 194.

21 See, for instance, the characters of Seamus in Macken, *I Am Alone* and Horse Roche in Patrick MacGill, *Children of the Dead End: The Autobiography of a Navvy* (London: Herbert Jenkins, 1914).

22 Timothy O'Grady and Steve Pyke, *I Could Read the Sky* (London: Harvill, 1997). Subsequent references to this text are cited in parentheses.

23 Ricoeur, *Time and Narrative, Vol. 3*, p. 246.

24 For a discussion of *dinnseanchas*, see Seamus Heaney, 'Sense of Place', in *Preoccupations: Selected Prose 1968–78* (London: Faber & Faber, 1980).

25 According to Ultan Cowley, 'working "on the lump" gave a man cash-in-hand on a daily basis' as well as a means of avoiding income tax. However, it left him open to exploitation, poor working conditions, abuse by agents and gangermen and 'the complete absence of any holiday, sickness, pension or unemployment benefits'. Cowley, *The Men Who Built Britain*, p. 191.

26 It is notable that Patrick MacGill used a pseudonym (Dermod Flynn) for his seminal 'navvy narrative', based on the author's experiences of railway construction work in Scotland at the beginning of the twentieth century. MacGill, *Children of the Dead End*.

27 For an account of this practice, see the interview with Noel Kelly in *I Only Came Over for a Couple of Years…*

28 Timothy O'Grady at the Irish Writers in London Summer School, 7 July 1999.

29 Aidan Arrowsmith, 'Photographic Memories: Nostalgia and Irish Diaspora Writing', *Textual Practice* 19.2 (2005), p. 308.

30 The novel was later adapted for cinema by Nichola Bruce, starring Dermot Healy in the lead role. See *I Could Read the Sky* (The Arts Council of England/Bord Scannán na hÉireann, 2000). Healy wrote a novel, partially set on a building site in London, which employs similar narrative devices. See Dermot Healy, *Sudden Times* (London: Harvill Press, 1999).

31 For examples of plays which have explored navvy experiences of exile and displacement in London, see Jimmy Murphy, *Kings of the Kilburn High Road*, in *Two Plays* (London: Oberon, 2001) and Owen McCafferty, *The Absence of Women* (London: Faber & Faber, 2010).

32 A newspaper report about the death of 'Elephant John' in 1999, containing tributes from friends and family of the deceased, provoked a flurry of letters from readers, insisting that he was quite the reverse of the benign person portrayed. See Ronan McGreevy, 'A Legend Dies', *Irish Post* (31 July,1999). For a more hagiographic account of his exploits, see Brendan Ward, *Builders Remembered* (Cavan: Abbey Printers, 1984), pp. 28–37.

33 For an almost identical appropriation of this story, see Peter Woods, *Hard Shoulder* (Dublin: New Island, 2003), p. 41.

34 Brian Behan, *With Breast Expanded* (London: MacGibbon & Kee, 1964), p. 117.

35 H. P. O'Brien, 'Irishmen in London (Old Style)' (unpublished article, Archive of the Irish in Britain, London, 1983). For a similar stand-off between Irish and Polish workers, see MacGill, *Children of the Dead End*, p. 197.

36 Marie Heaney, *Over Nine Waves: A Book of Irish Legends* (London: Faber & Faber, 1994), p. 221.

37 Patricia Monaghan, *The Encyclopedia of Celtic Mythology and Folklore* (New York: Infobase Publishing, 2004), p. 249. I am grateful to Fionna Murray for alerting me to this fact.

38 See Eamonn De Valera, 'St. Patrick's Day Address', Radio Éireann (17 March 1943). Available at www.rte.ie/laweb/ll/ll_t09b.html, accessed 17 November 2008.

4

Escape and its Discontents

Edna O'Brien is regarded today as one of Ireland's most eminent writers. Declan Kiberd, for instance, has referred to her prose style as one of 'surpassing beauty and exactitude'.[1] Such accolades, however, are a relatively recent phenomenon. It is only in the last ten to fifteen years that substantial critical attention has been paid to her work, largely due to the endeavours of feminist scholars.[2] Most criticism of O'Brien's work has been from the perspective of gender and sexuality, something which is not surprising given the subject-matter of her early work.[3] For critics who read her through psychoanalytical theory, it is an unresolved relationship with the mother that is the key to her work. Heather Ingman, for instance, has explored how the dual discourse of nation and motherhood in Ireland underpins many of O'Brien's characterizations.[4] This is something which resonates in her depictions of Irish migrant women, particularly in respect to how their love affairs often reignite unresolved issues in their relationships with their mothers.[5]

O'Brien's relationship with her own mother was a troubled one and in much of her work migration provides a backdrop against which relationships between mothers and daughters are closely examined. In this regard, the escape from Ireland which many of her protagonists enact through migration takes on a distinct maternal dimension, alluded to by O'Brien as 'another birth, a further breach of waters'.[6] The autobiographical content of her novels has long been a subject of interest, and in recent studies there has been a distinct focus on the subject of O'Brien's public persona and how this has affected the reception of her novels.[7] Issues of fact and fiction are particularly apparent in *The Country Girls Trilogy* (1960–64), which largely mirrors her own experiences of growing up and leaving Ireland in the post-war years. After marrying the Irish/Czech writer Ernest Gébler, O'Brien moved to London with her family in 1959, at which point she began to write *The Country Girls*

(1960), the first part of the trilogy. It is generally accepted that the relationship between Kate and Eugene Gaillard, who tellingly shares the same initials as O'Brien's husband, was closely modelled on her marriage, and it is tempting, therefore, to read Kate as a fictionalized version of the author.[8] But the parallel can only be taken so far. After all, if this was entirely the case, O'Brien would, as she has pointed out herself, 'be a goner now'.[9] Besides, she could also be legitimately read through Kate's close friend, Baba, something O'Brien appeared to suggest when she described the characters as 'two sides of the [same] coin'.[10] This is an analysis which is supported by Charlotte Nunes, who argues that 'Baba signifies the drive for self-preservation, which *necessitates* the maintenance of independent selfhood, whereas Kate represents the drive for union with others, which, particularly in a paternalistic society, demands the *submission* of independent selfhood'.[11] Another critic has argued that O'Brien's work can be seen as 'an effort to redeem herself, become whole',[12] and although, like many writers, O'Brien resists interpretations of her fiction that draw too readily on parallels with her private life, she contends that 'any book that is any good must be, to some extent, autobiographical'.[13] It would be myopic, therefore, to ignore the autobiographical content of her work. Migration was and still is a defining experience for O'Brien as a writer and this is also the case for many of her characters.[14] By analysing two of her early novels, *Girls in Their Married Bliss* (1964) and *Casualties of Peace* (1966), I argue that the experiences of O'Brien's migrant protagonists can be read as thought experiments on the part of their author and, by implication, a means by which she refigures her own identity from a combination of memory and imagination.

Since her divorce in 1964, O'Brien has continued to live in London, finding, like James Joyce (whose work she cites as a major inspiration), that physical distance and separation from her native land are imperative in order to write about it. 'I do not think,' she has confessed, 'that I would have written anything if I had stayed.'[15] However, given the persistent presence of migration in her work, it is surprising how marginal it is in the critical literature. The lives and loves of most of her female protagonists are deeply influenced or, at the very least, inflected by it. They almost always begin by escaping and usually continue to seek one form of escape or another for the rest of their lives. Sometimes the destination is London, at other times it is France or Spain or even Romania.[16] Migration also plays an important structural role in O'Brien's work by framing and accommodating the subtle shifts in

cultural perspective and consciousness that take place in her protagonists' lives. By migrating, her protagonists hope not just to live in a
different country but to become different people, and the catalyst for
this is very often romance, which usually enters their lives with an almost
primeval force. Most of them are unable to resist or control it and the
effect on their personal judgement and sense of self-image is often
profound. As a result, an emotional and psychological journey takes
place which, if initially an exciting one, invariably becomes tainted,
disrupted or truncated. The narrative diaspora space of these novels is
most apparent, therefore, in the psychological displacement of migration that, for O'Brien's protagonists, so often goes hand-in-hand with
ventures of the heart.

Girls in Their Married Bliss (1964) by Edna O'Brien

In *The Country Girls Trilogy*, of which *Girls in Their Married Bliss* is the
final instalment, migration is the central plot device. In the first part of
the trilogy, *The Country Girls*, the two protagonists leave their homes
in the west of Ireland in search of a new life in Dublin. By the close of
the second part, *Girl with Green Eyes* (1962), they have escaped again,
this time from unhappy personal relationships, by moving to London.
In the process, a shift in environment takes place from rural to urban,
from monocultural to multicultural and, most significantly of all, a move
from a deeply conservative society to a much more liberal and permis-
sive one. The latter provides the young women with one of their
strongest motivations to leave Ireland, but so does love. In this respect,
the 'push factor' is provided by their dissatisfaction with one affair and
the 'pull factor' is provided by the prospect of another, preferably in
another context and another place. During the course of the trilogy, we
also witness the gradual expurgation of a personality, from the change
of Caithleen's name to Kate, through the break-up of her marriage, the
loss of her son and finally the tragic self-erasure of suicide. As the story
progresses, Kate proves to have less and less control over her life and, as
a result, over how her identity is configured, something which becomes
graphically apparent by the final part of the trilogy when her narrative
voice is completely removed from the text.

The context for the two young women's departure from Ireland is
provided by the closing events of the second novel of the trilogy. Baba,
who is planning to have an abortion in London, discovers that the preg-

nancy is a false alarm, but decides to go to there anyway in order to leave 'this curse of a country', as she describes it.[17] Her ambition is to become a stripper in Soho – '"That's where I'll see life"' (198), she announces to Kate – but she tells her parents that she is going into nursing. Baba, like her male compatriots, discussed in the previous chapter, invents an identity as a decoy to disguise her true intentions. Nursing was a favoured occupation for young female Irish migrants in London in the post-war years and Baba, by exploiting this convincing persona to cloak a socially unacceptable alternative, demonstrates how one London Irish fictional persona can be overwritten by another.[18] Kate, on the other hand, has no real desire to leave Ireland, but she flirts with the idea of joining her friend as a means of snubbing her errant lover, Eugene. However, her attempt at constructing a similar fiction is unsuccessful. In an ill-judged and melodramatic ploy to shock him into declaring his loyalty to her, Kate sends Eugene a short letter explaining that she is leaving the country and won't be back (196). When the letter does not provoke the desired effect, she finds herself bound to the fiction she has constructed and, with Baba's encouragement, joins her friend at the embarkation point for the boat to Liverpool. After some prevarication, she is literally subject to a migration 'push factor' when propelled across the gangway by someone who shoves her from behind 'with the sharp corner of a suitcase' (208). As the boat moves 'steadily forward through the black night, towards the dawn of Liverpool', Kate, in the iconic exilic gesture of the 'backward glance', is more enraptured by what she is leaving behind than by what might await her across the Irish Sea. 'I could hardly believe that we were moving,' she thinks, 'that we were leaving Ireland […] And gradually the city of Dublin started receding in the mauve twilight of a May morning' (210–11). The traditional trope of exile as depicted here contrasts to that of escape in Baba's case, establishing a discursive opposition which continues throughout the rest of the trilogy.

By the opening of the ironically titled *Girls in Their Married Bliss*, both women are in unhappy marriages and it is clear that emotional disappointment has already become the keynote of their migrant adventure. Kate is married to Eugene and has a baby son, but husband and wife are estranged from each other after an ill-fated attempt to reignite their romance by returning to live in the Irish countryside. We witness a gradual unravelling of Kate's personality as a series of personal tragedies conspires finally to leave her in a state of emotional devastation. Apart from seeing her dream of a romantic marriage shattered by the realities of an inappropriate choice of partner, she is also forced to come to terms with the death of her mother and then her son. Like her friend, she resorts to extra-marital affairs in an attempt to escape her unhappiness. For Baba, the more emotionally robust and pragmatic of the two characters, the emotional effects of this are marginal. Kate's sexual adventures, however, are more damaging. It is debatable whether she is attempting to escape or find herself through these affairs, but what is certain are the emotional scars they leave on her psyche.

London proves to be an environment to which Kate is temperamentally ill-suited. She is unable to take advantage of the opportunities it presents for building a new life and identity. This is graphically evident in the way that she allows herself to be coerced by Eugene into forgoing her Irish name Caithleen (because he prefers the anglicized version, Kate).[19] Her loss of control over this crucial aspect of her identity stands in marked contrast to the more proactive use of name-changing described in the previous chapter. Kate's abdication of responsibility is made abundantly clear by a dramatic switch of narrative register in this final instalment of the trilogy. Up to this point, Kate has been the narrator of the story, but in *Girls in Their Married Bliss* the role is appropriated by a combination of her friend Baba and an omniscient third-person narrator. In other words, Kate's voice has been removed from the narrative because her identity has been effectively erased. Having arrived in London without any prior intention or purpose, she has not prefigured a narrative identity. Moreover, she is not as emotionally well-defended as Baba and, when an affair leads to the potential break-up of her marriage, her sense of guilt and fear of sudden abandonment lead her into increasingly self-abdicating gestures of marital duty:

> Upstairs she lay awake and planned a new, heroic role for herself. She would expiate all by sinking into domesticity. She would buy buttons, and spools of thread other than just black and white; she would scrape marrow from the bone and mix it with savoury Marmite to put on their bread; she would put her lily hand down into sewerages and save him the trouble of lifting up the ooze, and hairs, and grey slime that resulted from their daily lives.[20]

The conjunction of exile and martyrdom referred to earlier once again is clearly evident. Kate configures an idealized identity of dutiful wife and mother as a substitute for the role of romantic heroine, but neither is sufficient to arrest the disintegration of her inner sense of self. When

Eugene ruthlessly abandons her, taking their young son with him, Kate takes refuge in the home of Baba and her husband Frank, an Irish building contractor.

Although Baba is in a more stable relationship and has succeeded in marrying into money (as was her objective), she wryly reflects on how she has, nevertheless, ended up with '[an] Irishman; good at battles, sieges and massacres. Bad in bed' (11). As Brah points out in relation to diaspora space, differing subject positions can be 'proclaimed and disavowed' according to different circumstances, and the correlation between successful Irish navvy in Britain and Celtic hero, explored in the previous chapter, is subverted here in the context of personal relationships.[21] This highlights how a powerful configuration of identity within one dimension of narrative diaspora space (in this case, ethnic masculinity) can be rendered problematic or obsolete within another. Although Baba's home seems to offer Kate the prospect of protection in increasingly adverse circumstances, she must contend with the overbearing presence of Baba's husband. Fearing the consequences of being associated with a woman from a broken marriage, he threatens Kate in the following passage (narrated by Baba):

> 'You get out of here,' Frank said. She pleaded to be left until morning. It was really debasing to see her pleading. He said no. He said he didn't want to end up in the divorce courts, thank you very much, and that he had his reputation to think about. (54)

It is clear from the exchange that Baba and Frank's home, while potentially a form of cultural asylum in terms of ethnicity, is quite the reverse in terms of gender. For a separated and vulnerable Irish woman in London it is a deeply dysfunctional environment ridden with contested allegiances of patriotism and patriarchy. To quote Brah, 'the concept of diaspora centres on the *configurations of power which differentiate diasporas internally as well as situate them in relation to one another*'.[22] It is not only Kate's personal sense of identity, therefore, but the possibility of a collective sense of ethnic solidarity that is denied here by sanctimonious notions of respectability.

The novel ends with Kate's devastating decision to opt for sterilization, in effect a radical truncation of her identity as a woman. In this respect, the reaction of Baba, who no longer recognizes her closest friend as the person she once knew, is particularly telling and poignant: 'It was odd for Baba to see Kate like that, all the expected responses were missing, the guilt and doubt and sadnesses, she was looking at someone of whom too much had been cut away, some important region that they both knew nothing about' (160). The imagery here suggests that Kate has lost not only part of her body, but also part of her mind. The 'important region' reads like a prefigured sense of self which has been denied the opportunity to develop into something fully formed. Kate's narrative identity has, in other words, been foreclosed like an interrupted story. It comes as no surprise, therefore, when her eventual drowning, a form of suicide which earlier in the novel is portentously referred to as 'the gentlest way' of taking one's life (89), is confirmed in an epilogue, appended to the trilogy by O'Brien in 1986.[23]

Girls in Their Married Bliss points up a revealing opposition between two deeply entrenched discourses in Irish migration. While Baba's story reflects the trope of escape, Kate's is more representative of exile. However, in a further opposition, pragmatism wins out over romanticism, and becomes an important determinant in how Kate's and Baba's respective identities evolve over time. While the latter is able to adjust to changing circumstances and is prepared to compromise her ambitions in order to survive in a hostile and often misogynistic environment, the former is not, and is destroyed by forces beyond her control. Key factors in their respective fates are the differing extents to which they had, on the one hand, anticipated and prefigured appropriate narratives for their newly acquired status as migrants and, on the other, how (once in London) they had been able to reinvent themselves and their identities in a deeply conflicted arena of competing ethnic and patriarchal forces.

Casualties of Peace (1966) by Edna O'Brien

Similar conflicts are apparent in O'Brien's fifth novel, but this time they are subsumed into the consciousness of a single character. Like Kate, Willa McCord is the victim of an abusive relationship in a diasporic context. While she escapes her compatriot's fate by extricating herself from an unhappy marriage before it is too late, she eventually meets her demise as the unintended victim of a similarly dysfunctional relationship in a London Irish household. She has moved to London from Switzerland in a disturbed state after her sense of self-esteem has been systematically eroded by the tyrannical behaviour of her lover, Herod, whose name significantly suggests 'hero'. In a plot parallel to that of *Girls in Their Married Bliss*, Willa takes refuge in the company of a London

Irish couple, Patsy and Tom, to whom she rents a flat in her house in Peckham Rye. However, despite occasional oblique references to a shared sense of Irishness and Catholicism,[24] other discourses emerge with regard to race and gender in this household. Tom's dominance over his female co-habitants extends to beating and raping his wife and eventually murdering Willa, albeit in a case of mistaken identity. As in *Girls in Their Married Bliss*, the patriarch's sense of authority is linked to his position (in this case as a site foreman) in the building trade.[25] Unlike Frank, however, Tom's power is deployed in a racialized way. His attitude to his black workers belies a deep-seated contempt, seen in his referring to one of them as 'the darkie' who is 'all brawn and no brain' (50). But Tom's jibes have a special resonance for Willa, whose new lover is black. As a successful second-generation Jamaican film cameraman, Auro does not feel like an outsider in English society. He is an intelligent and well-educated man who belies the depiction of his race by Tom. Patsy's reaction to Auro, like her husband's attitude to 'darkies', is also unashamedly racist. She describes him as a 'coffee-coloured creep' who has 'the cheek' to call himself Auro after a Greek god, 'and he not white' (27). By disclosing these less savoury aspects to her characters' personalities, O'Brien highlights an important dimension to ethnic and racial identifications within London Irish experience. By the early 1960s, the Irish occupied an ambiguous position in multicultural relations in London. On the one hand, they were still subject to long-established discourses of anti-Irish racism, which had as much to do with religion as nationality.[26] On the other hand, with the arrival in the late 1950s and early 1960s of large numbers of black and Asian immigrants, they found themselves in a relatively advantageous position in the racial pecking order.[27]

Willa is no less willing than her compatriots to abuse such advantages. She recalls, at one point, how she refused accommodation to some Indian immigrants (despite knowing that there were free rooms available in the house) because they 'looked treacherous' (61). Victim of one form of abuse, Willa demonstrates that she is, nevertheless, capable of being the perpetrator of another. The relationship in this novel between Irish characters and other ethnic groups in London, therefore, is much more problematic than in the other texts discussed in this study. Avtar Brah points out that migrant identities are subject to a discursive relationship between different ethnic communities over time, something which can result in a particular migrant group being positioned in the ascendancy *vis-à-vis* another migrant group during one phase of its development but vice versa during another.[28] *Casualties of Peace* provides a rare fictional opportunity to see how these shifting social positions play out in a London migrant context and how, in the character of Willa, a particular identity is narrativized as a result.

Autobiography and memoir are the standard ways in which a personal identity is publicly narrativized, but the writing of letters and journals serves a similar purpose in the private domain. Letter-writing, in *Casualties of Peace*, provides a mechanism for Willa to negotiate her identity, and through these intensely personal narratives we gain access to her inner self. As the narrator explains: 'The letters saved her. They were at once her consolation and her nourishment'; like 'the streams and rivers in the limestone country [...] of Ireland' (36–39) that she alludes to, they provide a subterranean means by which Willa's personality finds expression. However, her sense of vulnerability is clearly apparent in an unsent letter to Auro in which she refers to her job as a glass ornament-maker with the lines: 'Glass breaks, glass is fragile, it does not endure. You can look at it, you can look through it, but you do not discover anything more the closer you look' (29). The suggestion of an imminent shattering of personality is clearly apparent in the reference to glass, which, while seemingly transparent, appears simply to reflect back other people's attempts to discover Willa's true character.

Most of Willa's letters record the course of her affair with Herod and how she manages to draw upon a deep survival instinct in order to escape from a psychologically destructive relationship. She describes the moment she finally walked out of the door in the following way: 'I started to walk. It was an hour of night I suppose when he thought I would not go far. I did not think it either. I am frightened of darkness but it was a question of choosing between two evils' (140). The nature of Willa's escape from Herod has some similarities with Kate's escape from Eugene. Rather than a premeditated act, it appears to happen spontaneously. What was clearly a subconscious prefiguration of herself as a free woman becomes, through the fundamentally migratory act of putting one foot in front of the other, its corporeal reality. Clues to Willa's identity, such as this, survive her in narrative form through her letters. Nevertheless, as literary constructions, they are dependent (as Ricoeur reminds us) on fictional as much as factual imperatives. We do not know for certain the precise nature of her relationship with Herod. As a result, the image we have of Willa's personality is arguably just as fictionalized as the somewhat heightened and romanticized image that Auro indulges in while courting her. It does, on the other hand, have the credibility of being her account rather than somebody else's. If identity is revealed, as H. Porter Abbott suggests, as much by the way a story is told as by the story itself, the means by which Willa has chosen to do so is instructive.[29] Although she is unable to talk about her past traumas, she *is* able to write about them, emphasizing the inherently narrativized manner in which her identity is configured. The letters are, in effect, her source of self, a form of narrative salvage from the wreckage of a failed relationship. In this regard, Willa is perhaps simply parallelling what the author herself is doing. O'Brien was still recovering from her broken marriage to Gébler at the time she wrote *Casualties of Peace*. The novel may have served the same therapeutic purpose that the letters do for her protagonist by enabling her to come to terms with her past and formulate an identity through the cathartic practice of writing.

The degree of personal transformation achieved by escaping to London in these novels is undeniably limited. Rather than offering a means of liberation for O'Brien's protagonists, the city threatens to be the site of their emotional exile or nemesis. Each of them uses migration as a means of flight from dysfunctional marriages or affairs only to find that this does not work because ultimately they are trying to escape from themselves. While the dream of a new future is what drives them to migrate in the first place, it is what they leave behind (or think they have left behind) that hinders their ability to find love and happiness abroad. These texts show, therefore, how the trope of exile can be embedded within the trope of escape through the loss of identity that takes place as a consequence of migrant dislocation. For Baba, her ability to configure a fictionalized persona by escaping to London helps engineer the partial fulfilment of her ambitions. But for Kate, her refusal to relinquish a romanticized notion of what is plainly a dysfunctional relationship leaves her subject to the debilitating effects of emotional exile. Meanwhile, in *Casualties of Peace,* the conflict between escape and exile is played out in the tension between Willa's hopes and fears. Although escape has facilitated the dream of a new life away from the destructive influence of a controlling lover, exile is evident in the way she falls into the dysfunctional and ultimately fatal trap of a supposedly supportive ethnic environment. While being a member of one migrant group subject to racism, Willa demonstrates that she is not above colluding in the subordination of another. So, rather than being a counter-discourse to negative media images perpetrated by the host community, this novel reflects equally unsavoury attitudes within the migrant community itself. As such, it is significant in relation not only to London Irish literature, but also to the inter-ethnic dimensions of migrant literature more generally.

Letter-writing in these novels also constitutes a distinct epistolary dimension to the narrative diaspora space of O'Brien's early work. Willa, for instance, comes to terms with the past by therapeutically recreating the narrative of her escape from an abusive relationship in unsent letters to her new lover. For Kate, her unsatisfactory relationship with Eugene is the push factor behind her migration, but the identity of escapee that she configures in her letter to him is disingenuous because it is designed to persuade him to call her back, rather than confirm her intentions. Meanwhile, as her protagonists are negotiating their narrative identities through letter-writing, O'Brien appears to be doing something similar through novel-writing. These early novels can be seen as her means of refiguring a sense of self in response to the experience of a failed marriage and her migration to London. Given O'Brien's success in extricating herself from a damaging marriage and building a successful career as a novelist in London, one might be tempted to read her principally through Baba's story. However, by exploring the themes of exile and self-erasure that permeate Kate's and Willa's stories, she continued to tend to 'unhealable' features of her own psyche and identity. Ultimately, while all three characters represent aspects of their author's personality, none of them should be read in a directly autobiographical way. Instead, they should be treated as fictional ventures into a narrative diaspora space which, as well as opening up new ways of understanding how migrant identities are configured, are also part of O'Brien's ongoing project of configuring an identity for herself as a writer. In broader terms, by exploring the trope of escape as well as exile, O'Brien opens up hitherto unexplored issues in post-war London Irish literature and lays the foundations for work by writers examined in Chapter 9.

Notes

1 Kiberd, *Inventing Ireland*, p. 566.
2 See, for instance, Jeanette Roberts Schumaker, 'Sacrificial Women in Short Stories by Mary Lavin and Edna O'Brien', *Studies in Short Fiction* 32.2 (Spring 1995), pp. 185–97; Amanda Graham, '"The Lovely Substance of the Mother": Food, Gender and Nation in the Work of Edna O'Brien', *Irish Studies Review* 15 (Summer 1996), pp. 16–20.
3 See, for instance, Mary Salmon, 'Edna O'Brien', in Rudiger Imhof (ed.), *Contemporary Irish Novelists* (Tübingen: Gunter Narr Verlag, 1990); Tamsin Hargreaves,

'Women's Consciousness and Identity in Four Irish Women Novelists', in Michael Kenneally (ed.), *Cultural Contexts and Idioms in Contemporary Irish Literature* (Gerrard's Cross: Colin Smythe, 1988); Sean MacMahon, 'A Sex by Themselves: An Interim Report on the Novels of Edna O'Brien', *Eire-Ireland* 2.1 (1967), pp. 79–87.

4 See Heather Ingman, 'Edna O'Brien: Stretching the Nation's Boundaries', *Irish Studies Review* 10.3 (2002), pp. 253–65.

5 For an example of how such tensions are brought to the surface when a young Irish woman in London is visited by her mother, see Edna O'Brien, 'Cords', in *The Love Object* (London: Jonathan Cape, 1968).

6 O'Brien, *Mother Ireland*, p. 45.

7 See, for instance, Rebecca Pelan, 'Reflections on a Connemara Dietrich', in Kathryn Laing, Sinéad Mooney and Maureen O'Connor (eds.), *Edna O'Brien: New Critical Perspectives* (Dublin: Carysfort Press, 2006); Maureen O'Connor, 'Edna O'Brien, Irish Dandy', *Irish Studies Review*, 13.4 (2005), pp. 469–77.

8 Gébler published a similarly autobiographical novel some years later. See Ernest Gébler, *Shall I Eat You Now?* (London: Macmillan, 1969).

9 A reference to Kate's eventual suicide. Julia Carlson (ed.), *Banned in Ireland: Censorship and the Irish Writer* (Athens, GA: University of Georgia Press, 1990), p. 73.

10 Edna O'Brien at Irish Writers in London Summer School, London Metropolitan University, 15 June 2005.

11 Charlotte Nunes, 'Return to the Lonely Self: Autonomy, Desire and the Evolution of Identity in "The Country Girls" Trilogy', *Canadian Journal of Irish Studies* 33.2 (Fall 2007), p. 39.

12 Peggy O'Brien, 'The Silly and the Serious: An Assessment of Edna O'Brien', *Massachusetts Review: A Quarterly of Literature* 28.3 (Autumn 1987), p. 484.

13 As quoted in Shusha Guppy, 'Edna O'Brien: The Art of Fiction, No. 82', *Paris Review* 92 (Summer 1984), p. 26.

14 There is a pronounced autobiographical and diasporic dimension to her most recent novel. See Edna O'Brien, *The Light of Evening* (London: Phoenix, 2007).

15 Philip Roth, 'Edna O'Brien', in *Shop Talk: A Writer and his Colleagues and their Work* (London: Jonathan Cape, 2001), p. 107.

16 See, respectively, Edna O'Brien, *August is a Wicked Month* (London: Jonathan Cape, 1965); *The High Road* (London: Weidenfeld & Nicolson, 1988); 'Epitaph', in *Lantern Slides* (London: Weidenfeld & Nicolson, 1990).

17 Edna O'Brien, *Girl with Green Eyes* (London: Penguin, 1964), p. 186. Subsequent references to this text are cited in parentheses. This novel was originally published as *The Lonely Girl*.

18 For a fictional account of a young Irish woman's experiences of nursing in post-war London, see Maeve Kelly, *Florrie's Girls* (London: Michael Joseph, 1989).

19 The practice of changing first names and surnames was relatively common among Irish migrants in Britain at this time. For an example of the former, see Morrison, *Things My Mother Never Told Me*. For examples of the latter, see interview with Noel Kelly in the film *I Only Came Over for a Couple of Years…*

20 Edna O'Brien, *Girls in Their Married Bliss* (London: Penguin, 1967), p. 31. Subsequent references to this text are cited in parentheses.

21 Brah, *Cartographies of Diaspora*, p. 208. For a more recent and more benign characterization of a London Irish navvy by the same author, see Edna O'Brien, 'Shovel

Kings', in *Saints and Sinners* (London: Faber & Faber, 2011).

22 Brah, *Cartographies of Diaspora*, p. 183, emphasis in original.

23 Edna O'Brien, *The Country Girls Trilogy* (London: Penguin, 1987), pp. 511–32.

24 See, for instance, the following description: 'Sometimes the house smelt like chapel but in the mornings it had the nice smell of grilled bacon.' Edna O'Brien, *Casualties of Peace* (London: Penguin, 1968), p. 29. Subsequent references to this text are cited in parentheses.

25 By the early 1960s, the Irish were very well established in the construction trade in Britain. Many building firms were Irish-run and wages were potentially very high. This was especially the case 'on the lump', which was a system whereby navvies, with the collusion of their employers, earned above-average wages by avoiding paying income tax. See Cowley, *The Men Who Built Britain*, p. 91.

26 Mary J. Hickman and Bronwen Walter, 'Deconstructing Whiteness', *Feminist Review* 50 (1995), p. 9.

27 For a discussion of this issue, see Donall Mac Amhlaigh, 'Irish Emigration', in *Terence MacSwiney Memorial Lectures* (London: Greater London Council, 1986).

28 Brah, *Cartographies of Diaspora*, pp. 182–83.

29 Abbott, *The Cambridge Introduction to Narrative*, p. 13.

5

Ersatz Exiles

The prospects for pursuing a literary career in the censorious moral climate of mid-twentieth-century Ireland were seriously circumscribed. Literature was a key target of the draconian censorship laws passed by the government of the Irish Free State and there were few opportunities and outlets for young aspiring writers, many of whom were forced (in time-honoured fashion) to seek fulfilment of their ambitions abroad.[1] For centuries, London had provided Irish writers with a potentially international market for their work. As a global hub of theatre and publishing, and by 1945 more physically accessible than hitherto, it became the favoured choice of destination for most migrant Irish writers of the time.[2] Members of the London Irish artistic and intellectual community were often already known to each other, having met in Dublin in pubs like McDaid's and the Palace Bar or drinking dens such as the legendary Catacombs.[3] As a result of this, there emerged a close circle of writers in London who cultivated a certain critical and ironic distance from the Irish literary establishment back home. For this new generation, the authority of the author had, in the wake of modernism, become seriously destabilized. This was best exemplified in Ireland by the appearance of Flann O'Brien's influential comic novel *At Swim-Two-Birds* (1939), in which the characters rebel against their author. As part of this reaction, the iconic figure of 'the Irish writer in exile', best represented by Yeats and Joyce, was considered a legitimate target for satire. The texts I analyse in this chapter are examples of how this was done in a migrant context and, as such, represent a vivid example of narrative diaspora space.

Anthony Cronin was a prominent member of the post-war generation of Irish writers and his memoir, *Dead as Doornails* (1976), provides an authoritative insight into the preoccupations and habits of his peers in both Dublin and London during the 1950s. Written some two decades after the period he is describing, it casts a wry, if somewhat jaded, eye on their pretentious and sometimes outrageous behaviour. Revealingly, however, its author maintains that London's 'literary bohemia' was merely a fictional construction itself and the product of the writers, publishers and media that had vested interests in colluding with such a myth.[4] If it had existed, he suggests, it was probably in the 1940s rather the 1950s, and by the time Irish writers and their fictional equivalents came looking for it after the war it had largely disappeared.[5] In this chapter, I argue that Irish writers, having not found quite what they had expected in the city, created an exilic and satirical London Irish version of the bohemian lifestyle they had left behind in Dublin. By way of contextualization, I begin the analysis by examining how this particular form of narrative diaspora space can be traced to two iconic members of this literary circle, Brendan Behan and Patrick Kavanagh, both of whom spent considerable periods of time in London. Firstly, I explain how Behan and Kavanagh both exploited a long-established trope of the stage Irishman to further their careers; I then go on to discuss how 'the exiled Irish writer in London' is satirized in two novels: *The Life of Riley* (1964) by Anthony Cronin and *Schnitzer O'Shea* (1985) by Donall Mac Amhlaigh.[6] Both novels draw on auto/biographical sources, respectively *Dead as Doornails* (1976) and *An Irish Navvy: The Diary of an Exile* (1964). By creating mock-autobiographical subjects in their novels, Cronin and Mac Amhlaigh display a shrewd awareness of the porous borders between fact and fiction in the construction of literary identities, exacting considerable comic purchase in the process.[7]

By reading the characters of Riley and O'Shea in relation to the lives of Behan and Kavanagh, such identities can be seen as part of a wider collective narrative of Irish exile and itinerancy in London. This is particularly evident with regard to their shared experiences of staying in Rowton House hostels or 'spikes' (as they were commonly known).[8] The connection between such establishments and the Irish is evident within the tradition of British itinerant autobiography. Two of the best known examples of this genre provide brief but illuminating glimpses into interactions between Irish and other itinerants in London. In *Autobiography of a Super-tramp* (1908), William Henry Davies describes how he made friends with Flanagan (an Irishman from County Mayo) in a Rowton House in Southwark.[9] Twenty-five years later, in *Down and Out in Paris and London* (1933), George Orwell describes how an Irish tramp helped him find a bed for the night at a sister establishment in the East End of London.[10] Behan and Kavanagh had a long-standing mutual antipathy and their differing recollections of such establishments were, in part, a product of their different personalities: the former, rumbustious and cocksure; the latter, more reserved if cantankerous. Despite their differences, however, they were both fully aware of how deeply embedded certain Irish stereotypes were in the British imagination and unashamedly took advantage of this to fashion their public personae abroad. By effectively behaving as 'stage Irishmen' in London, they tapped into a powerful discourse long established in the city's theatres. But within this highly attenuated form of narrative diaspora space, they also drew on the related and more recent motifs of 'the primitive Celtic poet', 'the republican bomber' and, most significantly, 'the migrant Irish navvy'.

Brendan Behan and Patrick Kavanagh

Although London itself did not provide a direct source of inspiration for his work, Brendan Behan successfully exploited the British appetite for stage-Irish stereotypes to further his literary career in the city.[11] London provided him with a cultural playground where he was able to indulge and perform a public persona away from the watchful eyes of his Dublin peers. This was nothing new. Oscar Wilde and George Bernard Shaw had deployed similar personae in London many years before. Instead of the figure of 'the witty and urbane Anglo-Irish writer in the metropolis', however, Behan's version drew for its effect on the more contemporary and controversial image of the working-class Irish migrant.[12] This was especially evident after the success of *The Quare Fellow* (1954), when Behan made frequent visits to the city, often staying with Irish friends with whom they had been acquainted in Dublin, such as Desmond MacNamara, Anthony Cronin and J. P. Donleavy. While Behan did not create any fictional London Irish characters of his own, he unwittingly became just such a character in Donleavy's work. After discovering that he had been granted a cameo appearance in *The Ginger Man* (1955), under the pseudonym of Barney Berry, Behan told the author, 'I'm proud to appear in your book, as fictionalized and as minor as I am.'[13] Despite a fractious relationship between the two writers (which, on one occasion, led to their brawling in Fleet Street), they shared a mutual admiration. Donleavy recalled how the playwright was a consummate mimic and 'embraced both the Irish rural brogue and the English cockney accent [...] stretching his point of identity to

72

absurdity'.[14] In the following passage, he describes how, while staying in a Rowton House in Hammersmith, Behan employed these linguistic facilities to maximum effect by

> waking the inmates from sleep in his thickest Irish brogue. 'You fucking bunch of British limey cunts, wake up the fucking lot of you. Bollocks to your fucking king. And if he's married to the fucking queen, bollocks to her too. Leave Ireland to the Irish. Up the Republic.' And the entrances to cubicles flew open and a plethora of patriotic Britishers poured out, the pounding feet would stop just outside Behan's door. And from within, Behan would let it be known, in his best Bow-bell cockney, that he was already up and ready to go looking for the Irish bastard who had insulted his king and country.[15]

By mischievously exploiting national rivalry between the English and the Irish, Behan simultaneously deploys the narrative identities of 'Irish republican' and 'patriotic Cockney' to maximum comic effect. This is something which, according to Donleavy, was also evident in his association with Irish navvies in the street. Aware that he might be the target of hostility from local residents due to his navvy-like appearance and boisterous manner, he adopted a Cockney accent when necessary in order to 'fool them into thinking he wasn't the Irishman they thought he was' but 'only imitating one'.[16] As an Irishman playing a Cockney playing an Irishman, Behan attempted, therefore, to double-bluff his neighbours and created in the process an audacious London Irish performative identity.

Those who knew Behan best believed that his greatest talent indeed lay in performance rather than in writing. Flann O'Brien wrote that 'he was much more a player than a playwright' and Anthony Cronin proclaimed that his real gift 'should have been as a cabaret entertainer'.[17] This was borne out when he attended performances of his own plays, and occasionally joined in the dialogue with the actors, making quips from the stalls and apparently delighting the audience.[18] After a performance of *The Hostage* (1958) at the Theatre Royal Stratford East, Behan allegedly got up on stage and began dancing a hornpipe.[19] According to his biographer Ulick O'Connor, he was 'in danger of becoming the victim of his own image'.[20] Behan, he observes, 'grasped greedily at the mask offered him. He began to play up to the role society demanded with a savage vigour'.[21] In retrospect, one can see O'Connor's point, but such performances, which by this stage were an integral part of

Behan's public persona, nevertheless constituted a remarkably astute manipulation of the 'stage Irishman' trope at a time when Irishness was by no means fashionable in London.

Like Behan, Patrick Kavanagh moved back and forth between Dublin and London, but spent longer living in the latter city than his compatriot. He first went to London in the late 1930s and returned there for lengthy spells of time in the 1950s and 60s. He, too, knew how to exploit a stereotypical Irish persona to further his ambitions and, coincidentally, chose the same institution as Behan in which to practise it. In his memoir, *The Green Fool* (1938), Kavanagh describes a sojourn at the Rowton House in Camden Town and recalls the 'soft voices of Mayo and Galway sounding in that gaunt impersonal place […] like warm rain on the arid patches of my imagination'.[22] The unashamedly exilic overtones of the soundscape that Kavanagh conjures up in this passage are strikingly different to those of Behan in the same environment. His use of the word 'imagination' suggests that such sounds might serve as inspiration for his poetry. But it also indicates that a degree of fictionalization is taking place here. This is evident in another incident later in the book when a fellow lodger and aspiring author, whom he describes as 'a sentimental dilettante […] unconscious of his own foolishness',[23] announces that a reputable London publisher is interested in a book he has written about his life. Puncturing the would-be writer's hubris, Kavanagh calls upon the same iconic persona that Behan would employ a few years later and explains that he, himself, is merely 'an illiterate Irish navvy in search of work'.[24] In other words, he camouflages his aspiration to become 'an Irish writer in London' with recourse to the mask of an equally stereotypical Irish persona and, by so doing, skilfully avoids a confrontation with a potential literary rival.[25]

Kavanagh's predilection for such manoeuvres is corroborated by accounts elsewhere. The Irish writer Bill Naughton, who socialized with the poet in London in the early 1950s, recalls that he 'exaggerated […] his accent, playing the part of the untamed savage genius for Londoners and the London Irish alike, earning him his keep by putting on a performance of otherness'.[26] According to his biographer, Antoinette Quinn, he also delighted in the subterfuge of having 'to pass himself off as Mr. Moloney' to his girlfriend's landlord, when staying at her flat near the Archway.[27] Kavanagh's strategy, like Behan's, was to manipulate various London Irish identities for the purpose of social and professional advantage.[28] However, despite his readiness to play the 'stage Irishman' in London, he had a more profound connection with the city than Behan, which expressed itself for the rest of his life in a curious form of unrequited love. In a letter to friends in 1959, Kavanagh stated that 'London is my city';[29] it appears that London represented a spiritual and aesthetic home for him, with the potential for conferring on him a literary reputation of greater international significance than that on offer in Dublin. Anthony Cronin knew Kavanagh well and recalls in *Dead as Doornails* how the poet described his differing relationships with the two cities as follows:

> Dublin, he said, was the cruellest city on the face of the earth because Dublin led you on. A city should ignore you, like London did, which gave you the English cold shoulder. A city should be impersonal, but Dublin was full of warm promises, like the worst kind of woman [...] London became the mythological counter world to Dublin in his thoughts, the hemisphere where the balance of what he knew was redressed. [...] Of course he was really conducting a very distant love affair with an organism that existed only in his own imagination; and, like many lovers who create their own illusion, he was creating a comedy of errors, as indeed he was to discover. (80, 86)

By pointing out how Kavanagh's view of London was framed by a gendered binary opposition with Dublin, Cronin illustrates how a centuries-old colonial relationship between the two cities did not just inform the poet's responses, but also exposed his personal prejudices with regard to women. In an unusual reversal of the way the two countries were represented in Irish nationalist discourse at the time, London becomes 'Madonna' and Dublin 'whore'. The fact that Kavanagh never fully settled in London was, possibly, his way of preserving such a romanticized image of the city in his mind, creating a necessary myth in order to distinguish his literary credentials and identity from his peers.

The Life of Riley (1964) and *Dead as Doornails* (1976) by Anthony Cronin

In the preface to *Dead as Doornails*, Anthony Cronin reveals a good deal about his own time as a writer in London and his reflections on his chosen profession. Some years before, he chose fiction to explore similar territory. In the preface to *The Life of Riley*, he assumes the role of his protagonist's literary executor by informing his readers that the ensuing text consists of the remnants of an autobiography by one Patrick Riley.

This 'apparent account of two years of his life', he reveals, was discovered amongst the writer's 'socks, rags and papers after his death'.[30] The operative word here is 'apparent', by which Cronin warns the reader about the partly fictional nature of autobiographical writing and, by implication, suggests we might want to draw comparisons between the self-mythologization of Riley's life and that of actual London Irish writers.[31]

Riley's journey across the Irish Sea begins after he is assured, by the socialist editor of a literary magazine in Dublin, that 'the doss-houses of London' (148) are the only places that the class struggle and the true political 'dialoctic' [sic] can be fully experienced and understood.[32] He is encouraged to believe that it is only by living the life of a 'down and out' amongst the dereliction of post-war Britain that he will produce anything of contemporary social and political significance. One is reminded here of Yeats' famous advice to Synge to go to the Aran Islands to find literary inspiration. In Riley's case, however, he is advised that such inspiration is to be found by going to the urban east rather than the rural west. Instead of being aligned with the Irish nationalist tradition, therefore, his literary identity is prefigured according to a more internationalist tradition of the socially aware itinerant writer, as represented in the texts referred to above. However, when he arrives in London, it is not so much the English working class that Riley discovers as the Irish underclass:

> The Irish were there in force and the dialoctic was in full swing; indeed it was all that the small group of harassed English officials who ran the place could do to prevent it getting out of hand altogether; it took all the immense pseudo-moral authority of the English lower middle classes to prevent large-scale massacre on Saturday nights. (150)

Riley's first impressions of the Rowton House in Camden Town where he stays are similar to Behan's. But, rather than performing the 'stage Irishman' himself, Riley prefers to observe from the wings. His description (which is reminiscent of scenes from John B. Keane's *The Contractors*) draws heavily on narratives of internecine violence among the Irish.[33] By colluding with such a discourse, Riley does not so much subvert the trope of 'the stage Irishman', but actively reinforces it.

During times of political tension between Ireland and Britain (as was the case in the 1950s following Ireland's neutrality during the war) anti-Irish racism often came to the surface.[34] It is something Riley experiences first-hand from an official at the National Assistance Board in Camden Town, who describes the writer's incomprehension of the British social security system as 'a bit too Irish' (178). In this regard, stereotypes in which Riley had earlier indulged come back to haunt him. Due to its significance from the mid-nineteenth century to the mid-twentieth century as a key site of settlement for Irish migrants in London, Camden Town (like Kilburn) has a mythical status in the Irish diaspora. But, as well as encountering anti-Irish racism for the first time, it is here that Riley has his first encounter with multicultural London. In the following passage he observes how each migrant group has its own habits and clearly defined domains to which it gravitates within the locality: 'the Irish to the Rowton and the adjacent pubs, there to continue their temporarily interrupted quarrels; the Cypriots to the room over the caff; the Maltese to check the girls' earnings' (171). Unlike the navvy characters explored earlier, who were arguably confined to a ghettoized ethnic hinterland, Riley does have some contact (if only tangentially) with other ethnic groups. In this regard, the narrative diaspora space of Cronin's novel not only reflects the status of the Irish as one of a number of such groups in this part of London, but also echoes the wider inter-ethnic discourses seen earlier in the work of Edna O'Brien.

By sending Riley to a Rowton House, Cronin positions his protagonist in an overtly mythologized site within the narrative diaspora space of London Irish literature. By sending him to the Stork (a fictional version of a pub near BBC Broadcasting House called the George), he places him in another equally mythologized location.[35] Described in *Dead as Doornails* as 'much frequented by Hibernophiles who worked for the corporation in various capacities' (93), the Stork is used by Cronin as an arena within which to ruthlessly satirize an incestuous clique of Anglo-Irish literati who drank there in the 1950s. The characters with which he populates it include Wally Coosins (based on H. A. L. Craig), a man given to flamboyant Hiberno-Irish idioms; Billy Boddells (based on W. R. Rodgers), who speaks in 'gnomic pseudo-proverbs, indecipherable to the rational mind' (154); and Casper McLoosh (based on Louis MacNeice), described as a 'dour, craggy and hard-headed' poet (156) who, according to Coosins, 'has the words to tear the bejasus out of reality' (165).[36] Coosins, who takes Riley under his wing, pays him ten shillings a day to buy drinks for members of the Anglo-Irish contingent, in the belief that by ingratiating himself with them, the aspiring young writer will secure work with the BBC.[37] But

Riley is somewhat reticent. Bemused by the Hibernophiles' intoxicated performance of Irishness, he reflects on their somewhat suspect ethnic credentials:

> far from hampering their style, or bringing a blush of shame to their cheeks, their membership of the traditionally oppressing class seemed to drive them on to a veritable frenzy, a sort of dervish dance of Irishry, which was to me a wonder to behold. The celticism of their speech sometimes resulted in a strange incoherence, not to say raving. The effect was of delirium. (154)

The Stork, like the Rowton House, therefore, is an arena for diasporic performance, its actors indulging in a collective form of stage Irishness whereby meaning becomes so subservient to linguistic pyrotechnics that the fictions they create become the London Irish literary equivalent of a hall of mirrors, in which fantasy and reality are virtually indistinguishable.

It is not long before Riley also begins to live out just such a fantasy. But it is a role with which he does not feel entirely comfortable, aware of the dangers of a personal identity being swamped by a public persona. 'We become,' he recalls, 'what we pretend to be, and I found myself, to my extreme confusion, metamorphosing under my own eyes' (166–67). Riley is clearly conscious of just how potent the narrative of 'the exiled Irish writer in London' can be and how the persona he indulges as a fiction today might become, regardless of his best intentions, a reality tomorrow. Despite these forebodings, however, he is unable to resist the offer of an invitation to dinner with Amelia, 'a lady in Hampstead' (186) with contacts at the BBC.[38] During the course of the evening, Riley agrees to dig a trench for her in the garden, which she promises to repay by providing him with food and lodging and a desk to write at. By accepting the deal, Riley adopts the persona of the 'Irish navvy writer', which extends back, via Jem Casey ('the poet of the pick') in *At Swim-Two-Birds* (1939), to the work of Patrick MacGill.[39] After finishing the job, he is charged to come up with scenarios for radio programmes, including a documentary about life in the Rowton House, something of which Cronin himself had direct experience.[40] However, fearing he is in danger of simply becoming 'Amelia's synopsising and pick-axe wielding slave' (216), Riley eventually manages to extricate himself from an underpaid and exploitative arrangement. In so doing, however, he succeeds in escaping from one narrative identity only to find himself entrapped by another. Consigned to the side-roads of

Hampstead, he must now follow in the footsteps of itinerant London Irish predecessors, such as Beckett's Murphy and Ó Conaire's Micil Ó Maoláin.[41] When, in the final lines of the novel, Riley states, 'It was high April, verging on May, and [...] I had absolutely no place to go' (222), one wonders if, on the streets, he may finally have found the anonymity he had always secretly craved. In this regard, Riley anticipates Ripley Bogle, a London Irish literary itinerant examined later; but his most immediate successor in terms of setting is the eponymous protagonist of a novel which appeared two decades later.

Schnitzer O'Shea (1985) and *An Irish Navvy: The Diary of an Exile* (1964) by Donall Mac Amhlaigh

Like Patrick Riley, Schnitzer O'Shea ultimately finds his sense of identity not so much in specific London Irish locations but in the anonymous territory of the streets.[42] The novel provides a generic bridge between three London Irish tropes analysed in this part of the study, i.e. the navvy, the writer and the itinerant.[43] Written in the style of a literary biography (complete with footnotes), it is a self-parody of the author's autobiography, *An Irish Navvy: The Diary of an Exile*, which traced his experiences as a migrant navvy in England between 1951 and 1957.[44] The storyline of *Schnitzer O'Shea* initially follows the events of the earlier text, but extends into the 1980s, thus providing a prelude to texts I examine in Part II. It also diverges dramatically from *An Irish Navvy* when Schnitzer falls down a lift-shaft, sustains a brain haemorrhage and, as a result, acquires a facility for producing torrents of Gaelic poetry. As in the 'navvy narratives', particular locations in the narrative diaspora space of London Irish literature are deliberately mythologized, including once again the Rowton House in Camden Town.[45] According to the narrator, it had

> many Irishmen among its rather down-at-heel inhabitants, most of whom, like the poet himself, wanted nothing more than to be left alone to plough their lonely furrows [...] and it was here [...] that Schnitzer grappled with strange new concepts, hewing poetic shape and form from the sometimes amorphous mass of ideas that simmered in his feverish brain. (141)

While Mac Amhlaigh, who stayed in the same hostel after first arriving in London in December 1952, was (as we know from his autobiog-

79

raphy) less than impressed,[46] his fictional alter ego hopes to find there the space and anonymity he needs in order to cogitate on his writing and 'the meaning of life'.

But such seclusion proves elusive when, like Kavanagh, Schnitzer encounters a fellow-writer in the hostel. If Anthony Cronin sends himself up through the character of Riley, Mac Amhlaigh does so through the self-deprecatingly named character of Awley MacDonnell (a clear inversion of his own name). MacDonnell is still living off the reputation of an autobiography (like Mac Amhlaigh's) written some years before about his life as an Irish navvy in Britain. Fearing a literary rival in his midst, he incessantly quizzes Schnitzer about his literary credentials. Schnitzer, in a tone reminiscent of Patrick Kavanagh's riposte in similar circumstances, displays nothing but contempt for MacDonnell, something which, as the following extract demonstrates, is shared by the narrator: 'If he unloaded six lorries of bricks in the course of the day, or shovelled ten yards of concrete, MacDonnell wrote it all down together with whatever piffling observations he wished to make on the excellence of modern working conditions' (137). Mac Amhlaigh, therefore, refigures a somewhat derogatory version of his past self through the character of MacDonnell, while through the character of O'Shea he prefigures, however comically, a more desirable literary career trajectory than he experienced himself.

Schnitzer's reputation quickly spreads. He is tracked down by the press and an Irish TV profile about the poet is followed by invitations to speak to London Irish community groups. Rather than providing the solitude he craves, Schnitzer's residence in the hostel becomes the subject of intense media attention and, like Riley, he finds he is in danger of having his identity configured by narratives beyond his control.[47] A feature article by Hank Folen entitled 'Camden Town Laureate' appears in the *Irish Post* newspaper. In it, Folen claims the poet for the Irish in Britain, rather than the Irish in Ireland, and urges 'the Irish community at large to honour him accordingly' (156).[48] Schnitzer, therefore, has an identity thrust upon him by his own community which is predicated on the aforementioned myth of Irish migrant hegemony in Camden Town. The poet is fêted by a community eager to see its diasporic credentials publicly acknowledged, but Schnitzer, in contrast to his forebears, is a reluctant celebrity.

The very notion of a literary diaspora is satirized by Mac Amhlaigh when word of Schnitzer travels across the Irish Sea. In a review of one of his poetry collections in the *Maynooth Magazine*, for instance, the myth of 'the exiled Irish writer in London' is deliberately invoked, but this time in relation to older literary and ecclesiastical narratives of exile:

> There is a profound spirituality in O'Shea's latest work: what the early Irish monks sought in retreat and solitude O'Shea seeks in the teeming heart of the city – the quest is the same and the Glenbeg poet can be as alone in Trafalgar Square or in Piccadilly Circus as Robinson Crusoe on his desert island. (153–54)

By arguing that Schnitzer is spiritually connected to a long and illustrious tradition of Irish religious emigrés,[49] the admiring reviewer emphasizes that a migrant can be as lonely in the heart of the big city as in any remote region of the world. It is a view which appears to be confirmed by Schnitzer's final book, an epic narrative poem running to over a thousand pages, entitled *A Cry from the Pit*. Written by hand (like a monk's manuscript) into an old ledger that the poet finds during one of his ventures into the West End, the work is compared to *Finnegans Wake* (1939) in scope and ambition and results in a flurry of academic interest in its apparently revolutionary literary import. However, the narrator/biographer of *Schnitzer O'Shea* reveals serious reservations about the degree to which the text has been 'dismembered and scrutinized' by critics and agrees with Professor Heinrich Mannerbaum of Stuttgart University, who scorns the 'propensity of the thesis-writers for discovering meanings which the poet never intended to convey' (161). This degree of critical attention proves too much for the self-effacing poet and, like Riley, he is forced to become not just an Irish exile in London, but an internal exile within Irish London itself. However, by going to live in a squat in Westbourne Grove, which happens to be very close to 'the medium-sized cage of north-western aspect'[50] occupied by an earlier fictional Irish migrant 'on the run' in London, he unwittingly enters yet another intertextualized zone of narrative diaspora space. From here, Schnitzer reduces 'the demands of existence to a minimum' and embarks upon a series of Beckettian peregrinations and Tube journeys whereby he aspires towards 'the "ecstasy of the infinitude of space"' (171). Even this does not shield him from the prying eye of the media, and eventually he is mistaken for an IRA bomber and imprisoned for life. Ironically, therefore, it is only as a consequence of mistaken identity that Schnitzer finally finds the solitude he requires for his writing and his ultimate artistic salvation.

The texts I have critiqued in this chapter demonstrate the ways in which a central motif in Irish literature, that of 'the exiled Irish writer', is parodied within the narrative diaspora space of post-war Irish London. While ballad, dream and oral history provided the means for such elaborations in the previous chapter, here it is discourses of biography, literary criticism and journalism. In the process, a comic interaction is produced between collective narratives of identity (including the stereotypical personae they are prone to reproduce) and the satirical counter-narratives that migrant writers create. As parodies of the 'exiled London Irish writer', who morph between navvy, poet and itinerant, Riley and O'Shea are dependent upon complex intertextual devices for their realization. Both Cronin and Mac Amhlaigh were well aware that such devices depended, to some degree, upon negative media stereotypes of the Irish in Britain. Rather than simply duplicating these stereotypes, however, they challenge and subvert many of the assumptions upon which they rested. Cronin and Mac Amhlaigh's literary creations prove to be recalcitrant London Irish heroes. Neither Riley nor O'Shea is as temperamentally suited to exploiting stage Irishness as Behan and Kavanagh, and it is this disparity which produces much of the comic purchase of the novels. For the most part, the action of the novels in this chapter is contained within the boundaries of a recognizably London Irish experience. Even when Riley and O'Shea escape from the ethnic milieu (the former to Hampstead, the latter to Westbourne Grove), they find their identities re-narrativized into stereotypical Irish personae (the former as navvy, the latter as an IRA bomber). Both novels, therefore, make an important contribution to the Irish comic tradition by parodying received notions of Irish writing and exile. However, they also reflect broader ways of conceptualizing migration as a creative itinerant enterprise, something which I look at in more detail in Chapter 8.

Notes

1 Wills, *That Neutral Island: A History of Ireland during the Second World War*, p. 284.
2 Prior to the war, Paris superseded London in this regard, becoming home not just to Joyce and Beckett but to other Irish writers such as Denis Devlin, Brian Coffey and Thomas MacGreevy.
3 The Catacombs was a unofficial nightclub that operated from the basement of 13 Fitzwilliam Place in the centre of Dublin and attracted many of the writers I refer to in this chapter.
4 Anthony Cronin, *Dead as Doornails* (Dublin: Lilliput Press, 1976), p. 131. Subse-

quent references to this text are cited in parentheses. For corroboration of this view, see Elizabeth Wilson, *Bohemians: The Glamorous Outcasts* (London: Tauris Parke Paperbacks, 2003), p. 6.

5   The pursuit of this literary milieu was not exclusive to the Irish. Afro-Caribbean writers in London also sought it out, but likewise found it to be 'more of an idea than a reality'. See Lynda Prescott, '"Coming to London" in the 1950s', *Wasafiri* 17.35 (2002), p. 21.

6   These are all typically male experiences, reflecting the extent to which women were confined at this time to playing a subsidiary role in literary life (e.g. as publishers' secretaries, supportive wives and lovers). Fictional representations of Irish women associated with the London literary world are rare, but see George Buchanan, *Rose Forbes* (London: Constable, 1937) and Leland Bardwell, *That London Winter* (Dublin: Co-Op Books, 1981), the latter of which features a middle-class female Irish migrant who mixes with the literary and bohemian set of Soho and Fitzrovia in the winter of 1959. See also Chapter 7 for my critique of a novel about an Irish woman in the 1980s' London publishing world.

7   For a later satire about an ambitious Irish writer in London (set in the early 1990s), see Michael Foley, *The Road to Notown* (Belfast: Blackstaff Press, 1996).

8   Rowton Houses were a chain of hostels built at the turn of the twentieth century by the philanthropist Lord Rowton, to provide decent accommodation for working men as an alternative to the squalid lodging-houses of the time.

9   W. H. Davies, *An Autobiography of a Super-tramp* (New York: Alfred A. Knopf, 1917), pp. 210–12.

10 George Orwell, *Down and Out in Paris and London* (London: Penguin, 1989), p. 144.

11 This is a technique which a more recent London Irish celebrity, Shane MacGowan, has successfully drawn upon for similar purposes. See Sean Campbell, *'Irish Blood, English Heart': Second-generation Irish Musicians in England* (Cork: Cork University Press, 2011), p. 69.

12 It is clear from Behan's autobiographical writings that this was a skill he had honed as a teenager while serving a three-year sentence for his part in the IRA's bombing campaign in England in 1939. See Brendan Behan, *Borstal Boy* (London: Hutchinson, 1958).

13 J. P. Donleavy, *The History of the Ginger Man* (London: Viking, 1994), pp. 391–92. For the relevant reference in the novel, see J. P. Donleavy, *The Ginger Man* (Paris: Olympia Press, 1955), p. 303.

14 Donleavy, *The History of the Ginger Man*, p. 68.

15 Donleavy, *The History of the Ginger Man*, p. 69.

16 Donleavy, *The History of the Ginger Man*, p. 390.

17 As cited in Ulick O'Connor, *Brendan Behan* (London: Coronet, 1972), p. 318; p. 93.

18 O'Connor, *Brendan Behan*, p. 229.

19 Donal Foley, 'His London Appearances', in Sean McCann (ed.), *The World of Brendan Behan* (London: Four Square Books, 1965), p. 154.

20 O'Connor, *Brendan Behan*, p. 277.

21 O'Connor, *Brendan Behan*, p. 278.

22 Patrick Kavanagh, *The Green Fool* (London: Penguin, 1975), p. 254.

23 Kavanagh, *The Green Fool*, p. 254.

24 Kavanagh, *The Green Fool*, p. 254.

25 There is a striking parallel between this incident and one recorded in the previously mentioned autobiography published thirty years before, where the author secures the support of a Rowton House lodger from County Mayo for similar literary ambitions. See Davies, *Autobiography of a Super-tramp*, p. 210.

26 Antoinette Quinn, *Patrick Kavanagh: A Biography* (Dublin: Gill & Macmillan, 2003), p. 318.

27 Quinn, *Patrick Kavanagh*, p. 407.

28 Not everyone was taken in by Kavanagh's 'fictions'. The poet Stevie Smith recorded how she found his adopted persona of the 'drunken Irish navvy' stereotypical and confessed she was bored by 'the owld Irish harp'. Frances Spalding, *Stevie Smith: A Critical Biography* (London: Faber & Faber, 1998), p. 263.

29 Letter to Elinor and Reggie Wiltshire (3 November 1959), as cited in Quinn, *Patrick Kavanagh*, p. 378.

30 Anthony Cronin, *The Life of Riley* (London: Faber & Faber, 1983), p. 5. Subsequent references to this text are cited in parentheses.

31 There is enough concordance between Cronin's and Kavanagh's lives at this time to read the character of Riley as a fictionalized amalgam of both writers. According to Cronin, Kavanagh regretted the fact that his old drinking partner had written a novel about their exploits in Dublin and London before he did. Cronin, *Dead as Doornails*, p. 190.

32 The editor in question, Prunshios McGonaghy, is a proxy for Peadar O'Donnell, under whom Cronin worked at the Irish journal *The Bell* in the 1950s. O'Donnell was from Donegal, hence the send-up of his regional accent.

33 Such depictions can be traced back as far as the twelfth century. See, for instance, illustrations of an account of the native Irish by the Welsh monk Giraldus Cambrensis, in Curtis, *Nothing but the Same Old Story*, p. 10.

34 Tim Pat Coogan, *Wherever Green is Worn: The Story of the Irish Diaspora* (London: Hutchinson, 2000), p. 122.

35 The George was popularly known as 'The Gluepot', a reference to the fact that once inside, many regulars (many of whom were writers and musicians with the BBC) found it difficult to leave.

36 H. A. L. Craig was an editor, with Sean O'Faolain, of *The Bell* during the 1940s and early 1950s, He moved to London in the mid-1950s, where he wrote and produced radio plays for the BBC's 'Third Programme'. See http://www.imdb.com/name/nm0185867/bio, accessed 6 March 2008. W. R. Rodgers was a poet and radio producer for the same station during the late 1940s and early 1950s. See http://www.pgileirdata.org/html/pgil_datasets/index.htm, accessed 6 March 2008. Louis MacNeice worked as a scriptwriter and producer for BBC Radio between 1941 and 1961. See http://www.pgil-eirdata.org/html/pgil_datasets/index.htm, accessed 6 March 2008.

37 For a similar plotline involving an Irish radio producer in the same location in the late 1960s, see Maurice Leitch, *Tell Me About It* (London: Absolute Audio Books, 2007).

38 'Amelia' is allegedly a pseudonym for Margaret Gardiner, a wealthy Hampstead socialist and patron of the arts. See Quinn, *Patrick Kavanagh*, p. 305.

39 See Flann O'Brien, *At Swim-Two-Birds* (London: Penguin, 1967), pp. 72–77.

MacGill was commonly known as 'the Navvy Poet'.

40 While in London, where he moved in 1954, Cronin worked as a freelance reviewer and 'devised ill-paid radio features for the BBC'. See Derek Mahon, 'Unflinching Gaze at the Real World', *Irish Times* (19 December 2004).

41 See Beckett, *Murphy* and Ó Conaire, *Deoraíocht*.

42 The novel is an extended version of the original Irish-language text published a decade before. See Dónall Mac Amhlaigh, *Schnitzer Ó Sé* (Baile Átha Cliath: An Clóchomhar Tta, 1974).

43 Donall Mac Amhlaigh, *Schnitzer O'Shea* (Dingle: Brandon, 1985). Subsequent references to this text are cited in parentheses.

44 While there are similarities with the tone and imagery of the texts examined in the previous chapter (e.g. the navvy Joyce, described as 'a great hound', p. 132), such Cuchulainoid references are largely absent from the work. The book has been described by the historian Roy Foster as 'a little known masterpiece'; see Foster, *Paddy and Mr. Punch*, pp. xii–xiii.

45 The Rowton House in Camden Town is referred to in this novel by its later name, Arlington House. For a history of Arlington House, see Jim McCool and Alex McDonnell, *One Better Day: A Profile of the Irish Tenants of Arlington House* (London: Bridge Housing Association, 1997).

46 Mac Amhlaigh describes the Rowton House as looking like 'a large barracks or prison'; of the residents he remarks: 'a worse looking crowd, you wouldn't see anywhere'. Mac Amhlaigh, *An Irish Navvy*, p. 47.

47 In an example of fact imitating fiction, the hostel became one of the locations where interviews were conducted for the TV documentary *Prime Time: Ireland's Forgotten Generation* (RTÉ, 22 December 2003). It also features in the film documentary *Men of Arlington* (Belfast: Hotshot Films, 2010).

48 Hank Folen is a thinly veiled play on the name of Frank Dolan, which was, in turn, a pseudonym used by the *Irish Post*'s long-serving editor and founder, Brendán Mac Lua.

49 For a discussion of this phenomenon, see Ward, *Exile, Emigration and Irish Writing*, p. 46; p. 32.

50 Beckett, *Murphy*, p. 5.

6
Departures and Returns

Emigration has been at the heart of Irish life for centuries, not least in the post-war years. Even if many men and women chose not to leave Ireland, nobody was entirely immune to the effects of migration. Most people knew at least one person, whether it was a relative or an acquaintance, who had decided to 'take the boat'. Conversation and, to some degree, preoccupations and way of life in Ireland during the post-war years were deeply underscored by emigration. Even if its economic and social ravages were sometimes consigned to the periphery of public debate by politicians and the media, the subject remained a persistent one in the private domain.[1] This discourse of emigration in everyday life during the post-war period is captured masterfully in the novels of John McGahern.

McGahern is generally seen as one of the last in a long line of twentieth-century Irish naturalist writers, and one who captures the moment of transition in Ireland from a largely rural and traditional society to a predominantly urban and modern one.[2] Migration, which played a vital role in this process, is a recurring feature of McGahern's fiction. However, it has been largely neglected by critics of his work. In this chapter I respond to this omission by looking at how the topic is treated in three of his novels: *The Barracks* (1963), *Amongst Women* (1990) and *That They Face the Rising Sun* (2002). In particular, I show how the treatment of diasporic relationships and attachments in these novels helps to illuminate the ways in which migration impacted on Irish people in the middle years of the century in a psychological as well as a socio-economic way. According to Martin Ryle, 'the self whose formation McGahern's novels portray comes to being not in "rural Ireland" alone, but in the relationship between marginal and metropolitan locations'.[3] London's role in the process of migration for McGahern's characters and the accompanying hopes and fears with which they are engaged is continually evident just below the surface of events in the novels. Rather than simply providing a backdrop to the social and emotional transformations of his characters, migration plays an active role in the configuration of their identities. McGahern lived in London for a number of years himself, first in the early 1950s and again in the 1960s.[4] The storylines of all his novels are informed by this experience and, as with Edna O'Brien, the biographical details of his life in the city sometimes match those of his protagonists. Although he was forced to leave Ireland, McGahern never saw himself as part of an ex-pat community, preferring to steer clear of other Irish writers in the city.[5] While his mid-career novels, such as *The Leavetaking* (1974) and *The Pornographer* (1979), are largely set in the city, it is, paradoxically, in work set predominantly in rural Ireland that London seems to exert the profoundest influence over his characters.

A key feature of Avtar Brah's concept of 'diaspora space' is the way that it incorporates those who choose 'to stay put' as much as those who leave, and in McGahern's work this is reflected in the social, familial and communal interconnections between home and away, coming and going, leaving and returning.[6] It is the consequent relationship, therefore, between his protagonists' sense of self and the discourses of identity through which their journeys are mediated that concern me in this chapter. London provides both the actual and the imaginative axis around which much of this process takes place. Its precise role differs according to the aspirations and preoccupations of the novels' protagonists, but the city is variously depicted as a nostalgic paradise, the gateway to modernity or a place of unhappy incarceration. The social and cultural discord of all three novels rests on an uneasy relationship between 'those who leave' and 'those who stay' and the resultant ways in which individuals are incorporated, often unwittingly, into the emotional dynamics of diaspora. As was the case in O'Brien's work, letters (whether sent or not) play a crucial role, emphasizing the ways in which texts sometimes literally configure migrant identities within the narrative diaspora space of London Irish literature.

The Barracks (1963) by John McGahern

In McGahern's debut novel the experience and aftermath of emigration is a central theme. Having returned home from London after the Second World War to marry and settle down in a village in rural Ireland, the novel's main protagonist, Elizabeth Reegan, continues to be haunted by memories of a migrant life and love affair in the city. London had enabled Elizabeth to discover and explore a sense of individuality denied her in the moral and religious confines of mid-twentieth-century Ireland. As a young nurse in the city, she came into contact with a much wider range of people than she would have in Ireland, including a doctor who became her lover and would change her life forever. Now, as she struggles to cope with the drudgery of the rural domestic routine she had originally gone to London to escape, the memory of a younger and more liberated urban self preoccupies her thoughts. A distinct tone of yearning is evident as she recalls 'the people in her life crowding into the vividness of the memory, shifting with each sudden change and she there at the heart of everything, alive, laughing and crying and calm'.[7]

Whitechapel, the area of London she settles in, plays a key role in this respect. As a neighbourhood which had accommodated migrants from many different countries over the centuries, it offers a place where Elizabeth can explore a multicultural world, unavailable to her in Ireland. Today, Whitechapel is most associated with the Bangladeshi and Somali communities, but during the early twentieth century it was home to a different community, the enduring presence of which Elizabeth encounters in the 'streets of London at all hours, groping for the Jewish names on the lintels – Frank, Levine, Lerner, Goldsberg, Botzmans – above the awnings in the little market off Commercial Road', while the sun glitters 'on the red-stained glass over the little Yiddish Theatre' (186). Elizabeth is clearly fascinated by the otherness of the neighbourhood in which she lives. It is a potential 'contact zone', a cosmopolitan space where people 'previously separated by geographic and historical disjunctures' might meet and their 'trajectories now intersect'.[8] She is unaware, however, that she is also following in the footsteps of her own migrant antecedents, as a century earlier the area was a favoured place of settlement for the Irish who found employment there on the docks.[9] The novel highlights, therefore, intra-ethnic as well as inter-ethnic dimensions of diaspora space. This is also illustrated by the way in which London provides Elizabeth with a romantic relationship with an Irishman that crosses class boundaries, something that would have been much less likely in Ireland at this time.

Her affair with Michael Halliday is described as 'the deepest relationship of her adult life' (65). After her return to Ireland, it lives on in her memories of 'enriched and indestructible days' (86). Through the novels, concerts and plays to which Halliday introduces her, Elizabeth is able to exercise a new sense of identity, informed by London culture and sophistication. When she realizes that 'suddenly, one morning, the first morning of the world, she had woken up to herself' (87), she discovers an identity for which she had always had the potential, but had lacked the opportunity to express. These feelings are nostalgically regenerated years later and she finds herself 'ecstatic with remembrance' (187), as elegiac images of an urban pastoral come to mind: 'long London evenings that were now lovely in the memory' (65) or 'the walks in the evening in the great parks' (88). In other words, while Elizabeth may have left London physically, the city continues to preoccupy her thoughts and emotions. It is notable, however, that the precise locations she frequents while living in London – the city's parks – represent an intermediate zone between her rural past and her urban future, signalling a deeper dichotomy. If the latter represents the enquiring and adventurous side to her personality, the former stands for her more conservative and fatalistic side. This rural/urban opposition which is so deeply embedded in her psyche produces a conflict of allegiance that she struggles for the rest of her life to resolve.

The extent to which Elizabeth has been acculturated to city life is vividly brought home when she first arrives back in Ireland. For friends and family, 'her age and years in London gave her position in their eyes' (50). While her experience of the city wins her a degree of grudging respect among her peers, it serves to distance her from them in moral as well as socio-economic terms. Perceptions of her sexual attractiveness are enhanced among friends and family by the fashionable clothes she now wears. However, this is not something she is at liberty to capitalize on in the loveless marriage and moral confines of the country to which she has returned to live out the rest of her life. As a consequence, Elizabeth tries to suppress her memories of London, graphically illustrated by the fact that she locks away the love-letters, books and money of her London years. By doing so, she metaphorically incarcerates her past and by implication that part of her identity. Each of these now-hidden possessions represents unresolved aspects of her self-image: the money, her now relative wealth; the books, which had 'grown in her life as if they had been grafted there' (39), aspirations towards an intellectual life; the love-letters and the narratives they contain, a potential threat to her marriage. The books and letters, in particular, represent two forms of textual liberation for Elizabeth. The former signify the love of literature she shared with Halliday and, through it, an intellectual relationship unavailable to her back home. The latter represent her deepest emotional desires and a place where she was able to realize her burgeoning sexuality. In an act of literary self-censorship (which mirrors Irish legislation of which McGahern was himself a victim) Elizabeth conceals the letters in a trunk and, by so doing, effectively condemns the London part of her identity to a form of narrative exile.

Yet, just as her rural identity had continued to assert itself while she was in London, her urban identity asserts itself when she returns to Ireland. It is clear, at the tragic close to the novel, that memories of her life in London will pursue her to the grave and become, as George O'Brien argues, 'a medium through which the mystery of death which she must now face can be contemplated and intensified'.[10] In the narrative circularity which is a general feature of McGahern's novels, Elizabeth's predicament mirrors a premonition (or prefiguration) that she had at the start of the novel when she had 'blanched before this vision of herself growing old and blind with the pain of ludicrous longing' (16). As she lies bedridden with cancer, attended by nurses who remind her of herself at their age, she imagines 'her heart and breasts laid bare on the lurid anatomy charts' at the London nursing hospital where she studied as a young woman (214). Perhaps, as Eamon Maher argues, she 'achieves peace when she stops fighting against what she cannot control',[11] but this disturbing image suggests that Elizabeth has fatalistically concluded that her physical condition is the result of the emotional damage she suffered when her love affair was abruptly curtailed by Halliday.

Amongst Women (1990) by John McGahern

In McGahern's penultimate novel, London once more plays a pivotal role. Despite being described by one critic as 'having only the sketchiest of existences in the novel',[12] the city nevertheless serves as the catalyst for much of the emotional purchase of the story. The novel consists of a series of leave-takings, homecomings and letters which weave a complex web of attachments, belongings and family ruptures, at the centre of which is the patriarchal figure of Moran. For this veteran of the War of Independence, the traditional narrative of national self-determination is paramount in his attitude to emigration. London, for Moran, is nothing more than the home of the enemy, somewhere 'a lot of our people go wrong' and the place he perceives as having stolen his children from him.[13] For his sons and daughters, however, the city provides a means of escape from economic penury and social isolation, thus overriding questions of national and familial allegiance. In her research into Irish women's migration to London, Louise Ryan found that 'familial networks offered mutual systems of support, loyalty and obligation but these often operated in particularly gendered ways'. She adds that 'the extent to which migrants engaged with these networks varied according to individual choices and circumstances'.[14] This is illustrated in the differing relationships between Moran and his children, which reveal how identities and attachments are gendered in the novel. The trope of 'Mother Ireland' and feminized representations of Ireland are well documented in Irish cultural studies and they have a particularly deep resonance in the context of diasporic literature. The role of the father-figure in *Amongst Women* provides a less explored, but equally revealing, aspect of Irishness and how it is affected by the experience of migration.

Like many of the events in his novels, the rift between father and son has strong autobiographical underpinnings, as confirmed in McGahern's memoirs.[15] For Luke and Michael, London holds out the prospect of economic and social freedom and provides the means of a conclusive break with their father and the past. This is especially the case for Luke, the eldest, who makes a concerted attempt to integrate into the life of the city: he works hard, takes night classes and qualifies as an accountant; he socializes with Londoners rather than with fellow migrants; he has an English girlfriend and an English business associate. He has, for all intents and purposes, become a Londoner and severed his links with Ireland. But his refusal to keep in touch with home, even by letter, is a source of increasing irritation for his father. When Moran confronts his son over the issue, we witness a struggle for supremacy between conflicting narratives of Irish identity. While Moran represents the conservative notion of nationhood, epitomized by de Valera, Luke represents the modernizing Ireland of the Lemass era.[16] After repeated lobbying from his siblings, Luke agrees to go home for his younger sister's wedding. However, the visit does nothing to improve the relationship with his father, which remains strained and detached. When confronted by Maggie about why he did not make more of an effort at rapprochement, he replies, "'I left Ireland a long time ago'" (155), a statement which confirms that, whatever efforts he might have made to reconnect with his family, Ireland (and by implication his sense of an Irish identity) is something he has given up for good. For the youngest son, Michael, the story is very similar. As he reaches adolescence, he begins to feel increasingly smothered by his father's overbearing presence in the home and eventually rebels, with predictable consequences.

Verbal confrontations between father and son become increasingly frequent and after Moran resorts to physically beating Michael, he runs away to London for good.

Despite sharing an urge to escape like their brothers, emigration proves to be a more ambivalent experience for Moran's daughters. Maggie, who is the first to leave, goes into nursing at the same hospital in Whitechapel as Elizabeth Reegan in *The Barracks* and marries Mark, an Irish navvy whom she meets at a Legion of Mary dance in Cricklewood. Moran does not approve of Mark, who dresses like a 'teddy boy' and appears to be anything but the heroic figure familiar from earlier texts. However, we do not learn a great deal about Maggie's life in London. Instead, her sense of belonging is directed much more towards Ireland. Although she finds diversion and opportunity in the big city, she makes frequent visits to Ireland (unlike her brothers) and her regular letters to her father help maintain for her a vital connection to family and nation. But, crucially, the letters also serve the same purpose for her father, who memorizes 'each phrase by heart' (65). As a result, their correspondence creates a narrative diaspora space within which Moran's and his daughters' identities are configured. Despite his disapproval of his daughter's choice of where and with whom she settles down, her letters and visits maintain for Moran a form of social discourse that would, otherwise, be absent from his life. By way of illustration, the following passage warrants quotation in full:

> These visits of his daughters from London and Dublin were to flow like relief through the house. They brought distraction, something to look forward to, something to mull over after they had gone. Above all they brought the bracing breath of the outside, an outside Moran refused to accept unless it came from the family. Without it there would have been an ingrown wilting. For the girls the regular comings and goings restored their superior sense of self, a superiority they had received intact from Moran and which was little acknowledged by the wide world in which they had to work and live. That unexamined notion of superiority was often badly shaken and in need of restoration each time they came home. Each time he met them at the station his very presence affirmed and reaffirmed again as he kissed them goodbye. Within the house the outside world was shut out. There was only Moran, their beloved father; within his shadow and the walls of the house they felt that they would never die; and each time they came to Great Meadow they grew again into the wholeness of being the unique and separate Morans. (93–94)

Moran, therefore, is the pivot around which his daughters' lives revolve, but at the same time he is incorporated into a collective narrative of migration which is reinforced each time they visit or write. Although he is intrinsically antipathetic to his country's oldest enemy, he is still drawn to its 'otherness', as the above passage shows, in the form of the 'bracing breath of the outside' that his daughters' letters and visits afford him. While they pay regular homage to their father by maintaining these links, it is also apparent that Moran's daughters no longer share all his values. Migration inevitably changes the attitudes and outlook of all of Moran's offspring, albeit more overtly in the case of his sons than in that of his daughters. Ultimately, the patriarch must reconcile himself to the fact that the country he fought for in his youth is no longer the country his descendants necessarily recognize as theirs.

That They May Face the Rising Sun (2002) by John McGahern

John McGahern's final novel recounts a year in the life of a small rural community in the north-west of Ireland. It is an ensemble piece with no single central character and is, as Eamonn Hughes observed, a novel as much about 'what does not happen' as about what does.[17] Although primarily set in Ireland, London plays an important role in the novel as the location where Johnny Murphy (a migrant of twenty years' standing) has lived for a large part of his life. It opens with preparations for Johnny's annual visit home and concludes with his funeral in Ireland, which is conducted according to the ancient custom from which the novel derives its title.[18] In this regard it is framed by the experience of return migration. By revealing how an emigré's sense of belonging to his homeland can be fatally affected by the actions of the community he leaves behind, it provides subtle insights into the psychological and cultural dynamics of diaspora. We learn that Johnny's original impetus for going to London was to follow a woman he was in love with, but who, he eventually discovers, did not reciprocate his feelings. In a symbolic act of severing his links with Ireland, he shoots his two gun-dogs and commits himself to a new life abroad. Johnny's experiences as a migrant in London very much resemble those of the immediate post-war generation. He works in the Ford car factory in Dagenham, socializes in the betting office or the local pub and shares digs with a group of Galway navvies.[19] The following description of his spartan accommodation would be familiar to many London Irishmen of the mail-boat generation:

> There was a table in the room, a high-backed chair, a single bed, an armchair for reading and listening to the radio, a gas fire in the small grate. In the mantel above the grate he always kept a pile of coins for the meter on the landing. A gas cooker and a sink were in the corner of the room inside the door. He didn't have a television.[20]

The similarities between the description of this room and that in *I Could Read the Sky* are striking, but, unlike the narrator of O'Grady's novel, Johnny has kept his social ties with Ireland intact and when he travels home each summer he is welcomed back wholeheartedly, even ritualistically, by the community he left behind.

In the opening scene of the novel, when he returns for one of his visits, Johnny is happy and the general mood is buoyant. He clearly feels more at home within the small rural community where he grew up than living the rather empty existence he now leads in the metropolis. In the following exchange, which opens with the voice of his friend, Patrick Ryan, he tries to be philosophical about the way his life has worked out:

> "People had to go. They had no choice. You went and had no need to go."
> "I know. I know. I know."
> "You'd be on the pig's back now, lad, if you'd stayed."
> "We'd all be rich if we knew the result of tomorrow's races." (77)

It is obvious that while Johnny regrets his original decision to leave Ireland, he has resigned himself to living out the rest of his life in London. However, the prospect of a permanent return to Ireland unexpectedly presents itself after he is made redundant at Ford's. Unfortunately, when he divulges his intentions to his family and friends back home, their reaction is not what he expects and reveals shortcomings in an otherwise mutually convenient annual arrangement. Doubts are cast on the wisdom of returning for good after such a long time away. His brother Jamesie proclaims, "'There's a big differ between visiting and belonging'" (95), a comment which suggests that Johnny might experience problems readjusting to Irish rural life after living so long in the city. However, it also implies that he relinquished his rights to full membership of the community once he left. As in *Amongst Women*, the narrative diaspora space of migrant correspondence acts as a domain within which configurations of personal and collective identity are radically contested. A diplomatically worded letter is sent to Johnny warning him of the difficulties he might encounter if he chooses to return permanently. Such is Johnny's naïve respect for their judgement, he fails to see that the letter (while well-meaning) represents the self-interests of those who stayed over those who left. The fact that Ruttledge, a central character in the novel, plays a key role in drafting the letter provides a somewhat ironic twist to these events. Upon returning from London himself, some years before, Ruttledge 'had been shunned by near-neighbours' (21), but eventually succeeded in reintegrating into the community from which he originally came.

Ultimately, Johnny is offered a new job by his landlord and he decides to stay in London after all. Although this is a new lease of life for him financially, he knows his hopes of a permanent return to Ireland have been dashed. Condemned never to achieve the home he desires, his identity appears to be adrift from its moorings on both sides of the Irish Sea. He is, as one interviewee described himself in a documentary film about the Irish in London, 'a lost Irishman'.[21] Johnny, nevertheless, is stoical in the face of disappointment. "'You don't get reruns in life like you do in a play'" he remarks, adding, "'There's no turning back now anyhow'" (263). Events, however, have taken their toll and Johnny's sudden death soon afterwards represents a poignant coda to the novel. Despite his philosophical attitude to his circumstances, it appears that his frustration at being denied the opportunity to determine his own destiny has accelerated his demise. It is left to the priest at his graveside to voice the words, which could be read as an indictment of the tragically finite generosity of Johnny's friends and family: "'These people forced into England through no fault of their own were often looked down on – most unjustly looked down upon – by some whose only good was that they managed to remain at home with little cause to look down on anybody'" (295). Regardless of his regular visits home, Johnny ultimately discovers that he is still classified as an outsider in Ireland because of his original decision to emigrate. Even though his body is finally buried there, Johnny is marginalized by the community to which he had hoped to return permanently, and his identity is left suspended and inconclusive in the narrative diaspora space of escape and return that defined his life.

Across the three novels I have discussed in this chapter, a collective diasporic dialogue takes place between 'those who go' and 'those who stay', differentially influencing how individual migrant identities are constructed according to personal circumstances. This is played out in a series of variations on the theme of leaving and returning. At one end of this spectrum there is Elizabeth Reegan, who returns to Ireland after a curtailed love affair, but finds that she is psychologically and emotionally still an exile. London (and the younger, freer self she associates with the city) accompanies her home through her thoughts and regrets and becomes a symbol for a life not followed. Conversely, Johnny Murphy, another victim of a failed love affair, desires to return permanently to Ireland, but finds his aspirations thwarted by the community he left, something which seems all the more tragic when set against the happiness he finds on his visits home each summer. Finally, in *Amongst Women*, the constant movement between home and away is clearly gendered and incorporates a patriarchal figure into a diasporic experience of which he never anticipated being a part. In relation to diaspora, these novels all demonstrate the importance, not only of the relationship between migrant and receiving community, but also of the relationship between migrant and sending community.

In lieu of visits, letters again constitute an epistolary form of narrative diaspora space in the novels. In *The Barracks*, Elizabeth's letters are not so much a link with home but a link with her life and love affair in London, and their concealment in a trunk acts as a metaphor for the suppression of a narrative identity she can no longer acknowledge. In *Amongst Women*, the contents of these letters do not necessarily please Moran, but they nevertheless serve to maintain an emotional link between parent and offspring. Finally, in *That They May Face the Rising Sun*, a single letter has a devastating effect because of its undue power to influence Johnny's decision whether or not to return to Ireland. Although written by a single individual, it represents the collective responsibility of a community for dissuading one of its members from realizing his desire for reunion. These novels highlight the ways in which migrant identities are configured in close if uneasy relationships between those who leave, those who stay and those who return. They demonstrate how a dialogue with home and family often continues for some time after a migrant has left and how migration is an open-ended process in which the significance of departure, arrival and return alter according to changing circumstances over time. The narrative diaspora space of McGahern's work offers a way of transforming our understanding of migration, therefore, from an essentially linear and autonomous process to one of dynamic interdependence between individuals and communities both at home and abroad.

Notes

1   Ryan, 'Irish Emigration to Britain since World War II', pp. 66–67.
2   Joe Cleary, *Outrageous Fortune: Capital and Culture in Modern Ireland* (Dublin: Field Day, 2007), pp. 154–65.
3   Martin Ryle, 'Place, Time and Perspective in John McGahern's Fiction'. Seminar paper given at the Institute for Study of European Transformations, London Metropolitan University (28 February 2007).
4   McGahern's time in London in the 1950s is recalled in a memoir by a close friend. See Tony Whelan, *The Last Chapter* (Leicester: Matador, 2010).
5   In a letter to Antoinette Quinn in 1997, McGahern recalled how, on Christmas Day 1965, he happened to see Patrick Kavanagh unsuccessfully trying to gain access to a pub in Westbourne Park, but avoided speaking to the poet and giving him 'an opportunity to practise his savagery on him'. Quinn, *Patrick Kavanagh*, p. 450.
6   Brah, *Cartographies of Diaspora*, p. 181.
7   John McGahern, *The Barracks* (London: Faber & Faber, 1983), pp. 186–87. Subsequent references to this text are cited in parentheses.
8   Mary Louise Pratt, *Imperial Eyes: Travel Writing and Transculturation* (London: Routledge, 1992), p. 7.
9   Lees, *Exiles of Erin*, p. 56.
10 O'Brien, 'The Aesthetics of Exile', p. 39.
11 Eamon Maher, *John McGahern: From the Local to the Universal* (Dublin: Liffey Press, 2003), p. 20.
12 Cleary, *Outrageous Fortune*, p. 217.
13 John McGahern, *Amongst Women* (London: Faber & Faber, 1990), p. 49. Subsequent references to this text are cited in parentheses. This is also the case for Mahony, the father of the boy protagonist in McGahern's second novel, who describes London as 'rotten, full of filth and dirt'. John McGahern, *The Dark* (London: Faber & Faber, 1983), p. 108.
14 Ryan, 'Family Matters', p. 357.
15 John McGahern, *Memoir* (Faber & Faber, 2005), pp. 213–14.
16 Sean Lemass's government is generally credited with modernizing the Irish economy in the late 1950s. See Lee, *Ireland 1912–1985*, pp. 187–95.
17 Eamonn Hughes, '"All That Surrounds Our Life": Time, Sex, and Death in *That They May Face the Rising Sun*', *Irish University Review* 35.1 (Spring/Summer 2005), p. 160.
18 It was the ancient Christian custom in parts of Ireland to bury the dead with their heads in the east so that they would face the rising sun when resurrected.
19 For a study of Irish workers in this particular car plant, see the chapter entitled 'The Dagenham Yanks' in Miriam Nyhan, *Are You Still Below? The Ford Marina Plant, Cork, 1917–1984* (Cork: Colllins Press, 2007), pp. 65–75.
20 John McGahern, *That They May Face the Rising Sun* (Faber & Faber, 2002), p. 80. Subsequent references to this text are cited in parentheses.
21 See interview with Patrick Hughes in *I Only Came Over for a Couple of Years…*

Part II

THE RYANAIR GENERATION

As Ireland slipped into severe recession in the late 1970s and early 1980s, unemployment rose dramatically. By 1984, it accounted for 16.4 per cent of the workforce and one in three out of work were under the age of twenty-five.[1] In parts of Dublin the figures were much higher, and it was here that the social consequences of unemployment were most marked, with a major drug and crime epidemic hitting the city. Meanwhile, in Northern Ireland, the intransigent position of the Thatcher government in relation to republican prisoners' demands for political status led to the hunger strikes of 1981. As a consequence of these events, attitudes north of the border became increasingly polarized and the economy continued to stagnate. Against this backdrop of economic and political stasis, large numbers of young people from both parts of Ireland once again began moving to Britain, especially London, in search of work.[2] By 1991, there were over a quarter of a million Irish-born in London and, as had been the case for most of the twentieth century, the majority were women.

This generation, however, was distinctly different from previous ones in important respects. While some migrants followed their predecessors by entering the unskilled and semi-skilled sectors of the economy, a new cohort of better educated, more self-confident and socially mobile migrants found jobs in the financial institutions of the City of London, the media and the professions.[3] The removal of foreign exchange controls in 1979 and the deregulation of the London Stock Exchange in 1986 were key factors in the growth of financial services in the city. By the end of the twentieth century, this sector of the economy was to account for 38 per cent of the city's GDP.[4] Although many migrants were attracted by this, most still went into jobs with which the Irish were more traditionally associated, such as construction, nursing and catering.[5] Others found no work whatsoever and ended up joining the ranks of London's increasing numbers of young homeless. When Joseph O'Connor coined the term 'Ryanair Generation' he was alluding to the fact that by the 1980s Irish migrants were able to avail themselves of cut-price air travel to Britain in a way that had not been the case before.[6] For a large number of migrants, however, more traditional modes of travel were the only affordable option.[7] The vicissitudes of demand and supply of migrant labour were part of a historical legacy between Ireland and Britain. The mutually dependent if uneasy economic relationship between the two countries is a perennial and important backdrop to almost all accounts of Irish migration to Britain. However, some of the literature I analyse in this part of the book also reveals that differences among Irish people themselves which may have been muted or tangential back home could be exposed in graphic relief once transposed to London.

Due to better standards of education and increased ambition, the expectations of many young Irish migrants in London by the 1980s were considerably greater than those of the previous mail-boat generation.[8] This generation was much more mobile than its predecessors and writers were no exception to this, moving back and forth between London and Ireland according to opportunity and demand. As Dermot Bolger observed at the time, 'Irish writers no longer go into exile, they simply commute'.[9] Nevertheless, while travelling between Ireland and Britain had become much easier, the literature about the experience indicates that the psychological consequences of migration were no less profound. An ethnographic study of middle-class Irish migrants in London during the 1980s found that their attitudes to migration were radically different from those of previous generations. By being ready to 'stress the variability, fluidity and contingency of ethnic self-representation'[10] they were less homogeneous than their predecessors. However, the study also noted that they sometimes expressed contradictory views about their identities, something reflected in the texts that I examine below.

While the effects of anti-terrorist legislation on the Irish community in Britain continued, the fortunes and the profile of the Irish in London took a distinct turn for the better in the 1980s. Largely as a result of the personal initiative of Ken Livingstone, the Greater London Council (GLC), of which Livingstone was leader from 1981 to its abolition in 1986, became the first municipal authority in Britain to recognize the Irish as an 'ethnic minority'. After an extensive consultation exercise with Irish community organizations in London, large sums of money were directed via the Irish Liaison Unit towards establishing and developing welfare and cultural projects, such as the Innisfree Housing Association, the Brent Irish Advisory Service and the London Irish Women's Centre.[11] For Irish people, this recognition, and the respect for Irish community concerns it implied, represented a profound shift in their relationship with authorities in the city. One of the consequences of this was that, along with many of their second-generation peers (born of Irish parents in the city), many of the Ryanair generation became active in Irish community activities. In cultural terms, there was a flowering of Irish literary, dramatic and artistic work across the capital, mirroring what had happened a century before at the time of the Irish Revival.[12] Events such as the Green Ink Bookfair and the Siol Phadraig Festival became annual showcases for Irish talent, and venues such as the Tricycle Theatre in Kilburn, the Battersea Arts Centre and the Riverside Studios in Hammersmith staged the latest productions from Ireland.

Literature played a central role in this renaissance, with a marked upturn in the number of novels and plays produced specifically about the contemporary experience of the Irish in London.[13] The short story was also prominent during this period, having made something of a comeback in Irish literature more generally, and in this part of the book I examine examples of the genre in work by Emma Donoghue, Sara Berkeley and Joseph O'Connor. The 1980s was a decade in which Irish women writers began to make a major impact. This was largely due to the growth of the women's movement, which gathered momentum in Ireland in the late 1970s and from which some of today's most respected female writers emerged. A key London Irish writer of the time was Margaret Mulvihill, whose novels I cover in the next chapter. A new generation of writers also emerged from Northern Ireland, and, alongside the work of Joseph O'Connor, I look at a novel by Robert McLiam Wilson which revisits some of the iconic sites of Irish London covered in Part I, but with a degree of postmodern reflexivity not seen in those earlier works.

Notes

1   Terence Brown, *Ireland: A Social and Cultural History 1922–2002* (London: Harper Perennial, 2004), p. 316.
2   By 1984, London was attracting 54.8 per cent of all Irish immigrants to the UK, compared to 31.9 per cent prior to 1955. See Ellen Hazelkorn, *Irish Immigrants Today: A Socio-economic Profile of Contemporary Irish Emigrants and Immigrants in the*

UK (London: Polytechnic of North London Press, 1990), p. 23.

3   Hazelkorn, *Irish Immigrants Today*, pp. 21–34. Between 1964 and 1979, participation in tertiary education in the Republic of Ireland rose by two thirds. See David B. Rottman and Philip O'Connell, 'The Changing Social Structure of Ireland', in F. Litton (ed.), *Unequal Achievement* (Dublin: Institute of Public Administration, 1982), p. 73.

4   Jerry White, *London in the Twentieth Century: A City and its People* (London: Viking, 2001), p. 211.

5   Hazelkorn, *Irish Immigrants Today*, pp. 33–34.

6   Ryanair was founded in 1985 and became the most successful 'low-cost' airline in the history of aviation.

7   Many migrants continued to travel by boat and train or, as was increasingly the case by the 1980s, boat and coach. Coach operators such as Slattery's undercut rail fares and became a popular option for poorer migrants.

8   Hazelkorn, *Irish Immigrants Today*, pp. 21–34.

9   Dermot Bolger, 'Foreword', in Dermot Bolger (ed.), *Ireland in Exile: Irish Writers Abroad* (Dublin: New Island, 1993), p. 7.

10 Mary Kells, *Ethnic Identity Amongst Young Middle-Class Irish Migrants in London* (London: University of North London Press, 1995), p. 36.

11 For the report which laid the foundations for this initiative, see *Policy Report on the Irish Community* (London: GLC, 1984).

12 The spirit of the 1980s' revival was captured in a touring exhibition and subsequent publication. See Liz Curtis, Jack O'Keefe, Claire Keatinge and Joanne O'Brien, *Hearts and Minds/Anam agus Intinn: The Cultural Life of London's Irish Community* (London: London Strategic Policy Unit, 1987).

13 Over twenty plays on this subject were staged during the 1980s. See Tony Murray, 'Irish Theatre in Britain 1981–91: A Survey' (unpublished undergraduate dissertation, University of North London, 1992), available in Archive of the Irish in Britain at London Metropolitan University.

7

Gendered Entanglements

Margaret Mulvihill is one of the few Irish women writers to have written consistently about the experiences of the post-war Irish in Britain. Her three novels are all period pieces set in London in the 1980s and early 1990s and her characterizations of young Irish migrants from this time mirror some of the satirical observations in earlier work by Anthony Cronin and Donall Mac Amhlaigh. However, for Mulvihill, who was born in Dublin in 1954 and came to London in her twenties, her perspective on the subject of migration was also imbued with a pronounced feminist sensibility. Apart from being a rare example of a writer from this time who explored Irish feminist issues in the context of migration, Mulvihill anticipated a genre of comic fiction about Irish women's experiences in London which writers such as Lana Citron, Marian Keyes and Anne Enright would develop in later years.[1] In this chapter, I focus on her first two novels, *Natural Selection* (1985) and *Low Overheads* (1987), which deal more fully with questions of London Irish identity than her third.[2]

Mulvihill's London Irish protagonists serve as vehicles for interrogating the experiences of the Ryanair generation in London and also as effective foils for the author's wry observations on the society within which they settled. Mulvihill uses satire to point up the ways in which personal shortcomings are graphically exposed by events beyond the control of individuals. While primarily comic in approach, *Natural Selection* and *Low Overheads* nevertheless provide valuable insights into the gendered entanglements of diaspora. A specific north London *milieu* provides a site for putting the relationship between the Irish and the English under the microscope and demonstrates the ways in which processes of integration and social cohesion are subject to resistances and complications even in the most supposedly liberal and progressive environments.

Natural Selection (1985) by Margaret Mulvihill

Mulvihill's debut novel has resemblances to *The Life of Riley* and *Schnitzer O'Shea* in so far as it is a comic portrayal of an Irish migrant caught up in the social and cultural machinations of the London literary world. The main protagonist of the novel is Maureen Ryan, a twenty-four-year-old Irish arts graduate from Dublin, who is described as 'the apple of her accountant father's eye' and 'a conscientious newcomer to London'.[3] She is typical of the generation of young, well-educated middle-class Irish migrants who left Ireland in the 1980s in order to pursue professional careers that had become increasingly scarce as their country plunged into recession.[4] She finds work at New Vision, a small publishing house in Covent Garden which is described as an 'enduring fruit of the cultural upheaval of the late 1960s' (5). If at first seemingly naïve and unworldly, Maureen provides the vehicle for a coruscating dissection of the professional shortcomings and personal peccadilloes of her colleagues. She is ambitious and 'fiercely suspicious of gender-specific virtues' (82) but is anxious that the disadvantages she has inherited as a result of her Irish upbringing will not prevent her from building a successful career in London:

> She wanted to be somebody or to do something, but she did not know who she should become or what she should try to do. It was difficult in London – a metropolitan density of talent and ambition – where she felt that, for a start, her flat and ordinary name was a handicap. (16)

Maureen's sense of self-image is primarily oriented to her occupation and future career. She does not reveal much about her past, her family or even why she left Ireland. In this sense, her narrative identity appears to be predominantly prefigured rather than refigured. Nevertheless, she feels disadvantaged by her background and, in particular, her Irishness. She is 'disappointed by evolution's failure to meet the metropolitan challenge on her behalf' (2) and as well as her name, she counts among her disadvantages her accent and her freckles.[5] This lack of self-confidence in her national identity must be seen in the context of the setting of the novel. In the early 1980s, the Irish were often vilified in the British media and anti-Irish prejudice was still common in London.[6] While Maureen is not a direct victim of such prejudice, she is conscious of its threat. She has nightmares about being persecuted by xenophobic thugs and avoids her local pub in Kentish Town when it displays Union Jack flags, assuming it has 'become an enclave of the racist lumpenproletariat' (24). Despite being aware of a long-established Irish community in her neighbourhood, Maureen is drawn more to the English middle classes, who appear to live 'denser lives, more, it seemed, about celebration than survival' (113). With this in mind, and armed with the benefit of a fortuitous entrée into this world through her job, she sets her sights on becoming part of an exclusive north London literary set. Untutored in its abstruse cultural codes, however, she finds this more difficult than she had anticipated until she discovers a valuable insider and 'emotional valet' (64) in the form of her flat-mate. Maureen knows she needs to 'find allies within the host culture' and Fabian, an amiable ne'er-do-well son of a literary baron, 'provided England with one of its most congenial faces'. This has a corollary, however, in terms of her Irishness. She is 'reluctant to fall in with her ethnic identity because of her vague but nagging ambitions'. This disinclination is also the result of 'her treacherous loss of the Faith' (24). Maureen's decision to suppress her Irishness, in other words, is not only due to her career ambitions, but also because she has disowned her Catholicism. However, the guilt she feels about doing so, which is ironically an intrinsic part of her religious upbringing itself, reveals the extent to which she is still emotionally bound to the cultural narratives of her past. The narrative diaspora space of the novel, therefore, is highly contested in terms of how personal and collective identities collide, and manifests itself in the conflicted juxtaposition of Maureen's former life in Ireland and her future life in London.

This is further illustrated by an affair she is having with Martin Kershaw, the managing editor of *Aspidistra*, 'a literary journal with a small circulation and great, if declining, prestige' (9). Despite her ambivalence towards her Irishness, Maureen is prepared, on occasions, to reveal to Martin her family connections to a migrant inheritance. En route with him to a clandestine liaison in Highgate, Maureen points out to Martin 'a gaunt Archway pub' which, she explains, is 'a landmark in her family history, a place where migrant Ryans had met and drunk the fruits of their labours in the days of the Empire' (60).[7] However, her trepidation about exposing her Irish ethnicity is warranted. Martin has no interest in Maureen's family history. He feels she should be espousing a rather more cerebral form of Irishness and patronisingly suggests she start by reading *Ulysses*. Maureen consents to reading Joyce's masterpiece because she 'did not think that she could continue in any comfort to nod in pseudo-informed amusement at his references to it' (6), but clearly has reservations about the idea. In other words, she follows

Martin's advice but only for the sake of her career prospects. As she observes, 'he and many other representatives of the British intelligentsia derived most of their knowledge of her country from this single source, it was obligatory reading' (6). Maureen's concern to assimilate into English society is such that she is prepared to suppress references to the much more grounded and immediate narrative of her migrant forebears in favour of what is, for her, a rather rarefied connection with Ireland. We see here the tension, common within narrative diaspora space, between the ways in which individuals choose to narrate their own identity and the ways in which it is narrated on their behalf.

During a meeting with Clive Riley, a successful author and presenter of a TV arts show, coincidentally called *The Life of Riley*, she has an even more revealing contretemps over the question of national identity. When Clive observes that she is not '"from this British isle"', Maureen imagines 'the double-edged stereotype that had risen up in his head: a drunken and irrational violence on the one side, and a verbose romanticism on the other' (37). Her subsequent reflections suggest that feminist as well as postcolonial theory has now become part of her reading diet. 'It was, she thought, rather like the woman/intuitive, man/logical antonym and resented the implicit condescension' (37). Clive's *faux pas* is aggravated by his clumsy attempt to compensate for it by claiming his own Irish heritage by way of 'distant (and therefore tolerable) Hibernian forebears'. He further exacerbates the situation by then referring to his erstwhile study of Gaelic, which he wryly claims he only abandoned due to his tutor's uncompromising insistence on correct accent and enunciation (37–38). The reactions Maureen provokes from her English acquaintances are highly ambivalent and, perhaps, indicative of wider attitudes among the host community at this time. On the one hand, they genuinely attempt to empathize with her Irishness by drawing on personal experiences and associations with her home country, but, on the other hand, they undermine these efforts by making ill-considered remarks which expose a fundamentally superficial and prejudicial understanding of the subject.[8]

Maureen's dismay is reinforced by the reactions she engenders at a party thrown by Clive. After a few drinks, which seem to galvanize her sense of nationality, she retires to the toilet to indulge in an inebriated rendition of 'Whack Fol the Diddle', a sarcastic song about Irish–British relations (43).[9] Shortly afterwards, she meets Lionel Trent, a bespectacled young man of Irish descent, who is introduced in Mulvihill's typically droll style as being 'like many of the unemployed [...]

unhealthily well-informed' (29). After his initial diffidence, he too proceeds to engage Maureen in the contentious topic of national origins:

"How did you get here?" he asked. She knew that he meant where did she come from and not what mode of transport had brought her to Tolpuddle Square, and she was considering how to duck an account of her arrival in London when he spoke again. "My dad came from Mayo. I can remember him telling me that the Duke of Wellington, the Waterloo star, once repudiated his Irish birth by saying that if you are born in a stable you are not necessarily a horse." "No," said Maureen. "You could be a rat." At this their conversation closed for a time, and so they moved towards the dancers. (45)

By employing this commonly quoted anecdote, Lionel implies that when it comes to the matter of national identity his own place of birth is equally insignificant in comparison to his bloodline. Maureen's pithy repost doesn't garner much appreciation from Lionel, who clearly regards the topic as unsuitable for mirth. As if to fortify his ethnic credentials, he claims to be the author of an unpublished novel based on the Celtic myth of 'Deirdre of the Sorrows' and presents the manuscript to Maureen for her opinion. When, some days later, she settles down to read it, she is disturbed to find that it is radically inconsistent with her interpretation of the tale she is familiar with from her schooldays. She notes, for instance, how the Deirdre character is portrayed as 'a coy and stupidly innocent *femme fatale*' and her favourite character from the story, the wise woman, Levorcam, is presented as 'a doting, dribbling crone' (80). When Maureen discovers that the novel is not, after all, the work of Lionel Trent at all, but an unpublished book by Clive Riley, she embarks upon a series of alterations to the manuscript in accordance with her feminist principles before returning it to its author. Aware, however, that there is a clear market for the reworked book, 'now that all this matriarchy stuff is preoccupying everyone' (118) and that 'green eyes and all that blarney' are 'a sound commercial proposition' (120), Riley agrees to relinquish his claim on authorship and have it published under Maureen's name.

Like Schnitzer O'Shea, Maureen finds herself thrust into the literary limelight as the author of a best-selling novel which subsequently attracts a large American advance and the promise of a feature film adaptation. One is reminded here, appropriately, of the eponymous protagonist of *The Life of Riley*, who declared, 'We become [...] what we pretend to be, and I found myself, to my extreme confusion, metamorphosing under my own eyes.'[10] The irony of Maureen Ryan's situation is that she had not set out to become a writer but, nevertheless, succeeds where many of her peers had failed. En route to Clive Riley's second home in the south of France, she reflects, philosophically, on the vagaries of literary ambition and the circumstances that led to her fame:

> As a defensive incantation she silently recited to herself the definition of plagiarism she had read before leaving London: "one who steals or passes off as his (or her) own the ideas or writings of another." But surely it was outrageously presumptuous to lay claim to originality anymore: nothing new could come out of the exhausted West. (116–17)

Maureen finds a convenient justification for her ethically suspect actions in poststructuralist claims about the 'death of the author'. But one is left feeling that while she has ironically established a public persona as a result of becoming an author herself, it is to some extent at the expense of her personal integrity.

The plotting of *Natural Selection* is undoubtedly rather unwieldy and was unkindly described by one reviewer at the time of publication as 'operetta-awkward'.[11] However, the novel is significant for the way in which it reveals the contested allegiances of migrant belonging with regard to ethnicity, gender, class and religion. It also highlights the intertextual nature of narrative diaspora space by reprising two key themes of London Irish literature. Firstly, it revisits and wittily reworks the narrative of the 'Irish writer in London' in the context of 1980s' migration. It shows how an Irish migrant in London with literary ambitions encounters many of the same prejudices as her predecessors, but must also negotiate equally objectionable attitudes with regard to her gender. Secondly, like the 'navvy narratives', it employs Celtic mythology as a central plotting device. But, rather than revealing any collective sense of London Irish identity, here the process is more individualized. Three key characters appropriate and redefine a traditional Celtic narrative as a means of establishing their literary/cultural credentials. For Clive Riley, it is a means by which he can express his claim to an Irish inheritance but in an indirect and therefore politically unthreatening way. For Lionel Trent, it is an opportunity to assert a national identity he feels is unfairly ignored due to his place of birth. Finally, for Maureen Ryan, it is the means by which she is able to satisfy her need 'to be somebody'. By negotiating the entangled nature both of the relationship with her peers and of the novel in question, Maureen fulfils her career ambition in accord with her feminist principles. Furthermore, it enables her to renew her affiliation to Irishness once she realizes, to her dismay, that criticisms of her 'deficiencies', which she had attributed solely to patriarchal attitudes back home, are in London more likely to stem from prejudice against her nationality than from sexism.

Low Overheads (1987) by Margaret Mulvihill

Natural Selection demonstrates Margaret Mulvihill's capacity as an outsider to recognize and satirize the pretensions of British society. This is evident again in her second novel, which portrays the lives and preoccupations of a group of middle-class north Londoners centred around Deborah Lieberman, 'an entrepreneurial guru on alternative obstetric practices' and founder of Nativities Ltd, 'London's first "all-in" home birth agency'.[12] In the course of the novel a wide spectrum of attitudes to the Irish are revealed, from outright racism through varying degrees of condescension to genuine benevolence. The novel also examines the social implications for women of unwanted pregnancy, which was a hot topic of debate in Ireland at this time.

Once again a young newly arrived female migrant provides the hub around which the novel's themes revolve. Like Maureen Ryan, Cora Mangan leaves Ireland in the 1980s to carve out a new life for herself across the water. Her journey 'past the misty Telford Bridge and down to London through the grimy heart of old industrial England' is described as 'no different from that undertaken by her illiterate great grand-aunts' (9). Cora comes from a somewhat different social background to Maureen, having grown up in the rural south-west of Ireland, and is described as 'a girl whose head still reverberated with [...] the head nun's doleful deliberations on her lack of "drive"' (10). Cora's principal motivation for leaving is not the desire for career advancement but an unwanted pregnancy.[13] Unlike Britain, where abortion was legalized in 1967, no such legislation was passed in Ireland. Given its proximity and potential for anonymity, London offered a convenient destination for women who wished to circumnavigate such constraints.[14] According to the sociologist Breda Gray, migration operated both as 'a resource in concealing pregnancy' and as a 'regulating practice that helped eliminate evidence of non-marital sexual activity in the space of the Republic of Ireland'.[15] When a referendum on abortion was held in 1983, not only did a majority vote in favour of retaining existing prohibitions, but the outcome resulted in an amendment to the Irish constitution which bestowed an explicit right to life upon 'the unborn'. The generational divide in attitudes to the subject at the time is illustrated by Cora's reaction to

> her Auntie Eileen's frenzied involvement with an organization that worried more about the unborn than living women, let alone the millions of unwanted children born into suffering. So effectively had this aunt's propaganda boomeranged on Cora that she was almost disappointed not to see women 'sleeping around' all over London, laying down their languorous heads whenever they could and now and then tossing babies into the incinerators placed at every street corner. (25)

Pregnancy, and perhaps more importantly her family's reaction to it, represents a major turning point for Cora in the development of her attitudes and beliefs. Growing up in Ireland, she had been a dutiful and rather overlooked member of an extended rural family. During her journey across the Irish Sea, however, she 'had decided for definite that she was going to terminate her pregnancy' and 'had begun to make her own history' (82). In other words, Cora commits herself to a new identity. But, as was the case for Maureen, this takes place within the context of pre-defined narratives. Where, for Maureen, this is literary, for Cora it is religious. She decides to confront this head-on. We learn that she had 'hardened and stopped asking God to shift fate in her favour' (91). Instead, Cora takes control of her future, a key part of which is taking the boat to England.

Despite her lack of qualifications and experience at a time of rising unemployment in London, Cora finds work immediately. Ironically, given her maternal predicament, she secures a job as a nanny minding Orlando, Deborah Lieberman's baby son. Deborah's husband Gordon, who interviews Cora for the job, supposes that the Irish are 'good with children' and employs her on the spot. Like his peers in Mulvihill's previous novel, Gordon's actions are motivated by a revealing prejudice about the Irish. Referring to babies, for instance, he tells himself: '"They had so many of them after all"' (5). Deborah has equally suspect attitudes, describing Cora as 'a sweet little Irish girl' (36), while her friend Leonie refers to the newly appointed nanny in condescending terms as 'a docile colleen' (70). Like Maureen in *Natural Selection*, Cora worries that her Irish background might prejudice her chances of building a new life in London. Her home town of Rathbwee has been the location of

a recent IRA siege, but despite her fears that her background will disad-
vantage her, the Liebermans have a surprisingly *laissez-faire* attitude
towards Irish republicanism. Mulvihill exacts considerable satirical
purchase, however, from the fact that the Liebermans and their circle,
despite their liberal attitudes, frequently position Cora in the traditional
role of subservient woman in discussions about household management.
She is 'a person whose statements were the sounding board against
which the thought processes of the more masterful personality could
bounce' (100) and, even more pointedly, is the one who, after one of
the family's regular debates about domestic politics, finds herself left with
'a sinkful of washing-up to be done' (81). As an Irish female migrant,
therefore, Cora finds herself doubly subordinated by the power-play of
discourses within English society, which are so deeply embedded that
even their most supposedly enlightened members fail to recognize them.
As was the case for Maureen, therefore, Cora's identity is subject to the
vagaries of a narrative diaspora space in which the personal affirmation
of a sense of self is continually challenged by definitions imposed by
others from without.

If Cora is circumspect about her true feelings with regard to the
Liebermans, she is equally so with her own family about her choice of
employment. When she tells her Auntie Eileen that she has 'an
extremely interesting job as an administrative assistant to a lady
authoress' (26), she engages in a form of fictionalization now familiar in
the narrative diaspora space of post-war London Irish literature. In
particular, one is reminded of Baba (in Edna O'Brien's *Girls in Their
Married Bliss*), who also fabricates an alternative occupation in order to
withhold information from her family about the true purpose of her
emigration. But migration involves a major life-change for Cora and
she relies, to some degree, on her family for emotional support. This
falls to her older brother, Patrick, who left Ireland when he was seventeen and has lived in London for some time. However, despite sharing
the experience of migration with his sister, he has misgivings about her
career prospects in the city:

> Patrick Mangan, whose potential as a carrier of the patrilineal bad blood had
> yet to be assessed, had expected a qualified, marketable sister to join him in
> London. Instead he found her on his doorstep within a matter of months,
> without a certificate declaring her competence on some kind of keyboard
> and with a tendency to sudden nausea. (25)

Patrick lives close to the Liebermans' home, but on the other side of 'a sociological Equator' in a multicultural working-class estate described as a 'latterday rookery' (40–41). His longer absence from Ireland is marked by his 'more neutral mid-Atlantic accent', in contrast to Cora, whose speech still retains colloquialisms such as 'the "hot press"', which her employer is 'still learning to translate' (27). The reaction he provokes in the Liebermans is as benign as that provoked by Cora, if no less clichéd. For Deborah's sister Vivien, for instance, he is 'a real door-dark-ener of a man' and 'the very picture of your romantic, rugged Celt' (26). During her pursuit of Patrick, Vivien learns about his dubious connec-tions to the Irish republican movement in London, but this only seems to enhance his appeal. Like his sister, Patrick's identity is subject to narra-tives imposed from without, but in his case, distinct personal advantages are immediately apparent from colluding with the Celticist discourses upon which such glamorized perceptions rely.[16] However, this does not stop him from eventually disagreeing with Vivien over questions of ethnic identity. During one exchange on the topic, Patrick exclaims, '"you know fuck-all about us. That's why we have to keep harping on about our history"', to which Vivien counter-attacks by informing him that her '"grandparents came from Latvia you know, and so you're prob-ably more British than I am."' '"It's true,"' she continues, '"you drink tea and form queues, just like the English, and just emphasize these petty differences as a form of narcissism. […] It's like families. To assert your individuality, you have to play up differences, but you're more the same than you're different"' (108–09). The exchange is indicative of the kind of ethnic point-scoring which had become a feature of identity politics in London in the 1980s. By making reference to her Latvian back-ground, Vivien attempts to trump Patrick in the ethnicity stakes by distancing herself from her Englishness and the attitudes Patrick alludes to. However, by disparaging Patrick's grievances in the process, she shows herself guilty of precisely the dismissive attitude to Irish ethnicity that was a common feature of the Englishness she is disavowing.

In this regard, the conflict in Northern Ireland forms another impor-tant backdrop to this novel. Most English people had little or no knowledge about the shared history of Ireland and England.[17] This was partly a consequence of the virtual absence of the subject from the secondary school curriculum and partly due to the highly partisan British media coverage of the Troubles.[18] In the denouement to the novel, events take place which reflect a lack of appreciation of the negative effects of the Prevention of Terrorism Act (1974) on the Irish community. When a riot breaks out in the Liebermans' neighbourhood, Deborah's car is burnt out and suspicions are aroused among neighbours that subversive links between disaffected black youths and Irish terrorists might be the cause (144). On his return from a trip to New York, Patrick is arrested under the PTA and cross-examined at Paddington Green police station.[19] He is later released, albeit with a face that 'was suspiciously puffy on one side', once they discover that it is his associate, Enda (a local contact with the republican movement), whom they really need to question (164). However, Deborah's *blasé* attitude to Patrick's arrest exposes a clear attitudinal gap between her and Cora over the way the police deal with Irish people.

Cora's support of her brother is unequivocal and this appears to be largely mutual. Patrick takes a pragmatic position on her decision to have the abortion and takes her on weekend outings in his van to Epping Forest. His actions, however, prove to have ulterior motives. Despite the fact that he knows the Lieberman house is being watched, he cajoles Cora into hiding a pistol in her room until Enda requires it. By putting her at risk in this way, Patrick shows very little concern for his sister's personal safety and reveals a mercenary and cowardly side to his character. The fact that Cora agrees so readily to the plan demonstrates not only her naïvety about the potential consequences but the extent to which she still defers to other members of her family despite the danger to her well-being. During a discussion with Cora about Irish people's historical predilection for migration, Patrick says, '"maybe I will go back sometime, when I'm thirty-five and I've found the right wee woman"' (45). Here he alludes to an ambition which many of his compatriots before him had shared yet rarely fulfilled, but by choosing not to respond to the patriarchal nature of the remark, Cora shows that she is still not confident enough to openly challenge such attitudes. On the other hand, she is sufficiently aware of her feelings to want to find her own sense of self and place in London, now that she has left behind her sense of anonymity. As the narrator explains: 'It was not that Cora Mangan wanted to stand out in a crowd. Rather, she desperately wanted to stand in with some group. She was tired of being invisible' (55).

In this respect, Patrick and Cora are at quite different stages in their journeys of migration, the former away long enough to know he would rather be back, the latter away for too short a time to know one way or the other. Both of them, however, share a sense of ambivalence about their identities. For Patrick, being an emigrant is 'neither flesh nor fowl, never quite at home in the host country and forever contaminated by foreign influences when back in the old country' (79). For Cora, her Irishness makes her feel like 'a visitor from another planet'. Her status as a surrogate mother, however, puts her 'at another remove', rendering her 'invisible' on the streets of the city (56). 'Somehow,' she reflects, 'she was always stuck in the middle, neither a mother nor a proper nanny, neither a girl nor a woman' (79). The narrative diaspora space of the novel, therefore, is profoundly contingent and intersectional. For both siblings, the in–between state in which they find themselves is partly due to the fact they have not yet found a suitable narrative within which to couch their identities.

Cora's predicament is, perhaps, the more complex of the two. Questions of ethnicity are not, or not yet at any rate, Cora's primary concern, and while her maternal and occupational status is more pressing, she has no serious plans in either respect. Having had the abortion, Cora has taken charge of her destiny, but this does not necessarily mean that she has yet configured a longer-term identity for herself. As nanny for another woman's child, she proves to have all the skills of an exemplary mother, but with none of the biological or legal rights normally associated with the role. The extent to which nannying is emotional compensation for the trauma of abortion is not something that is seriously explored in the novel. But the fact that Cora has recurring nightmares about transporting a baby in a parcel across the Irish Sea to an undercover agent in London suggests that the deeper psychological impact of her pregnancy is something with which she is yet to come to terms.

Mulvihill's second novel, like its predecessor, ends on a wry note, with its main protagonist reflecting on the ability of human beings to overlook the disparity between their political convictions and their actual behaviour:

> Orlando's first year as a social being had been Cora's first as an adult, the year when she realised that people never grow up. All around her were the betrayals and contradictions that proved any belief in maturity to be childish: the Deborah who was quite happy, despite all of her rhetoric, to construct something very like the odious nuclear family; the Vivien who was prepared to be monogamous with a man who had said he'd never settle down. (178)

Because of her unwanted pregnancy, Cora is more a product of forced migration than her middle-class peer in *Natural Selection*. Her socio-economic background also means she does not have the same level of education or career options as Maureen. However, despite these disadvantages she survives in the rarefied world of a politically liberal yet socially exclusive 'alternative' community in 1980s' north London. By using Cora as a window through which to observe this *milieu*, Mulvihill makes some incisive critiques of the contradictory attitudes and lifestyles of its inhabitants. This highlights starkly contradictory positions within the narrative diaspora space of the novel. While, on the one hand, the Liebermans' position on Irish republicanism is remarkably tolerant for the time, their understanding of the negative effects of the Prevention of Terrorism Act on Irish people in Britain is seriously deficient. Cora, however, proves to have contradictions of her own. While she has been brave enough to make the break from the socially stifling environment of her family in Ireland by emigrating to London, she still defers, ill-advisedly, to her elder brother's suspect authority once she gets there. Finally, while her choice of occupation appears to reveal maternal predispositions rather than simply opportunist instincts, her attitude to motherhood is still unclear by the close of the novel.

Maureen Ryan and Cora Mangan share many characteristics. For both of them, their migration is the consequence of feeling trapped in a country where social and moral attitudes continue to regulate and restrict the lives of women. They are both independent and self-sufficient to the extent that they quickly find employment in London. They are also very adept at negotiating the often convoluted intersectionalities of diaspora space and they both emerge from their experiences of life in the city more mature and more aware of the potential pitfalls of emigration. Yet they differ considerably in other ways. While they both encounter varying degrees of ethnic and gender stereotyping, Maureen seems better able to exploit the discourses upon which they are predicated for personal advancement. She is able to draw on resources of self-confidence which Cora does not have. For the most part, she appears to be in control of her destiny and, by the end of *Natural Selection*, has configured a clear if somewhat unforeseen identity as a best-selling author. Cora, on the other hand, is subject to aspects of her past which continue to frustrate her attempts at independence and, as *Low Overheads* closes, the question of her future path in life and consequent identity is still very uncertain.

Notes

1   See, respectively, Lana Citron, *Sucker* (London: Secker & Warburg, 1998); Marian Keyes, *Last Chance Saloon* (London: Michael Joseph, 1999); Anne Enright, *What Are You Like* (London: Jonathan Cape, 2000).

2   Jacinta, the London Irish female protagonist of Mulvihill's third novel, is not as comprehensively drawn as those of the previous novels and does not offer the same possibilities for exploring questions of migrant identity. See Margaret Mulvihill, *St. Patrick's Daughter* (London: Hodder & Stoughton, 1993).

3   Margaret Mulvihill, *Natural Selection* (London: Pandora, 1985), p. 26, p. 23. Subsequent references to this text are cited in parentheses.

4   For a study of this particular cohort, see Kells, *Ethnic Identity*.

5   Freckles are often read as a signifier of Irishness by virtue of their association with red hair.

6   See Curtis, *Nothing but the Same Old Story*.

7   The pub referred to is the Archway Tavern, which has long been a well-known meeting place for the Irish in north London. In a curious example of diasporic circularity, a pub of the same name now exists in Gort, Co. Galway.

8   Peter Gavin, the protagonist of a satirical novel about an aspiring literary Irishman in 1950s' London, has a similar experience. See Michael Campbell, *Oh Mary, This London* (London: Heinemann, 1959).

9   'Whack Fol the Diddle' (a.k.a. 'God Bless England') was composed by Peadar Kearney and popularized in the 1960s by one of Ireland's most successful ballad bands. See the Clancy Brothers and Tommy Makem, 'Whack Fol the Diddle', on *The Rising of the Moon: Irish Songs of Rebellion* (New York: Tradition Records, 1959). For a stage-play about the plight of a lonely middle-class Irish woman suffering cultural isolation in 1980s' London, see Jonathan Moore, *This Other Eden*, in *Three Plays* (Twickenham: Aurora Metro, 2002).

10 Cronin, *The Life of Riley*, pp. 166–67.

11 Eden Ross Lipson, 'Review of Maureen Mulvihill, *Natural Selection*', *New York Times*, 4 May 1986, p. 40.

12 Margaret Mulvihill, *Low Overheads* (London: Pandora, 1987), pp. 1–2. Subsequent references to this text are cited in parentheses.

13 There is a small sub-genre of literature about Irish women's experiences of abortion in London. See, for instance, Maeve Binchy, 'Shepherds Bush', in *Central Line* (London: Quartet Books, 1978); Deirdre Shanahan, 'Dancehall', in *Green Ink Writers: Anthology of Short Stories* (London: Green Ink Writers Group, 1982); Edna O'Brien, *Down by the River* (London: Weidenfeld & Nicolson, 1996).

14 For a study of Irish women's experiences of coming to London for abortions at this time, see Ann Rossiter, *Ireland's Hidden Diaspora: The 'Abortion Trial' and the Making of a London-Irish Underground, 1980–2000* (London: Iasc Publishing, 2009).

15 Breda Gray, *Women and the Irish Diaspora* (London: Routledge, 2004), p. 27.

16 For early notions of the 'romantic Celt' in English discourse, see Matthew Arnold, *On the Study of Celtic Literaure* (London: Smith, Elder & Co., 1867) and Ernest Renan, *The Poetry of the Celtic Races*, trans. W. G. Hutchinson (London: Walter Scott, 1897).

17 For an example of how a Northern Ireland Protestant woman encounters this in 1980s' London, see Linda Anderson, *Cuckoo* (London: The Bodley Head, 1986).

18 See, respectively, Hickman, *Religion, Class and Identity* and Liz Curtis, *Ireland: The Propaganda War: The British Media and the 'Battle for Hearts and Minds'* (London: Pluto Press, 1984).

19 For a stage-play about a suspected IRA bomber who is interrogated in Paddington Green police station, see Ron Hutchinson, *Rat in the Skull* (London: Methuen, 1984).

8

Ex-Pat Pastiche

In the economic and political circumstances of 1980s' Ireland, emigration presented an attractive option – and in some cases the only option – for young people north and south of the border. The two key protagonists of the works I examine in this chapter, the first from Dublin and the second from Belfast, are representative of these changes. Their authors, Joseph O'Connor and Robert McLiam Wilson respectively, were typical of a new generation of Irish authors at the time who brought a renewed youthful iconoclasm to the pages of Irish fiction. Here, familiar locations of Irish London (the building site; Euston station; the local Irish pub) metamorphose from iconic to ironic sites. Rather than being merely parodied (as was the case in the texts I explored in Chapter 5), in these texts the experience of the Irish migrant in London is subjected to a degree of postmodern pastiche not seen before. However, while London's streets provide (sometimes literally) an arena for the expression of a more individualized, if solipsistic, sense of self beyond questions of national allegiance, personal identity ultimately proves to be something over which O'Connor's and Wilson's protagonists have less control than they might think. Eddie Virago, a key figure in O'Connor's early fiction, and the eponymous protagonist of Wilson's novel *Ripley Bogle* (1989), leave Ireland because they feel constrained by traditional notions of Irishness and an attendant nationalist/republican rhetoric to which they feel no sense of allegiance. But after being in London for some time, their sense of exile becomes evident, albeit experienced in radically different ways. Rather than issues of ethnicity, they discover (sometimes through altered states of consciousness) that their identities are ultimately subject to more fundamental questions about fact and fiction, sanity and madness, and life and death.

Cowboys and Indians (1991) and related short stories
by Joseph O'Connor

The character of Eddie Virago, who first appeared in Joseph O'Connor's debut novel and later in a number of his subsequent short stories, is one of the most memorable fictional portrayals of the Ryanair generation. London offers the former English literature student a convenient way of escaping the recession-ridden country of his birth and, as 'the fetid birthplace of punk', promises this would-be rock-star a career and lifestyle still only dreamed of back home.[1] Gerry Smyth points out that one of the salient themes of the novel is 'the way in which old narratives are negotiated by new subjects',[2] and Eddie serves as a fictional vehicle for invoking a very broad range of dichotomies concerning migrant identity. This includes postcolonial discrepancies within multicultural London, intra-ethnic clashes between those who left Ireland and those who stayed and, perhaps most tellingly of all, the disparity between individual occupational aspirations and economic realities. This very complexity, by the close of the novel, appears to be the cause of Eddie's attempts to escape from the *cul-de-sac* of his social circumstances into the inner space of his sensory perceptions.

During the course of *Cowboys and Indians*, a small hotel in King's Cross becomes something of a surrogate home for Eddie. It is run by Mr Patel, a Pakistani, who is initially wary of the young Dubliner with the Mohican haircut, but gradually warms to his lodger after discovering that they share an interest in Oscar Wilde. He begins to take Eddie into his confidence, revealing details about his own difficulties when he first arrived in England in 1974 and his attitude to racism:

> He said it was better not to get too obsessed with all that racism stuff. Better to put your energies into work. Nobody could work like an Asian could work. Nobody at all, and he'd met people from all over the world. "You see, that's why the English don't like us, Eddie," he said. "We can out-shopkeeper the nation of shopkeepers." (67–68)

Mr Patel is anxious to explain to Eddie how his sense of identity differs from that of the host community not so much by virtue of race and colour, but because of his work ethic. By imparting this information, he hopes to incorporate Eddie, whom he sees as a somewhat naïve, if likeable, young man from another corner of the former British Empire, into his particular narrative of migrant aspiration. However, Mr Patel's and Eddie's experiences of diaspora, while similar in relation to a shared postcolonial history, are qualitatively different in terms of hopes and desires. This is a generational difference as much as an attitudinal one. Eddie has come to London to fulfil his youthful ambitions and become a rock star. He doesn't see the city as necessarily a place where he will put down roots and work steadily to build a career. Instead, he sees it much more as a short-cut to fame, unavailable to him in Dublin. Despite a strong personal rapport with his Pakistani landlord, Eddie's experience suggests that a narrative disjunction exists in relation to the ways in which the two men prefigure their migrant ambitions, thus limiting the prospect of inter-ethnic solidarity.

The novel reveals that an equally conflicted 'confluence of narra-tivity' can be apparent *within* ethnic communities as well as between them. As was the case in John B. Keane's *The Contractors*, regional factors play a role in the way ethnic allegiances are differentially asserted within Irish London. Eddie's girlfriend, Marion, is from the rural north-west of Ireland and her idea of a good night out is very different from that of the Dubliner. During a visit to the local Pride of Erin pub, Eddie is repelled by the traditional and, in his view, phoney sense of Irishness celebrated by his girlfriend's peer-group:

> Marion's friends got on his nerves. They were all gossiping culchies, from Donegal like her, and the Pride felt more Irish than any pub he'd ever been to in Ireland. It was Irish in the same way that Disneyland is American. Something about it just bugged him, and after the first night he said he didn't want to go again. (87)

The Pride of Erin incorporates 'traditional Ireland' into the texture of ethnic London life. However, in so doing, it brings with it the associ-ated dichotomy between rural and urban conceptions of Irishness that became institutionalized after independence and still had purchase at the end of the twentieth century. Marion is content to indulge a much more traditional form of Irish migrant culture than her boyfriend, but for Eddie such behaviour amounts to nothing more than an outmoded and now obsolete exhibition of cloying Irish exile. Looked at from a socio-economic perspective, the Pride of Erin could perhaps represent what David Lloyd describes as 'the inseparable double of an aesthetic culture which continues to pose as a site of redemption for those who are subject to the economic laws of modernity, even in the spaces of recreation that pretend to emancipate them from labour'.[3] However, one could equally well argue that Marion is smarter than she lets on and, unlike Eddie, is happy to knowingly indulge such unashamedly Irish pastiche rather than take it too seriously. Ultimately, the incident reveals how, regardless of their differing attitudes, narratives of exile and the identities associated with them impact on these two members of the Ryanair generation as much as they did on their migrant predecessors.

This is evident, in another form, in O'Connor's short story 'Four Green Fields' (1993), where, once more, regional and generational factors exert a direct influence on how personal identity is negotiated in a London Irish context. In particular, the story demonstrates how radically different perspectives on 'the Troubles' commonly associated with Dubliners and Northerners are heightened when political value judgements about identity are read within the frame of ethnic solidarity. In this story, Eddie is with Evelyn (another girlfriend from a northern Irish background) at a friend's wedding reception at the Irish Centre in Camden Town. It is the day after an IRA bomb has gone off in the City of London and he finds himself drawn into an argument about the ethics of, as he puts it, 'blowing up chartered accountants for a United Ireland'.[4] After a rendition of the republican ballad that gives the story its title, a discordant note is sounded when Eddie proclaims that young Irish people don't care for such sentiments any more. He is immediately taken aside by an old IRA activist who says to him quietly, '"Well sure, maybe that's what we fought for [...]. So you'd have the right not to care, if ye didn't want to"' (145). The 1980s marked a turning point for the Irish in London. In the wake of the abuses of the Prevention of Terrorism Act over the previous decade, the issue of the hunger strikes politicized and galvanized large sections of the London Irish in a manner not seen since the Irish War of Independence.[5] Despite Eddie's understandable frustrations, it is clear that he has badly misread the collective narrative at play here. In his impatience to attack what he considers to be a redundant form of nationalism, he not only succeeds in isolating himself from his girlfriend but ironically (given his stance in the Pride of Erin) finds himself exiled from a potentially supportive circle of compatriots. In the process, Eddie learns that collective (if somewhat mythologized) narratives of nationalist and republican identity paradoxically find a more readily available space for expression in London than they might have at home. Once more, therefore, he must come to terms with the realities, rather than his perceptions, of how Irish migrant identities are configured in the diaspora.

Allusions to these telling gaps between the promises of migration and its often divergent reality are typical of O'Connor's work from this period. His London Irish fiction is, on one level, a light-hearted take on the often comic contradictions between such aspirations and actual economic circumstances. But it also casts a serious light on the ways in which narratives of migrant identity are played out at a key juncture in the history of Irish migration to London. The overt disparities of opportunity available to different sectors of the London Irish community in the 1980s are clearly apparent in *Cowboys and Indians*. After being refused entry to a select Covent Garden bar where two friends from Dublin are drinking, Eddie feels, once again, like an exile among his own people. Feeling as alienated from this equally exclusive sub-group of the Irish in London as he did from Marion's friends, he mischievously christens them 'Nipples', i.e. New Irish Professional People in London. By inventing this acronym, O'Connor established an unforgettable and subsequently oft-repeated term to describe the Irish migrant 'yuppies' who found employment in London's financial services sector. Another portrayal of this particular breed of 1980s' London Irish migrant is found in O'Connor's short story 'The Wizard of Oz' (1991). Ed Murphy is a Trinity-educated, BMW-driving advertising executive with a warehouse apartment in London's docklands. Dave, the narrator of the story, initially chooses to ignore the insult of being offered an office cleaning job by Ed, but, after being chastised by him for not 'hacking it', takes his revenge by leaving his compatriot's car-phone connected to the speaking clock in Australia and dropping his keys down a nearby drain.[6] A similar form of intra-ethnic disjunction is illustrated in the following passage from *Cowboys and Indians*, where Eddie is buying a Ryanair ticket in a travel agency near Hyde Park and recognizes a familiar face:

> Eddie knew the guy behind the counter, some bright spark hot shot who used to be auditor of the UCD History Society. He pretended not to know Eddie but it was him alright. […] He looked embarrassed. He looked like he didn't want anybody to know he was working here. (42)

Regardless of when and where a migrant chooses to travel, an element of risk is inevitable in the enterprise. When the gamble fails for one individual, the untoward consequences can act as a warning of what might be in store for others. O'Connor was well acquainted with the reality of loneliness for the London Irish, having lived in the city in the late 1980s and early 1990s. In an essay, ironically titled 'How to be Irish in London', which first appeared in 1994, he describes how, on the way home from a party one night, he encountered a young Irish down-and-out in Charing Cross. After O'Connor had bought him a cup of tea, the man broke down and kept repeating, "'I'm only hanging on by my shoe laces'".[7] The account illustrates how, while one set of Irish migrants in London were acquiring the skills that would be brought back home to contribute to the birth of the 'Celtic Tiger' a few years later, another set were living very different lives as part of a rapidly growing underclass in the city. The subtext of this anecdote reads, 'there, but for the grace of God, go I'. This echoes Eddie's encounter with the former UCD student and highlights, once again, revealing intertextualities between autobiography and fiction in the narrative diaspora space of London Irish literature.

Such interactions in O'Connor's work show how configurations of identity can take place concurrently for individuals who are not necessarily aware of a shared experience. This is apparent in *Cowboys and Indians* when, early one morning, Eddie decides to find work as a navvy in Cricklewood and encounters a familiar image of post-war London Irish life:

> lines of silent men with red Irish faces and stained overalls and World Cup T-shirts, coughing up phlegm and pulling on cheap cigarettes. The bosses arrived in Mercs and Jags, fat greasy bastards with dandruff all over their Savile Row suits. They looked like the kind of guys who would have been urban district councillors back home in Ireland. The type who've got hand-made Italian shoes but never change their socks. That type. (183)

By going to Cricklewood, Eddie travels a considerable distance across the city, but by visiting such an iconic location of Irish London, he also makes an important journey across the narrative diaspora space of post-war London Irish literature. Here, he encounters the heroic figures from the 'navvy narratives', but such paragons of Irish masculinity take on a much less attractive hue when seen from the sceptical perspective of a 1980s' migrant. However, it is not long before Eddie realizes that his position in the London migrant economy may not be as different from that of the navvies in Cricklewood as he had assumed. As his hopes of making it as a rock star are gradually eroded, Eddie must reconcile himself to a life which merely skirts the periphery of the social set he had aspired to join. As the prospect of fulfilling his ambitions recedes, the option of returning to Ireland starts to appeal. The return visit, however, is often the site at which migrants' own mythologized narratives about their lives abroad begin to assert themselves. Stories about 'the good life' elsewhere, imparted to old friends who chose not to migrate, are a typical example of this, and during a trip back to Dublin for Christmas Eddie indulges in precisely this diasporic form of blarney:

> He did his best to consume as much free drink as was humanly possible, chatting up women, laying down the bullshit about what he was up to in London. Sometimes he was a roadie for Terence Trent D'Arby, other times a trainee designer for Katherine Hamnett, other times an investigative journalist for *New Statesman and Society*. (118)

Fictions such as this, paradoxically, achieve their maximum impact back home in Ireland, where mythologized accounts of the capital's music and fashion business would have found more resonance than in London itself.

The relationship in diaspora space between those who stay and those who go has, of course, long been a feature of Irish migrant culture, and its manifestation in literature goes back at least as far as George Moore's short story 'Homesickness' (1903). Like Moore's protagonist, James Bryden, Eddie discovers that the longer he is away, the less at home he feels when he finally returns, leaving him with an acute sense of double exile. Once again, autobiographical parallels are evident. O'Connor described his own experience of this in 1993:

> Suddenly, about half an hour before closing time, you find yourself looking around the pub and becoming frantically uptight. You're feeling completely out of place, you don't know why. It's weird. You don't get it. But somehow, despite the *ceol* and the *caint* and the *craic*, something is wrong. You're home in Ireland, but you're not home really […] and you realize in that moment that you really are an emigrant now. And that being an emigrant isn't just an address. You realize that it's actually a way of thinking about Ireland.[8]

Perspective, here, is all-important. The account neatly captures the way in which the phenomenon of return and the configuration of identity that accompanies its narrativization can transform a sense of cultural belonging from something fixed and reliable into something much more uncertain and provisional. In other words, return can play as significant a part in the evolution of a sense of belonging in diaspora space as leaving. Even for those who are unable or unwilling to return, its possibility at some point in the future exerts some influence on how a migrant identity evolves, a theme I explore further in the next chapter. The comparison between Eddie's experience of living in London and his attitude to migration upon leaving Ireland is also instructive. At the beginning of *Cowboys and Indians*, he situates his own departure in the historical context of previous migrant generations:

> Eddie tried to feel the way an emigrant is supposed to feel. Sentimental songs and snatches of poetry drifted like remembered smells into his consciousness and then eluded him. And although he was vaguely aware of the thousands of petulant Paddies who had crossed the same stretch of sea over the decades, and over the centuries too, he couldn't actually feel anything. (6)

Eddie attempts, unsuccessfully, to configure a narrative of migrant identity by relying on a trope which, though familiar, is at odds with his instincts and sensibilities and is no longer applicable to his generation's circumstances. His rather half-hearted attempt at framing his experience in terms of exile seems premature anyway, given that he has not yet even reached his destination. More importantly, however, it is bound to fail because, as the phrase 'couldn't actually feel anything' reveals, Eddie has conclusively suppressed his emotional response to leaving Ireland. However, the very fact that he engages with the idea of exile, if only in a flippant way, highlights the continuing influence of this powerful trope in Irish migrant fiction and foreshadows a more pronounced manifestation later in the novel.

First, however, Eddie must come to terms with the bureaucracy involved in moving from one country to another. While waiting for his break in the music business to materialize, he is forced to 'sign on' at his local unemployment office in King's Cross, where he is confronted with a dizzying array of form-filling and impenetrable red tape:

> Income Support. Supplementary Benefit. Social Fund. Unemployment Allowance. What the fuck was the difference? And how could he get a social security number when he'd never worked here? And why hadn't he sussed all this out before he'd left home? The Students' Union never stopped ranting on about it, *Your Rights in London*, all of that – the brochure was almost handed out to you with a copy of your degree when you graduated. (49)

Eddie's confusion and frustration with the British benefits system has its parallel in Patrick Riley's encounter with it thirty years before in *The Life of Riley*. His consternation at attitudes in English society is reinforced when he eventually gets a steady job as a salesman with a company manufacturing bin bags. He is taken aback by how quickly his English workmates resort to anti-Irish abuse during a drunken argument about religion and nationality (101), and, like his counterparts in Margaret Mulvihill's novels, he is forced to come to terms with the deep-set prejudices of the host community. This has clear implications for his livelihood. The longer Eddie is in London, the more he is confronted with the bald social and economic realities of his situation, and *Cowboys and Indians* closes with him wandering, disconsolately, around the centre of the city. Crossing over Waterloo Bridge, he drops a tab of acid and calls Marion in Donegal from a phone-box. However, when the voice on the other end of the line innocently asks, "'Is there anybody out there?'", he cannot muster the courage to answer (249–50). In a surreal moment of tragi-comedy, Eddie interprets the question as an existential enquiry about his very being in the world and breaks down in tears. Instead of assuaging the feeling of exile, the phone-call home seems only to have exacerbated his sense of dislocation. Alone and astray in the metropolis, the hallucinogenic effects of the LSD take effect:

> And when he turned hot-eyed into the Strand the lights were on, all priestly purple and Mohican red and beer can yellow and acid house blue, glowing in the rain, running together. The whole street was a river of light. It looked like a time-lapse photograph, streaks of fluorescent colour all flowing up and down, as though they had a life of their own. (250)

When Yeats walked down the same thoroughfare in London, almost a hundred years earlier, the sound of running water prompted memories of his Sligo childhood and inspired 'The Lake Isle of Innisfree' (1897).[9] Similarly aqueous images are induced by the rain and the tears in Eddie's eyes, and combine with the effects of the drug to produce a psychedelic re-enactment of this quintessential moment of Irish exile. The Strand is transformed from an iconic London landmark into a placeless and timeless swell of light and colour. For Eddie, the prospect of narrativizing an identity seems momentarily lost as his consciousness dissolves into a textless zone of the senses.

When we meet Eddie Virago three years later, in the short story, 'Last of the Mohicans' (1991), he has begun to realize that he is more of an exile than he could ever have imagined before he left Dublin. This is confirmed by the only job he is now able to hold down, 'sweating behind the burger bar in Euston Station, a vision in polyester and fluorescent light'.[10] Such a location, at the diasporic axis between departure and arrival for so many Irish migrants over the years, seems appropriate given how indeterminate Eddie's status has now become.[11] Lonely and frustrated, he revisits the notion with which he had failed to connect emotionally on the boat to England three years before. 'It was hard being an exile,' he complains. 'He didn't want to be pretentious or anything, but he knew how Sam Beckett must have felt' (12).[12] O'Connor appears to take pleasure here in sending up his migrant protagonist (and perhaps himself) and, by so doing, engages in a satirical practice which has clear antecedents in the work of Cronin and Mac Amhlaigh. By resorting to one of the most powerful narratives of Irish diasporic experience, the 'exiled Irish writer in London', Eddie aligns himself not only with his peers but also with a collective Irish migrant imaginary re-mythologized within the narrative diaspora space of London Irish literature.

Ripley Bogle (1989) by Robert McLiam Wilson

Exile, writing and identity are also central to Robert McLiam Wilson's debut, which was one of the most critically acclaimed Irish novels of its day. Its postmodern approach to these themes is particularly noticeable in the way that the experiences of its eponymous anti-hero are mediated through intertextual references to Irish literature and how his identity is collapsed into a kaleidoscope of allusions to characters from novels by James Joyce, Flann O'Brien and others. In a resolutely self-reflexive account, Bogle becomes the protagonist of his own literary aspirations and, rather than his identity being grounded in a single migrant metanarrative, it is fragmented into a multi-discursive form of narrative diaspora space. Given Wilson's own biography, one is tempted to read Bogle as a vehicle for the narrative identity of the author.[13] Much of the novel consists of Bogle's reflections on his upbringing in Belfast and the impact of the Troubles. However, by focussing predominantly on these sections of the novel, most critics have undervalued the way that his migration and experiences in London shape his attitudes to life and identity.[14] By addressing this, I demonstrate how events in the city shape the identity of Bogle and lend an important diasporic dimension to the novel.

Bogle is a solipsistic itinerant in his early twenties, who takes his readers on a vicarious four-day tramp through London's streets. This is accompanied by acerbic observations on human nature, prompted by memories of his childhood and adolescence in Belfast, his failed relationships with women and his encounters with other tramps. At the opening of the novel, Bogle has been living rough for six months and has not eaten for three days but, despite this, he repeatedly finds time to allude to his love of literature, claiming (with a penchant for hyperbole that becomes a key-signature of the novel) to have read the entire works of Thackeray by the time he was five years old. Such has been their influence that he wonders, with a mixture of self-indulgence and self-mockery, whether this might be why his style is 'so florid, so rotund, so fucking courtly'.[15] In drawing parallels between his love of literature and his life on the streets he regularly alludes to a shared sense of exile experienced through writing and walking. He unashamedly makes direct comparisons between himself and certain novelists, drawing attention to the itinerant context of their inspiration and, by association, appropriating an intrinsically writerly identity for himself. He claims, for instance, that being a down-and-out is 'vital to the formation of a truly incisive intellectual mien'. Where would Dickens and Orwell have been, he asks, 'without all that early fruitful pavement-licking?' (7). At the outset, therefore, Bogle configures his identity in an explicitly narrative manner, suggesting that we are dependent on language and the flow of words to provide meaning to our lives.

As for many of the protagonists I analyse in this book, escape is the initial driving force behind Bogle's decision to migrate from Ireland. In his particular case, the impact of the Troubles on his childhood is a key 'push factor'. He recalls how, when younger, he 'began to memorise the ferry timetables for Holyhead, Stranraer and Liverpool' (84), indicating just how early this prefiguration of a migrant identity had begun. As a consequence of this, the moment of leaving itself has an air of inevitability, as well as liberation, about it: 'I prepared to depart, to embark. My eyes were green again, I had younged up again. I was feeling trim and tremendous once more. All was ready. My city was packed and labelled. Nothing there nomore. All was ready now. Departure. Bye bye Ireland' (158). This exuberant assertion of escape from Ireland and things Irish is, however, short-lived.[16] When he gets to England, he discovers that his Irishness has stowed away in his baggage and makes an unwelcome reappearance at university. Having secured a place at Cambridge University, Bogle had hoped to immerse himself in an environment where he could forget his past. To his dismay, he discovers that his national identity is precisely what distinguishes him most from his fellow students. However, he gradually realizes that it furnishes him with an unexpected appeal. Like Brendan Behan, Bogle quickly learns that by playing the part of the 'exiled Celtic rogue', he can present a mixture of cultural affront and allure to upper-middle-class English sensibilities. By resurrecting and renarrativizing the trope of the 'stage Irishman', Bogle begins to configure a public persona which protects him in a sometimes hostile environment. When Laura, a female admirer, persuades him to move to London with her, he discovers that this performative apprenticeship has served him well. In order to prosper financially and socially, he lives the double life of a navvy in Brixton by day and a Chelsea socialite by night: 'After a week of bare-chested ribaldry and laddishness with my boisterous chums on the building site, I would nip back home, put on my posh gear, brush my teeth and hose down my language and rendezvous with my own personal child of ease and privilege' (227). Bogle, therefore, straddles a divide between an occupational identity associated with working-class Irishness and a recreational identity associated with upper-class Englishness.

Bogle's penchant for performance is also evident in his role as narrator. 'It's time for me to show you around', he announces (45), before leading us, flamboyantly, into a theatrical journey through a homeless night on the streets. As quasi-autobiographer, Bogle is acutely aware of how 'narratival depth' (100), as he describes it, is crucial to maintaining the attention of his audience.[17] 'Obviously, we're lacking action here,' he states at one point, 'we're losing thrust and pace' (90). At other times, he makes self-deprecating comments about his literary abilities, reminiscent of Thackeray's Irish migrant hero in the novel *The Luck of Barry Lyndon* (1844). 'I don't quite know why I bother with all this ballsaching fire and semi-satire,' he complains, 'it doesn't really suit me and I'm not terribly good at it' (8). The relationship between diaspora space and narrative identity becomes most pronounced when we are introduced to the netherworld of a Kilburn drinking den, where events take place that amount to a London Irish variant on the 'Cyclops' episode of *Ulysses*. The following description of Bogle's entrance, as protagonist of his own self-reflexive third-person narration, warrants quotation in full:

A dark low-ceilinged chamber; wall mirrors reflect other fictional chambers, conjuring wide spaces bereft of glamour and generally confounding the eye. The cluttered butterthick air is filled with long troughs of tobacco smoke which spirals around the groups of drinking men like some ghostly foliage sprouting from the mangled, match-thin stubs of rolled paper clamped between their wicked yellow fingers. There is a constant clamour – the sottish riot of Irishmen arguing, bawling, singing and shouting in rational, national disharmony. The odour of the place is a verminous, cloying blend of stingsweet whisky fumes, stale spilt beer and rotting carpets. It is heady and warming – a homely fragrance. Confusion is nourished; stomachs bubble and babble burgeons. A young man enters from the left-hand side of this diverting scene, skulking through the lower and smaller of the two street doors. He is shabby and hunted, his face is pale and unshaven. Grime rings his collapsing shoes and his eyes are hollow and mirthless. Ripley Bogle, he is. On dead feet, he slouches through the Celtic mêlée, heading obliquely towards the bar. "So, what do I do?" he asks. "Get a job? Find somewhere to sleep? Retrieve my sliding life? No, of course not, I come to Kilburn to see if I can cadge a few drinks off some Irish dickhead like myself!" (128)

The narrative diaspora space described here, if similar in some ways to that of the Stork in *The Life of Riley* and the Pride of Erin in *Cowboys and Indians*, differs radically in others. The smoke and mirrors, referred to in the opening sentences, parallel the distorting effects of Bogle's skewed consciousness. What in reality may well be an ordinary London Irish bar is transformed through his 'hollow and mirthless' eyes into a phantasmagorical and dystopian vision of a migrant underworld, suspended between fact and fiction. Meanwhile, the reference to 'other fictional chambers', by mirroring the intertextuality of his own narrative, suggests that the precise nature of this particular microcosm of London Irish life is just as confounding and unrepresentable as his own identity. The sequence is prefaced by an exhortation on the significance of naming and, like the navvies who have preceded him, Bogle has accumulated a catalogue of pseudonyms, including Armand Lefevre, Boges, Ikey Moses and 'Shitface the Third'.[18] After a drunken display of self-criticism in which he describes his life-story as 'bad yankee fiction' (129), he indulges in a degrading sexual encounter with an older female drunk and loses an after-hours verse contest with the formidable Murphy brothers in a scene reminiscent of *At Swim-Two-Birds* (1939). From here on, the action becomes increasingly surreal, with the ghosts of Bogle's father and best friend appearing to him and, grotesquely, the baby that he helped his girlfriend abort in Belfast emerging from a toilet bowl to plead for his help. Finally, Bogle is unceremoniously ejected from the pub like a London Irish analogue of Leopold Bloom in Barney Kiernan's hostelry in Dublin and exiled from the community wherein he had hoped to take refuge.

Such encounters may explain why, rather than mixing with his ethnic peers, Bogle ultimately feels more at home on the streets. While itinerancy has its obvious drawbacks, he finds, nevertheless, that it offers qualities previously lacking in his life. Paramount among these is a guarantee of personal anonymity. This was something absent in his youth in Belfast, where religious and political divisions and allegiances severely constrained the development of his individuality, but it is absent also in the claustrophobic Irish company he finds in Kilburn. In the following passage he elaborates on the anonymity provided by his adopted home:

> The nicest thing about London is that London doesn't care. In Belfast I was fettered like all the Irish by the soft mastery of my country, by its mulch of nationhood and its austere, parental beauty. London will play ball if you make the effort but the city will leave you mostly unmolested. It provokes the pleasant spur of loneliness yet populates your dreams, despair or solitude. In dark suit striped with ancient grey London remains polite but distant. This is admirable behaviour on the part of any city and should be loudly commended. (271)

In a manner reminiscent of Patrick Kavanagh's personification of the city, Bogle celebrates London as a place where he can divest himself of the cultural straitjacket of his past and discover unexplored aspects of both his own identity and that of the city. He enjoys being on the margins of society and revels in the urban omniscience this affords him. As an Irishman, he already brings a certain perspective to bear on English society, but through the experience of exile on the streets, he acquires an additional degree of objectivity. He is not simply a migrant by virtue of his transplantation from Ireland to England, but also by virtue of his itinerant status on London's streets. In this sense, his identity is the product not just of the relationship between two nations, but of a more localized affiliation with the neighbourhoods and streets that he frequents in the metropolis. Although Bogle's past life in Belfast does provide a counterpoint to (and some explanation of) his present predicament, his fundamentally peripatetic and writerly identity finds its most emphatic voice through the narrativization of his London itinerant experience.

In contrast, the past and therefore Ireland is another country for Bogle. The loss of his father and his best friend at the hands of republican paramilitaries does not appear to have had any obvious emotional effects on him. Instead, his only signs of grief are reserved for the death of Perry, an older London Polish tramp, with whom he develops a cross-ethnic father–son relationship. However, their shared sense of migrant identity is rooted not so much in a multicultural 'confluence of narrativity', but in their shared freedom of movement and the lack of social and civic constraints that life on the streets affords them. Perry has long since disowned his nationality because of a strong distaste for his own countrymen, a sentiment which Bogle also vents on a regular basis, as in the following vitriolic diatribe:

> We Irish, we're all fucking idiots. No other people can rival us for the sense-less sentimentality in which we wallow. [...] As a people we're a shambles; as a nation – a disgrace; as a culture we're a bore ... individually we're often repellent. But we love it, us Irish fellows. We just slurp it up. The worse we are, the better we like it. We love old Ireland and it loves us. (160)

Bogle, therefore, rejects all allegiance to a sense of nationhood or ethnicity. Instead, through his status as a London itinerant, he finds he has more in common with a fellow migrant from Poland than with his own compatriots.[19] It is by tramping the streets that Bogle learns to read the narrative of the city. Dickens, with his 'nightly perambulations of grotty old London' (51), serves as his key reference point. He discovers that, like Victorian novels, the city and its identity are best read in narrative instalments, opening up a microscopic world in 'its smallest essence [...] its stones, its pipes and bricks and doorways and pavements' (17). Sheer size is often cited as a prime reason for why London is difficult to identify with, and Bogle describes it as 'wholly too vast' for his 'provincial compass' (165). His personal touchstone, therefore, is not so much the city as a whole, but more the journeys between particular locations, a phenomenon which Jonathan Raban describes in his memoir of London as 'unique as a footprint'.[20]

The pride Bogle takes in his adopted role as social geographer is apparent when he proclaims, 'I know these places as a tramp. As a watcher. That's what trampdom gives you – audience status; the observer's, the artist's overview. We tramps, we watch you all – and listen too. Rude perhaps but we've got bugger all else to do' (17). This role as the writer on the sidelines of mainstream society allows Bogle, like the figure of 'the fool' in Shakespearean drama, to pass astringent and incisive judgements on human nature proscribed elsewhere.

Foucault defines 'heterotopia' as a zone between the factual and the fictional, beyond conventional social structures of power and power relations, where an individual's behaviour is 'deviant in relation to the required mean or norm'.[21] In *Ripley Bogle*, this manifests itself as a sphere between the public and the private, made possible by the cosmopolitan and often anonymous nature of London street-life. As more and more of the conventional coordinates for anchoring a sense of identity elude him, wandering becomes Bogle's *raison d'être* and the domain of the streets provides him with his most secure sense of place.

As illustrated earlier in his description of the Kilburn drinking den, Bogle's writerly sense of exile appears to take its cue from Joyce. As with Stephen Dedalus, his persistently self-reflexive attitude to narration inevitably results in his 'fret[ting] in the shadow' of language. 'Where will I find the words I need?' he asks. 'I try. I try very hard. For wisdom and benevolence, for comprehension and resolution' (270). Bogle fears that he is ill-served by the tools of the storyteller's trade, but failing and 'failing better' in the face of the inadequacies of language seems to provide both his tramping and his writing with a sense of obstinate purpose. By ensuring that he puts one foot in front of the other, Bogle guarantees that he will always be moving on, making progress of sorts and, according to the principle of the *dérive* (the aimless stroll), turning the absence of a destination or an objective into a virtue rather than a failing.[22] When he states that '[p]erambulation's the name of my game' (201), he is alluding to the inherently linear practice of writing as much as walking. Michel de Certeau stated that 'every story is a travel story, a spatial practice',[23] and for Bogle too, a word is a step, a sentence is a movement, until a peripatetic narrative and attendant identity have been configured through words and the movement of a pen across a page. Bogle subscribes, by implication, to the cult of psychogeography, which Merlin Coverley describes as the realm where the 'figure[s] of writer and walker merge'.[24] In this respect, *Ripley Bogle* illustrates how migrant identity can be embodied, as well as enunciated, within the diaspora space of Irish London.

In the novels and short stories I have critiqued in this chapter, Irish migrant identity is narrativized in the form of high pastiche. Written with a postmodern sensibility, these texts do not give precedence to any single metanarrative; they evince, instead, a mult-dimensional form of narrative diaspora space. They are inhabited by a new, more self-confident generation of Irish migrants who find that the affirmation or performance of Irishness in London no longer has the same mythical or satirical purchase that it had for the previous generations. They are products of a society which, even as it was exporting its youth due to economic shortcomings and political strife, provided them with an education which ensured that they no longer saw themselves as simply the latest wave of an inevitable historical process. In this respect, they are more immune to the hegemonic discourses of the host community than were their predecessors, and to some extent those of their own community also. Like their forebears, they exploit their status as Irish migrants in London when it is to their advantage. But they are also aware that there are limitations on how far such a strategy can satisfy their search for a credible personal identity and, as a consequence, they employ other devices to assuage their sense of exile. This is evident in two ways: first, in how they move beyond the boundaries of their own ethnic communities and aspire to become part of the multicultural metropolis; secondly, in the way that they attempt to project themselves out of narrative into a realm of sensory perceptions devoid of textual meaning.

Neither of these strategies is wholly successful. Despite the fact that they belong to a more urbanized and better educated cohort of migrants than their parents' generation, O'Connor's and Wilson's anti-heroes still find that they must interact with their predecessors, and it is notable how the iconic figure of the Irish navvy makes a significant, if peripheral, reappearance in both texts. Ultimately, like members of the 'mail-boat generation', they must come to terms with the reality of their economic and cultural displacement and what this means for their own sense of self. In experiencing an existential form of exile beyond nation and migration, in the atemporal zone of the 'here and now', Eddie Virago and Ripley Bogle go further than their compatriots by rejecting the very premises upon which traditional exilic Irish migrant identity is constructed. By challenging the cultural polarities of home and away and of past and present they highlight the discursive nuances of diaspora space and deepen our understanding of the relationship between individual migrant identities and the historical narratives within which they are configured.

Notes

1   Joseph O'Connor, *Cowboys and Indians* (London: Flamingo, 1992), p. 2. Subsequent references to this text are cited in parentheses.

2   Gerry Smyth, *The Novel and the Nation: Studies in the New Irish Fiction* (London: Pluto Press, 1997), p. 151.

3   David Lloyd, *Ireland after History* (Cork: Cork University Press, 1999), p. 91.

4   Joseph O'Connor, 'Four Green Fields', in Dermot Bolger (ed.), *Ireland in Exile: Irish Writers Abroad* (Dublin: New Island, 1993), p. 144. Subsequent references to this text are cited in parentheses.

5   Curtis et al., *Hearts and Minds*, p. 16.

6   Joseph O'Connor, 'The Wizard of Oz', in *True Believers* (London: Flamingo, 1992), pp. 33–48.

7   Joseph O'Connor, 'Getting to Know the English', in *The Secret Life of the Irish Male* (London: Minerva, 1995), p. 42. 'How to be Irish in London' appears as a subsection of this essay.

8   O'Connor, 'Introduction', p. 14.

9   For a discussion of the precise circumstances which inspired this poem, see Timothy Webb, 'Yeats and the English', in Joseph McMinn (ed.), *The Internationalism of Irish Literature and Drama* (Gerrards Cross: Colin Smythe, 1992), pp. 246–47. For another reference to this precise location of diaspora space, see the contemporaneous ballad 'The Mountains of Mourne' (1896) by Percy French.

10 Joseph O'Connor, 'Last of the Mohicans', in *True Believers* (London: Flamingo, 1992), p. 3. Subsequent references to this text are cited in parentheses.

11 For a postmodern interpretation of Eddie Virago's sense of alienation in London, see Linden Peach, *The Contemporary Irish Novel: Critical Readings* (Basingstoke: Palgrave Macmillan, 2004), pp. 30–34.

12 It comes as little surprise that when Eddie Virago appears again ten years later, he has returned to live in Dublin and has developed a somewhat cynical perspective on his time in London. See Joseph O'Connor, 'Two Little Clouds', in Oona Frawley (ed.), *New Dubliners: Celebrating 100 Years of Joyce's Dubliners* (London: Pegasus Books, 2006), pp. 1–18.

13 Wilson lived rough on the streets of Belfast for a time and also studied at Cambridge University. For further details, see Richard Mills, '"All Stories Are Love Stories": Robert McLiam Wilson Interviewed by Richard Mills', *Irish Studies Review* 7.1 (1999), pp. 73–77.

14 See, for instance, Eamonn Hughes, '"Town of Shadows": Representations of Belfast in Recent Fiction', *Religion and Literature* 28.2–3 (Summer–Autumn 1996), pp. 141–60; Cleary, *Outrageous Fortune*, pp. 159–66; Esther Aliago Rodrigo, 'Glenn Patterson and Robert McLiam Wilson: Two Contemporary Northern Irish Writers and the Question of National Identity', in Marisol Morales Ladrón (ed.), *Postcolonial and Gender Perspectives in Irish Studies* (La Coruña: Netbiblo, 2007).

15 Robert McLiam Wilson, *Ripley Bogle* (London: Picador, 1989), p. 23. Subsequent references to this text are cited in parentheses.

16 Bogle makes a cameo appearance in one of Wilson's later novels, indicating that he eventually returns to live in Belfast. See *Eureka Street: A Novel of Ireland Like No Other* (London: Secker & Warburg, 1996), p. 346.

17 Such meta-discursive practices have a long tradition in Irish literature, directly linking this late-twentieth-century novel with similar texts from as early as the mid-eighteenth century, such as Laurence Sterne, *The Life and Opinions of Tristram Shandy, Gentleman* (1759–67).

18 The first of these pseudonyms is a possible reference to the French philosopher Henri Lefebvre, whose work on the production of social and cultural space was an influence on the practice of 'psychogeography' with which *Ripley Bogle* could be associated. The third, Ikey Moses, is an anti-Semitic name used in the nineteenth century to refer to a Jewish con-man. There are repeated references to the name in connection with the character of Leopold Bloom. See James Joyce, *Ulysses* (Oxford: Oxford University Press, 1998), p. 55, p. 192, p. 491.

19 The character of Micil Ó Maoláin experiences similar disillusionment with his own countrymen and (despite his tragic death) finds his only real sense of belonging with London's community of down-and-outs. See Ó Conaire, *Deoraíocht*.

20 Jonathan Raban, *Soft City* (London: Fontana, 1975), p. 94.

21 Michel Foucault, 'Of Other Spaces', *Diacritics* 16.1 (1967), p. 25.

22 See Guy Debord, 'Theory of the *Dérive*', in Ken Knabb (ed.), *Situationist International Anthology* (Berkeley: Bureau of Public Secrets, 1981), pp. 50–54. The original article was published in 1958 in *Internationale Situationniste #2*.

23 Michel de Certeau, *The Practice of Everyday Life* (Berkeley: University of California Press, 2002), p. 115.

24 Merlin Coverley, *Psychogeography* (Harpenden: Pocket Essentials, 2006), p. 49. With its roots in the work of Daniel Defoe, William Blake and Thomas de Quincey, psychogeography is the notion of inscribing the topography of the city through the mythical and potentially transcendent powers of writing. For an exemplar of the genre, see Iain Sinclair, *Lights Out for the Territory* (London: Granta, 1997).

9

Transit and Transgression

In her inaugural address as President of Ireland in 1990, Mary Robinson stated that she saw her election as an opportunity for Irish people world-wide to 'tell diverse stories [...] stories of celebration through the arts and stories of conscience and social justice'.[1] Seven years later Gerry Smyth argued that

> something fundamentally different has overtaken novelistic discourse in Ireland since the mid-1980s [...] a willingness to confront the formal and conceptual legacies of a received literary (and wider social) tradition along-side a self-awareness of the role played by cultural narratives in mediating modern (or perhaps it would be better now to say *postmodern*) Ireland's changing circumstances.[2]

Arguably, there had not been a generation of Irish writers so conscious of the contribution they were making to the redefinition of Irish iden-tities since the Literary Revival a century before. Part of this development was the rapidly increasing number of short stories by female Irish writers which began to appear during the 1980s. This was largely the result of the social and cultural changes that had taken place in Ireland over the previous two decades, as the country slowly moved away from the old certainties of Catholicism, nationalism and patriarchy. The changing role of women in Irish society was a pronounced feature of this transformation and the women's movement a key catalyst in the process. In the literary world, this was evidenced by the emergence of small feminist presses such as Attic Press and Arlen House. Despite these changes, women's rights in Ireland experienced setbacks such as the results of the abortion and divorce referenda in 1983 and 1986. As a result, large numbers of women continued to leave the country, the majority choosing to migrate to London and the south-east of England.

The more positive changes for women that had taken place in Ireland, however, were reflected in the London Irish community, with a marked expansion and diversification of women's involvement in cultural and political activities. A series of London Irish women's conferences in the mid-1980s were crucial in this regard and led to, for instance, the establishment of Fine Lines, an Irish women writers' group.[3]

The two writers I focus on in this chapter, Emma Donoghue and Sara Berkeley, both lived in the south-east of England at this time. Donoghue is now one of Ireland's best-known female writers. She first came to public prominence in the early 1990s with novels about lesbian sexuality, based on her experiences in Dublin, where she grew up, and Cambridge, where she studied for her PhD. Berkeley, who was also born in Dublin, is now better known as a poet but in her early career wrote fiction, which was influenced by her experience of living in London in the late 1980s. The protagonists of Donoghue's and Berkeley's short stories are, in many ways, typical of the Ryanair generation, but I demonstrate how the temporary nature of their adopted home in London contributes to a distinct sense of provisionality in the way their diasporic identities are narrativized. Some years ago, Iain Chambers noted how the migrant is 'cut off from the homelands of tradition, experiencing a constantly challenged identity' and is 'perpetually required to make herself at home in the interminable discussion between a scattered historical inheritance and a heterogeneous present'.[4] This discursive dimension to the configuration of identities in narrative diaspora space is captured well in the work of both authors. Their protagonists have escaped from the social constraints of 1980s' Ireland, but have not found their new lives in London entirely satisfactory. Instead the city represents a form of limbo, where, as for Edna O'Brien's protagonists, the initial elation of escape from Ireland has worn off but hopes of an alternative life have not yet materialized. On reading these stories one is reminded of John Berger's assertion that 'in his imagination every migrant worker is in transit. He remembers the past: he anticipates the future: his aims and his reconciliations make his thoughts a train between the two'.[5] By the close of both short stories, the leading protagonists are considering the prospect of either returning home or migrating further afield. In this respect, these stories pick up on the theme of return examined earlier in the work of John McGahern, but they also engage with the topic of re-migration, something which both authors eventually experienced themselves.[6]

'Going Back' (1993) by Emma Donoghue

This short story is Donoghue's earliest published work, and is notable for its highlighting of the ways in which cultural allegiances and their often shifting signifiers come into conflict in the 'confluence of narrativity' that characterizes diaspora space. Cyn, the lesbian protagonist of the story, is a former step-dance instructor who left Ireland in 1978 and is now working in London as a secretarial temp. "'I felt more of an exile for twenty years in Ireland,'" she tells Lou, a gay male friend, "'than I ever have in the twelve I've been out of it.'"[7] Her comment highlights how exile can manifest itself internally as well as externally and how, by leaving Ireland, she has attempted to escape from exile rather than (in the more traditional sense) been projected into it. In the process, traditional notions of nation and sexual orientation are questioned and challenged by Cyn as she veers increasingly towards a non-essentialized, performative and queered sense of self.

The action takes place over a period of approximately one year (1990–91) and during this time, which sees the election of Mary Robinson as President, these two young migrants discuss whether Ireland has changed sufficiently (particularly with regard to homosexuality) for them to consider returning. Lou, who gave up a vocation for the priesthood, now works as a set-painter with a community theatre group at the Rainbow Centre in Brixton. He is less alienated from his home country than Cyn and flaunts a 'shamrock in relief on the back of his No. 2 shave' to prove it (158). He is more amenable to the idea of return and attempts to persuade Cyn to consider it. However, like many of her generation of migrants, she continues to feel a sense of disappointment and frustration with the Irish state for not acknowledging her sexuality. "'I don't know, Lou-Lou,'" she says, "'the very idea makes me tired. Wake me up when Ireland starts consenting to us instead of kicking us in the teeth'" (170). This feeling of exclusion, which had been the original reason for her migration, continues to assert itself abroad, so much so that she now feels fundamentally alienated from her nationality:

> "I mean, I don't seem to remember ever being consulted. Correct if I'm wrong." She pointed a stubby finger. "Were you ever asked if you agreed to be Irish?" He shook his head carefully, once. "All that cultural baggage foisted" – Cyn paused, checking the word – "absolutely *foisted* upon us without a by your leave." She continued, her finger dipping on every impor-

tant word like a conductor's baton. "And what happens if you try and refuse it or leave it behind? Everybody freaks out as if you've dumped a baby in a carrier bag at the airport." (161)

By alluding to the way in which national identity in Ireland has been historically determined, Cyn argues that its constructedness is only revealed when challenged in this fundamental way. However, Cyn's choice of destination inevitably means that she is faced with addressing the legacy of Britain's historical relationship with Ireland and the notion of national identity which is one of its products.

This is illustrated by the way she is branded by her accent in London. Lou notices, for instance, how her voice 'relaxed and dipped' (158) and how it had become more Irish-sounding over the period of their friend-ship in London. After agreeing to teach Irish step-dance to children in the local community centre, Cyn notices that keeping time in English is less satisfactory than doing so in Gaelic (159). Despite her reservations about her nationality, therefore, she feels compelled to assert it in certain circumstances. Cyn's predicament illustrates Ricoeur's point that narra-tive identities are not only determined by individuals but also by historical and political circumstances. As Margret Somers has observed, 'we come to be who we are (however ephemeral, multiple and changing) by being located or locating ourselves (usually unconsciously) in social narratives rarely of our own making'.[8] The role that uncon-scious signifiers such as accent play in this process is highlighted here, illustrating how aural and performative as well as narrative dimensions of language can have an impact on how an identity is configured. Differing subject positions within the frame of ethnicity are, as Brah points out, proclaimed or disavowed according to circumstances, and this is apparent when Cyn explains to Lou that her precise sense of Irish-ness may be different to his. "'Dublin's not home," she says, "'I grew up a hundred and fifty miles away. I've been to Manchester more often than Dublin.'" When he responds by saying, "'Well, think of it as a halfway point [...] between the Rainbow Centre and your parish hall'" (168), one assumes that she comes from the geographical periphery of Ireland (perhaps a Gaeltacht). Cyn's remarks about Dublin suggest that she is dissociating herself from the capital city and any national claims it might have on her identity. The exact location of her place of birth is not confirmed, but the distinction she makes between it and Dublin implies that, by comparison, her regional identity is more important to her. However, her reference to Manchester also suggests that she is as familiar with British society as she is with Irish society and that her past experiences of travelling between the two have, in her view, somewhat diminished their supposed cultural differences. These may be passing and rather ambiguous remarks in a spontaneous exchange about identity, but what they do clearly reveal is the extent to which Cyn is determined not to be pigeon-holed into a preconceived identity category of any kind.

This is corroborated by her reaction to Lou when he first realizes she is a lesbian. When he congratulates her on being one of the '"little green fairies"', she rebukes him by saying, '"I've never felt like one of an us"' (158). This comment can be read as a reaction to the term 'fairies' as much as to the term 'green', that is, to her assumed inclusion into a category of sexual preference as much as one of national identity. Cyn, therefore, is someone who has begun to challenge not only the heterosexual and patriarchal bias of the society she grew up in but also the essentializing tendencies of her peers with regard to the politics of sexuality.[9] Lesbian and gay identities in the 1970s and 1980s were predicated on quite rigid ideas of sexual difference. Public expressions of bisexuality and transgenderism were not common (at least outside theatrical circles) and it was not until the late 1980s that the boundaries of homosexuality were challenged in this way.[10] In other words, Cyn is not prepared to be the victim of a binary opposition between narratives of sexuality any more than of that between narratives of nationality. Her sense of identity, therefore, is 'queered' and resistant to monocultural categorizations of any kind. Despite her indecisions and the 'troubling insecurity and uncertainty of identity' that Aidan Arrowsmith identifies in the story,[11] Cyn has developed a sophisticated and assertive sense of self by rejecting any form of homogeneity.

Lou, if less perturbed by cultural categorizations, largely shares her position. Like Cyn, he appears to be more at home when testing the boundaries of such domains rather than reinforcing them, something demonstrated when the story opens with the two protagonists playacting at being a 'straight' couple in the presence of their co-workers at the community centre: 'Cyn kicked the machine systematically. She glanced down at Lou, who was scrabbling under the radiator for a pound coin. "Come on, wimp, help me kick," she told him. "I'm not letting you deflower me without a packet of Thick-Ribbed Ultras"' (157). By provoking quizzical reactions from their peers, they enjoy challenging assumptions about their sexuality in a mischievous and performative manner. Moreover, by so doing, they demonstrate that narrative is not only intrinsic to the construction of identity but can also act as a means of relief and escape from pre-given and more rigid categorizations imposed from without. On another occasion, Cyn takes Lou to a 'dyke' club which does not admit men (gay or straight). Wearing 'matching Pervert t-shirts' and dancing 'like lunatics under a full moon' (164), Cyn passes Lou off as her 'slave' and then tells a curious woman that he is her son. Both of them not only take a roguish pleasure in breaching controls imposed by one minority group over another, but again construct a fictional narrative as a means of asserting rights to a proscribed cultural space. By deploying such narratives, Cyn and Lou are able to express the nuances of their sexuality in a way which is closed to them by more conventional and static classifications.

This shared predilection for iconoclastic and rebellious behaviour is what brings the two migrants increasingly close, and Cyn tells Lou how nice it has been '"getting to know someone who was gay but of the opposite sex, like having so much in common yet being so far apart"'. '"How brilliant it was,"' she adds, with some self-irony, '"that the two of them could sort of share their thoughts without having them sort of curdled by heteropatriarchal patterns"' (165). Cyn's use of the term 'curdled' suggests stasis and stultification, something she is determined to avoid at all costs, even if it requires her being disloyal to her lesbian constituency. However, the experience of sleeping together leaves both of them feeling sexually frustrated and somewhat embarrassed. When they accept it was an experiment that didn't work and pledge to stay 'just good friends', this marks a crucial turning point in the story. When Cyn tells herself that 'she wouldn't have to unearth that "Bi Any Other Name" badge after all' (168), one assumes that she has acknowledged certain limits on her sexuality and that any aspiration she might have had to a hybrid sexual identity is something she is happy to let go. By the close of the story, she is still unsure of where she should live but she does appear to have a clearer sense of her personal identity. London, and her relationship with Lou there, has provided her with an opportunity to explore a number of different configurations of identity. Self-knowledge, Cyn seems to conclude, is as much about coming to terms, refiguratively, with who she is as much as it is about pursuing, prefiguratively, what she aspires to be.

'The Swimmer' (1991) by Sara Berkeley

A similar reconciliation takes place in Sara Berkeley's short story. Cam migrates to London to escape from an incestuous sexual relationship with her brother, Rene, which has left her emotionally damaged and lacking in self-confidence.[12] 'Life,' she declares, 'was too big and I wasn't enough to fill it'.[13] She is puzzled by how major changes in people's lives can seem so matter-of-fact to them. 'How do people live their lives?' she ponders. 'Is this it? Is this how the decisions come about?' (112). Although Cam's decision to migrate, rather like Kate's in *Girls in Their Married Bliss,* appears to have been spontaneous, it proves to have been germinating in her subconscious for some time, something illustrated by the following description of a dream she had prior to leaving:

> I dreamed I was swimming. Out against the small choppy waves. The wind was warm against my face, that quick wind that came up in the early evening. The boys were shouting from the beach, I could hear them, but I was swimming and swimming, through the deep blue, over to the other side. Maybe they're calling me back, I thought, but the swimming didn't leave much time for thinking. Maybe I should look back, I thought, or maybe I can just keep swimming, over to the other side. After that I thought nothing at all. I just swam. (114–15)

The act of swimming appears to be a metaphor for Cam's escape from Ireland; the dream, by implication, a warning about how difficult it is for a migrant to change her decision to leave once the physical act of boarding a ferry or a plane has been undertaken. Cam chooses to go to London because she knows she can stay with her uncle Hugh there, but otherwise her choice of destination seems to have been quite arbitrary.[14] She confesses, 'there hadn't been much thinking – not of what would happen after … after I boarded the ferry. Thought had stopped there' (120). In other words, so strong is her drive to escape that just being gone is sufficient achievement. Even during the train journey from Holyhead to London she remains in a state of emotional limbo. She recalls staring down at a river from the train window and of having 'felt suspended, way up there with nothing below my feet'. 'It was a dangerous feeling,' she continues, 'and I half relaxed into the danger as though it was my only friend' (115). This in-between state, literally one of suspension, mirrors Cam's state of indecision about her future life and identity. Rather than inducing a sense of anxiety, Cam (like Elizabeth

Bowen) finds comfort in being on the cusp between leaving and arriving, halfway between Ireland and London.[15] The passage, however, also gestures towards possible suicide. Anne-Marie Fortier notes that 'the space and time when bodies "hover perilously" between two "moments" is lived at once as eternal and momentary for it is inhabited by living embodiments and embodied memories of continuity, presence and change'.[16] By inhabiting such a state, Cam appears to strive for a transcendental sense of identity beyond mere territory and even her own corporeality.

Like thousands of Irish people before her, Cam arrives in London through the migrant threshold of Euston station. Caught once more on a diasporic axis between departure and arrival, she has second thoughts about her decision. 'Turn back!' she tells herself. 'You can go back now! None of this has to happen!' (116). As was the case for Eddie Virago, Euston station is not simply a physical crossing point but a psychological intersection in diaspora space. As the prospect of dislocation in an unknown city confronts her, Cam finds herself culturally immobilized by conflicting narratives of escape, exile and possible return. Despite this, she finds a job and moves in with her uncle, with whom she shares a love of books and reading. She takes refuge in literary allusions as a means of assuaging her fears about what the city might have in store. 'It's like Dickens,' she thinks. 'So much crowding and noise. I let the crowds dull my thoughts. I let them trample down my rising heart' (115–16). Like Eddie Virago and Ripley Bogle, she welcomes the opportunity to dissolve her worries in the anonymity of the metropolis and finds a way to 'shut the avenues off, to close down thought and memory' (121). Gradually, Cam discovers that London offers her a more effective means of escape from her past than she had anticipated. During a visit to the British Museum, however, the motif of the threshold emerges again in another context when she records the following lines of poetry in her guidebook: '"They are not long, the weeping and the laughter, love and desire and hate. I think they have no portion in us after we pass the gate"' (123).[17] The gate here is quite clearly a metaphor for death, but given the traditional association between death and exile in Irish culture, it can equally be read as the Rubicon on an irreversible psychological journey that she has taken by becoming a migrant.[18]

Cam's relationship with literature and writing provides her with a cathartic means of coming to terms with past trauma. This is illustrated during a regular exchange of letters between her and Rene, which provides a narrative conduit to past events and the means of configuring, however tentatively, a new identity. Despite the psychological damage she has suffered from the relationship with her brother, Cam is still very close to Rene. She clearly draws some emotional sustenance from the correspondence, which is conducted in what she describes as their 'own cryptic tongue' (130). However, when John, an old college friend, arrives in London, this bond is tested. 'The letters,' Cam recalls, 'were becoming harder as the edge wore off' (130). John attempts to persuade her to follow him to Australia, something she initially resists. In the following exchange, he reveals a distinctly fatalistic attitude to the subject of migration:

> "I mean it," he leaned forward, suddenly aggressive. "They're dead people back there, all of them, and I'm a dead man. It all starts tomorrow at eleven when I step on that plane." "So I'm dead too." "No." He sat back. "You're not dead." Finishing his drink, he got up to go to the bar. "You're just asleep." (132)

John's comments about migration as a form of death echo the exilic association referred to above. But his attempt to configure an identity along these lines is devoid of any real meaning, other than a somewhat spurious and self-indulgent association with martyrdom. His description of Cam being 'asleep', on the other hand, has more resonance, given earlier references to her sense of diasporic suspension. Eventually, she opts to take his advice. 'John was right,' she decides. 'It was as if I'd been leaving all along, and London was a stopover. I glanced down at the globe, then lifted it onto my lap. Australia' (141). By choosing a desti-nation so far from home Cam not only demonstrates how powerful the impulse to escape continues to be for her, but how determined she is never to return.

As she spends her last few days with her uncle Hugh and they resume their shared love of literature, the metaphor from the beginning of the story recurs when he asks her to read him John Cheever's short story 'The Swimmer' (1964). Set in the middle-class suburbs of mid-twen-tieth-century New York State, it is about a man who decides to make his way home one day by swimming through the private pools of his friends and neighbours.[19] However, at each pool he visits *en route*, time begins to play tricks on him; hours turn to days and days to months. As his strength diminishes, his friends become increasingly distant and when, finally, he reaches his own home, he finds to his consternation that the house is locked and empty. If read as an extended metaphor for

Cam's predicament, each swimming pool represents another hurdle on her journey of migration and constant desire to find a sense of home. But the deeper implication of the story is that, if Cam does finally decide to return to Ireland, she may discover that it no longer feels like the home she left in the first place. In this respect, the story serves as an allegory for Cam's relationship with migration, in which the narrativization of her identity is affected by the temporal, as well as the spatial, dimensions of diaspora space.

The texts I have critiqued in this chapter illustrate how, for the Ryanair generation, the decision to leave Ireland was often based upon social and cultural as much as economic imperatives. As was the case with texts previously discussed, national identity is inflected and often displaced by regional, generational or political factors, but most apparent is the decisive shift away from essentialized notions of identity *per se*. In Cyn's case, this is the idea of identity as queered, while in Cam's case, it is the notion of identity in a form of suspension. The belief in a foundational narrative upon which to construct an identity has little purchase in these texts. In one respect, this is clearly because the discourses of nationhood appear to have less authority over these individuals than they had over those from previous decades. However, Cyn and Cam both come to realize that, ultimately, they do not have complete authority over their own personal identities either. Cyn discovers that, despite her best efforts, her identity has been configured not so much by narratives beyond her control as by language itself, whether in the form of accent or the persistent traces of her Gaelic-speaking past. In the case of Cam, control appears to have been relinquished even before departure. Importantly, her identity is configured as much by undisclosed stories from the past as by the narrative of migration and re-migration that defines her present situation. In contrast to the texts from the mail-boat generation, these texts barely acknowledge discourses about the Irish in London produced by the host community, which remain peripheral or non-existent. The focus is less on the external relationship between migrant and host community and more on the internal relationship these migrants have not just with where they have come from, but also with where they plan to go next.

Rather like the experience of Edna O'Brien's protagonists, escape for Donoghue's and Berkeley's London Irish protagonists is, ultimately, a somewhat unfulfilling experience. The narrative diaspora space of these stories is, as a consequence, a highly ambivalent one. Cyn hopes to find in London a freedom to express her identity in a way that is not possible in Ireland, but discovers that her ability to achieve this is prescribed by the extent to which narratives of sexuality are politicized at the time. Cam, on the other hand, has (like Willa McCord in *Casualties of Peace*) migrated to escape an abusive relationship, and has the emotional scars to show for it. As a consequence, she struggles to build a new life and identity for herself abroad. Both women are caught in a diasporic limbo between leaving, arriving and leaving again. London, therefore, is not so much a destination or home for these women as a place of temporary refuge in a longer, more open-ended journey of migration and transformation which, once embarked upon, may or may not be satisfactorily concluded.

Notes

1 As cited in Katie Donovan, Norman A. Jeffares and Brendan Kennelly (eds.), *Ireland's Women: Writings Past and Present* (London: Kyle Cathie Ltd, 1994), pp. 253–54.

2 Smyth, *The Novel and the Nation*, p. 7.

3 Interview conducted by the author with Áine Collins, one of the founders of Fine Lines, 19 May 1991.

4 Iain Chambers, *Migrancy, Culture, Identity* (London: Routledge, 1994), p. 6.

5 John Berger and John Mohr, *A Seventh Man* (New York: Viking Press, 1975), p. 64.

6 Donoghue now lives in Canada while Berkeley lives in California.

7 Emma Donoghue, 'Going Back', in Dermot Bolger (ed.), *Ireland in Exile: Irish Writers Abroad* (Dublin: New Island, 1993), p. 160. Subsequent references to this text are cited in parentheses.

8 Margret Somers, 'The Narrative Constitution of Identity', *Theory and Society* 23.5 (October 1994), p. 606.

9 Donoghue herself has referred to such attitudes as 'rather doctrinaire'. See Stacia Bensyl, 'Swings and Roundabouts: An Interview with Emma Donoghue', *Irish Studies Review* 8.1 (2000), p. 4.

10 The London-based Irish writer Cherry Smyth was at the forefront of such debates. See Cherry Smyth, *Lesbians Talk Queer Notions* (London: Scarlet Press, 1992).

11 Aidan Arrowsmith, 'Inside-Out: Literature, Cultural Identity and Irish Migration to England', in Ashok Bery and Patricia Murray (eds.), *Comparing Postcolonial Literatures: Dislocations* (Basingstoke: Palgrave, 2000), p. 67.

12 Berkeley explored similar themes at greater length in a subsequent novel. However, the novel does not feature the subject of return and re-migration to the same extent as the short story and, for this reason, I have chosen to focus on the latter for the purposes of this chapter. See Sara Berkeley, *Shadowing Hannah* (Dublin: New Island Books, 1999).

13 Sara Berkeley, 'The Swimmer', in *The Swimmer in the Deep Blue Dream* (Dublin:

Raven Arts Press, 1991), pp. 111–12. Subsequent references to this text are cited in parentheses.

14 Hugh moved to London in the 1960s, but there is little reference in the text to his experience of migration.

15 Bowen reputedly claimed that she felt most at home in the middle of the Irish Sea. See Foster, *Paddy and Mr. Punch*, p. 107.

16 Anne-Marie Fortier, *Migrant Belongings : Memory, Space, Identity* (Oxford: Berg, 2000), p. 174.

17 The lines are taken from the following poem, first published in 1896: Ernest Dowson, 'Vitae summa brevis spem nos vetat incohare longam' ('How should hopes be long, when life is short'), in *The Poems of Ernest Dowson* (London: John Lane, 1902), p. 2.

18 Farewell parties held the night before migrants' departure, for instance, were referred to as 'American Wakes'. See Lawrence J. Taylor, 'Bás In Eirinn: Cultural Constructions of Death in Ireland', *Anthropological Quarterly* 62.4 (October 1989), pp. 175–87.

19 John Cheever, 'The Swimmer', in *The Brigadier and the Golf Widow* (London: Gollancz, 1965).

Part III

THE SECOND GENERATION

After a lapse of time, the past becomes a mythical country – a dreamscape. Memory is a literary exercise: it shapes our yesterdays into narrative form, an inevitably fictionalizing process.[1]

In the British census of 2001, which for the first time allowed respondents to indicate their 'cultural background', only seven to eight per cent of an estimated two to two and a half million second-generation Irish people in Britain ticked the box marked 'Irish'. Researchers have offered a number of reasons why such a small percentage of second-generation migrants were disinclined to identify themselves in this way, among them being a tendency to read the concept of 'cultural background' (or ethnicity) as equivalent to formal nationality.[2] The outcome of the census illustrates just how difficult it is to quantify or categorize something as elusive as personal identity. Qualitative and ethnographic approaches appear to be better able to elicit and reflect the subtleties and nuances of cultural orientations and allegiances, and interviews conducted with second-generation Irish subjects demonstrate this.[3] Research by Philip Ullah on schoolchildren from Irish backgrounds in London and Birmingham in the 1980s discovered that they were remarkably adroit at adapting their cultural identities to differing circumstances and had developed sophisticated approaches to negotiating conflicts of allegiance in the public and private domains. As Ullah says of his subjects, 'the very flexibility of their identities means they can actually respond to competing situational demands when such a response is required. They are not doomed to remain on the boundaries of two cultures but are able to take an active part in both'.[4] This ability to develop a dual identity seems crucial for second-generation children and is illustrated by Patrick Joyce's essay about growing up with Irish parents in north London in the 1940s and 1950s. Joyce describes how his Irishness and Catholicism provided him with a 'structure of meaning' while, at the same time, he was 'versed in the ways of London and [moved] in the city like fish through water'.[5] For others, the process is more conflicted. In the foreword to his study on exile in Irish literature, Patrick Ward describes how his parents used the term 'home' to refer to Ireland rather than London and explains the effects of this on him in the following way:

> For us children this emphasis on 'Home' by those we loved and admired was both intensely appealing and oddly alienating. It appealed at a primary instinctual level in that it gave us a history. We could make the connection in the narrative of our lives [...] At the same time that involvement in the past of our parents was peculiar and estranging – their 'Home' was theirs – most of us had never been to Ireland. The Ireland we identified with was largely imaginary.[6]

Like many second-generation Irish children, Ward grew up having an ambivalent relationship with the term 'home', but his use of the phrases 'narrative of our lives' and 'largely imaginary' indicates how the process of identity formation entails a storytelling dimension. As Ricoeur points out, each of us constructs our own personal biography on a daily basis, regardless of whether we choose to consign it to paper or not, but memoir and autobiography are particularly interesting for the way they reveal how such an interior sense of narrative identity is re-narrativized in textual form.

Given that the Irish are one of the oldest ethnic minority groups in Britain and that London has been the favoured destination of Irish migrants since the Second World War, literary accounts by and about the descendants of Irish migrants in the city have not been as common as one would expect. The second-generation literature of other ethnic groups, such as Jews and Asians, is generally better known.[7] In reference to this, Shane Connaughton predicted, in 1991, that 'the second-generation Irish conflict of identity is a cultural time bomb waiting to go off'.[8] However, if such an explosion did take place, it certainly was not widely heard. A writer of second-generation Irish experience has not yet emerged who can be compared to, for instance, Arnold Wesker, Hanif Kureishi or Zadie Smith. The dramatist Martin McDonagh is the best known second-generation London Irish writer of recent years but, although Aidan Arrowsmith has persuasively read his plays as 'a working through of the processes and obstacles of second-generation identity construction', none of his work directly addresses the lives and preoccupations of second-generation people in the diaspora.[9]

The experience of growing up in London of Irish parents has historically been recounted more often in memoir than in fiction, and the five texts I analyse here (only one of which is classified as fiction) reflect this.[10] All the subjects of these texts, which were published between the late 1980s and the turn of the millennium, grew up in London Irish families during the first three decades after the Second World War. By returning to the immediate post-war decades, these texts also provide a rare example of how the lives and attitudes of first-generation Irish migrants during that period impacted on their children. The accounts portray the conflicts and contradictions of such experiences and highlight how themes and tropes explored earlier in the work of first-generation migrant writers are regenerated by the London-born Irish. The period covered in Part I is revisited, therefore, but from the perspective of middle age, highlighting the distinctly generational relationship between the period in which texts are written and the period in which they are set.

Memoir and autobiographical fiction would appear to confirm the poststructuralist notion that subjectivity is discursively produced. Such texts engage not only with the past and the events that shaped the identities of their subjects, but with the narratives and discourses within which those identities were configured. Childhood memories play a crucial role in this process. Because they are recalled from the distant rather than the recent past and are prone to reinterpretation and renarrativization over time, they provide particularly good sources for examining how fact and fiction interact during the storytelling process. As George O'Brien has stated, 'childhood as a subject is more effectively treated as an imaginative reservoir to be plumbed rather than an archaeological dig yielding trophies to be displayed'.[11] Also useful here is Marianne Hirsch's concept of 'postmemory', which she describes as

> a powerful and very particular form of memory precisely because its connection to its object or source is mediated not through recollection but through an imaginative investment and creation. [...] Postmemory characterizes the experience of those who grow up dominated by narratives that preceded their birth, whose own belated stories are evacuated by the stories of the previous generation shaped by traumatic events that can be neither understood nor recreated.[12]

The narrative diaspora space of second-generation London Irish literature might, therefore, be conceived of as a collective form of postmemory, a body of work which regenerates and refigures events from 'family mythology' and the associated cultural discourses and ideologies which pre-date the birth of its authors. For this reason, a key aspect of the analysis in this part of the book is the way in which tropes of migration and diaspora, explored earlier, are renarrativized through the selected texts.

A further aim is to investigate literary representations of the experience of the second-generation Irish in the specificity of their London setting.[13] Rather than just being a stage for the performance of identity or even a catalyst in the production of identity, in these texts London and Londonness are intrinsic to the narrativization of identity itself. The common experience of the annual summer holiday in Ireland is recognized as an important ingredient in the development of second-generation Irish identity. However, I only cover the topic here in so far as it impacts on the experiences of subjects in London. I have not, therefore, been able to examine novels about female second-generation experience such as those by Maude Casey and Brian Keaney, for instance, because neither of them explore in any detail their protagonists' experiences in the city.[14] In Chapter 10, I examine three memoirs which attempt to negotiate competing registers of cultural allegiance within Irish working-class families in post-war London. In Chapter 11, I compare a memoir and an autobiographical novel. While experiences of cultural disjunction are equally apparent in these texts, the way their authors mediate this experience is more self-reflexive than the approach of the authors in the previous chapter and the conclusions arrived at, with regard to questions of identity, declaredly more provisional and ambivalent.

Notes

1   Emanuel Litvinoff, *Journey Through a Small Planet* (London: Penguin, 2008), p. vii.
2   See Bronwen Walter, 'English/Irish Hybridity: Second-generation Diasporic Identities', *International Journal of Diversity in Organisations, Communities and Nations* 5.7 (2005/2006), pp. 17–24.
3   See, for instance, Philip Ullah, 'Second-generation Irish Youth: Identity and Ethnicity', *New Community* 12 (Summer 1985), pp. 310–20; Bronwen Walter, Sarah Morgan, Mary J. Hickman and Joseph Bradley, 'Family Stories, Public Silence: Irish Identity Construction Amongst the Second Generation Irish in England', *Scottish*

Geographical Journal 118.3 (2002), pp. 201–17.

4   Ullah, 'Second-generation Irish Youth', p. 319.

5   Patrick Joyce, 'More Secondary Modern than Postmodern', *Rethinking History* 5.3 (2001), p. 375; p. 369.

6   Ward, *Exile, Emigration and Irish Writing*, p. viii.

7   For examples of second-generation London Jewish literature, see Israel Zangwill, *Children of the Ghetto* (London: Heinemann, 1892); Simon Blumenfeld, *Jew Boy* (London: Jonathan Cape, 1935). For examples of second-generation London Asian literature, see Hanif Kureishi, *The Buddha of Suburbia* (London: Faber & Faber, 1990); Gautam Malkani, *Londonstani* (London: Fourth Estate, 2006). For examples of literature about 'mixed race' Londoners, see Bernadine Evaristo, *Lara* (Tunbridge Wells: Angela Royal Publishing, 1997); Zadie Smith, *White Teeth* (London: Hamish Hamilton, 2000).

8   Interview conducted by the author with Shane Connaughton, 16 May 1991. The best-known example of a literary portrayal of the second-generation London Irish is a stage-play, which is beyond the scope of this research. See Mary O'Malley, *Once a Catholic* (London: Amber Press, 1978).

9   Arrowsmith, 'Plastic Paddy'. For a play which explores the subject more directly through the conflicting memories of two second-generation London Irish siblings about their recently deceased father, see Darren Murphy, *Irish Blood, English Heart* (London: Oberon, 2011).

10   For earlier accounts of growing up second-generation Irish in London, see Sheila Wingfield, *Real People* (London: Cresset Press, 1952), set in Marylebone at the time of the First World War; Bridget Boland, *At My Mother's Knee* (London: Bodley Head, 1978), set in Pimlico in the 1920s; Seán MacStíofáin, *Memoirs of a Revolutionary* (London: Gordon Cremonesi, 1975), set in Islington in the 1930s.

11   George O'Brien, 'Memoirs of an Autobiographer', in Liam Harte (ed.), *Modern Irish Autobiography: Self, Nation and Society* (Basingstoke: Palgrave Macmillan, 2007), p. 234.

12   Marianne Hirsch, *Family Frames: Photography, Narrative and Postmemory* (Cambridge, MA: Harvard University Press, 1997), p. 22.

13   For studies of second-generation literature in a wider English context, see Arrowsmith, 'Plastic Paddy', and Harte, '"Somewhere beyond England and Ireland"'.

14   Casey, *Over the Water*; Brian Keaney, *Family Secrets* (London: Orchard Books, 1997). The following memoir, which is one the few about a female London Irish upbringing, unfortunately appeared too recently for me to examine it in this study: Anna May Mangan, *Me and Mine: A Warm-hearted Memoir of a London Irish Family* (London: Virago, 2011).

10
Irish Cockney Rebels

The authors of the three memoirs I analyse in this chapter are all second-generation Irish men who grew up in working-class neighbourhoods of post-war London and explore this experience from the perspective of middle age. In the course of writing about their backgrounds, they regenerate themes and tropes familiar from texts in the previous two parts of this study. These occur in relation to narratives of nationality and gender, and also with regard to religion, class and sexuality. The conflicts and disjunctions of belonging that ensue are in part common experiences of childhood and adolescence, but in other ways they are specific to the way in which these different narratives of identity intersect for subjects of Irish descent. They are apparent in both the public and private domains but also at locations such as church and school, which are neither wholly public nor wholly private but contain elements of both. The 'confluence of narrativity' between personal and collective notions of identity is often most pronounced in such intermediate zones, graphically illustrating a crisis of belonging for the subject concerned. Where the accounts differ from each other is in the extent to which the individuals concerned overcome such disjunctions, something which, in turn, influences the attitude of each author to his own memories and the nature of the identities configured in each text. These are not just personal testimonies, therefore, but interventions in a much broader spectrum of narrative diaspora space. Ien Ang argues that such interventions amount to the 'rhetorical construction of a "self" for *public* not private purposes: the displayed self is a strategically fabricated performance'.[1] For this reason, I pay particular attention to the ways in which each memoir is 'driven by its own fictive conventions'[2] and employs performative strategies to configure identities through narrative.

The Grass Arena (1988) by John Healy

John Healy's prize-winning autobiography is a harrowing account of the destitution and violence he experienced as a down-and-out. As Colin McCabe remarks in his introduction: 'Beside it, a book like Orwell's *Down and Out in Paris and London* seems a rather inaccurate tourist guide.'[3] In the early chapters, which I focus on here, Healy describes his childhood as the youngest son of a poor Irish immigrant family in Kentish Town in the late 1940s and 1950s and his eventual descent into alcoholism, prison and vagrancy. McCabe argues that 'Healy's writing rejects totally any of those rhetorical personalities which so much of our culture mistakes for a sense of self' (ix), and it is true that his account is less self-reflexive than the other texts I examine. Healy does objectify himself as the boy protagonist of his own memories, however, something that is evident from the sequences of dialogue within the text. By so doing, he not only exacts considerable dramatic effect but configures a retrospective narrative of his identity in the light of subsequent experience.

Healy's mother and father came from small farms within twenty miles of each other near Boyle, Co. Roscommon, and met in London in the 1930s. His father was a violent drunk who physically assaulted his son at regular intervals, a particularly vicious example of which opens the book when he punches the boy of six in the face for making an innocent yet apparently inflammatory remark. Healy was, understandably, much closer to his mother. However, here too he was denied the affection he craved as a child. While his mother was 'a kindly and attractive woman', Healy explains that he was not encouraged to 'show [his] feelings' for her. 'She would defend me physically with her own life,' he recalls, 'but she would recoil if I tried to cuddle or kiss her' (2). Because he grew up in a tough working-class neighbourhood, Healy had to learn to defend himself physically as well as verbally from an early age. In the immediate post-war years in London, such encounters often had an anti-Irish or anti-Catholic dimension. The vast majority of Irish migrants who came to London at this time were Roman Catholics. They were concerned to raise their children in the faith and did so even within mixed marriages. In a technically Protestant (if largely non-practising) country, this marked second-generation Irish children with a cultural signifier distinctly at odds with their peers. 'Being immigrants,' Healy states, 'we were treated as lepers' (2). However, after telling his parents about one particular beating he had received from boys in the neighbourhood, Healy's father imposes a strict regime of religious observation, rather than sympathizing with his son. One example of this was putting him through nightly tests of the Catechism,[4] which are described as follows:

> "I believe in the Immaculate Conception ... I believe in the Holy Ghost ..." and on and on. I believed in anything just to get to bed. Six questions had to be learnt each night; to get one wrong resulted in a good beating. I should have been a priest! One night I forgot all the answers to the questions. I just couldn't remember a thing. My father's eyes started to narrow. I tried to explain, making some excuse or other. He interrupted, imitating my London accent. It was making his temper boil. [...] I wished my father would die, then I could get rid of this scared feeling and I'd be happy. (4–5)

Healy learns early on, therefore, how religion and ethnicity are fused in his upbringing. His father's insistence on bringing him up as a strict Catholic appears designed to ensure that he is distinguished from the host community by his religious piety as much as his nationality. When his anger is provoked, however, he mimics his son's cockney accent, utilizing a potent signifier of cultural difference for the purpose of ridicule. In doing so, Healy's father undermines any claims his son might have on Irishness, further confusing the boy's sense of identity.

Regular recitation of the Holy Rosary constitutes another form of indoctrination.[5] The repetition of the prayer cycle ensures that its declaration of belief is embedded in Healy's psyche from infancy. Because it requires him to kneel in an uncomfortable position for half an hour, it proves to be as much a physical ordeal as a psychological trial. As a result, his faith is literally embodied in the domestic arena of the family home as well as in the more public arena of the church. By the same token, it is also coloured by the particular ethnic environment within which it is enacted, thus reinforcing the apparent synonymy of Irishness and Catholicism. Later, he refers to the way in which the image of the Virgin Mary aroused in him the early rumblings of sexual desire, and at Benediction he is distracted by equally devout 'flesh and blood' examples of the opposite sex.[6] 'Waves of sadness would all but overwhelm me,' he recalls, 'until the girls' voices, united in prayer vowing purity and modesty, would send a surge of desire racing through me' (17). The onset of adolescence and a growing awareness of his sexuality bring a new dimension to Healy's sense of identity. What is most striking and ironic about this passage, however, is the way he objectifies his female peers within the context of a powerful Marian trope of desexualized Irish Catholic femininity. The use of such a trope, with its connotations and conflations of the national and the maternal, has a long heritage in Irish literature and culture.[7] However, the way in which it is mediated here is specific to the narrative diaspora space of second-generation Irish memoir. In the intermediate zone between the public and private (in this case, the church) a confluence of narrativity between the personal and the collective takes place across discourses of religion, nationality and sexuality.

Another example of such a confluence is when Healy returns from an extended holiday in Ireland, where, for the first time, he felt welcomed as part of an extended family. Having acquired a slight Irish brogue while away, he finds he is the victim of verbal abuse from his peers, who, he records, 'would start putting on an Irish accent,' in order to 'take the mickey' out of him (11). The full consequences of this become apparent for Healy when verbal baiting turns to physical abuse at the hands of one particular boy called Ronnie:

> I was playing with his brother and a few other kids one day when he came up. 'Top of the morning to you, Paddy,' he said. All the happiness went out of me but I pretended to smile. 'What you laughing at, you Irish cunt?' 'Nothing,' I said. 'You better not be laughing at me, you cunt,' and grabbing me by the collar he kneed me in the bollocks. (11)

So, despite having felt accepted by his extended family in Ireland while on holiday there, Healy discovers how much of a liability his Irishness is when he returns to London. Regardless of which accent he adopts, he is subject to a binary opposition between Irishness and Englishness which is beyond his power to control. Healy's sense of home is problematized by such encounters and the development of his cultural identity arrested, therefore, by conflicting signals of belonging.

As Healy grows older, his life descends into one dictated by crime and alcoholism and, before long, he literally has no home to go to. His sense of Irishness partially recedes into the background as his links with family and Ireland are loosened. However, it is clear from later passages in the memoir, where motifs and parallels with previous London Irish literature emerge, that it does not disappear altogether. When he gets a labouring job in Hampstead, for instance, one is reminded of Patrick Riley digging a trench in the same part of the city (53). On another occasion, there are familiar signs of self-fictionalization at work when, in order to extort money from the nuns, he passes himself off as a mute newly arrived Irish migrant (74–76). The community of down-and-outs with whom Healy mixes are mostly Irish or of Irish descent. This partially, if inadequately, makes up for the lack of a social/ethnic network he experienced when growing up. Figures such as Kelly, Hogan, Finnegan and Mad Rafferty are hardly positive role-models for Healy, but by introducing him to the various dodges and pitfalls associated with life on the streets, they do at least help ensure his survival in a hostile environment. He learns, for instance, to employ a number of methods for avoiding the police. When he calls himself 'John Murphy' in order to get a bed for the night at a homeless hostel, which he describes as somewhere 'not even Oliver Twist would have wanted seconds' (155), a string of intertextual links spring to mind: the navvy practice of name-changing in *The Contractors*, the role of the Rowton House in *The Life of Riley* and *Schnitzer O'Shea* and the Dickensian references of *Ripley Bogle*.

Ultimately, it seems that Healy's experiences as a child led to the kind of psychological problems that have been identified by researchers as disproportionately high among second-generation Irish people compared to the host population.[8] He had little contact with other London Irish children during his upbringing and, as a result, he did not have the opportunity to nurture the sense of ethnic belonging he experienced in Ireland. However, by writing his memoir, Healy provides a stark exposition of the cultural disjunctions and potential problems of second-generation Irish upbringing and, by so doing, configures an unforgettable narrative of diasporic identity in the process.

Rotten: No Irish, No Blacks, No Dogs (1994)
by John Lydon

John Lydon (a.k.a. Johnny Rotten) is approximately ten years younger than Healy and also grew up in a London working-class neighbourhood. Lydon, whose mother was from Cork and father from Galway, was the eldest of three brothers. He suffered from a serious bout of spinal meningitis when he was seven, which led to a loss of memory from which he did not recover for some years. He was bullied at school by his classmates, but in his teenage years he eventually learnt how to win the admiration of his peers through his iconoclastic and rebellious behaviour. After being expelled from secondary school, he left home and was eventually auditioned for lead singer with the embryonic Sex Pistols. His numerous interviews over the years demonstrate how he has self-historicized his role in the group, something which has become the subject of scholarly analysis. Sean Albeiz, for instance, views him as 'a cultural agent continually re-configuring and performing his identity through a process of self-transformation'.[9] As I demonstrate, this applies as much to his sense of ethnic and class identity in childhood and adolescence as it does to his status as a popular music icon. For this reason, Lydon provides a fascinating case study of how a second-generation London Irish identity may be configured.

This is most apparent in his memoir, *Rotten: No Irish, No Blacks, No Dogs* (1994). The book was an attempt to chronicle his role in the punk revolution, which was one of the most controversial and mythologized movements in late twentieth-century popular culture.[10] Written in conjunction with Keith and Kent Zimmerman after he had moved to live in Los Angeles, it was aimed mainly at an American readership and is an unusual amalgam of first-hand accounts from Lydon himself and his friends and associates. The clearly contradictory nature of these accounts is something that Lydon celebrates, but inevitably this presents certain difficulties when attempting to distinguish fact from fiction. In a comment about the memoir on his website, Lydon states, 'I'm not saying I'm completely correct, because in reading the book, you'll notice more than a few contradictions. That is what makes the book valid. Contradiction is the art form.'[11] A porous border between fact and fiction has characterized many of the texts I have analysed so far, but what is striking about this account is the way such ambiguity is deliberately foregrounded by its author as something of intrinsic merit.

The early chapters ('Segments', as they are described) cover Lydon's childhood and adolescence. My analysis focuses, particularly, on Segment 2, which is entitled 'Child of the Ashes'. Anticipating, in title and in content, Frank McCourt's famous memoir of Irish childhood published later in the decade, it describes Lydon's childhood in Holloway and Finsbury Park in the late 1950s and 1960s.[12] According to Lydon, the term 'Child of the Ashes' refers to an ancient Irish initiation ceremony in which a child is positioned in front of a coal fire and is only considered a true Gael if it chooses (as Lydon did himself) to touch the ashes rather than the flames. Building on this reference, Lydon's descriptions of his early childhood help to configure an unashamedly mythologized narrative. He deliberately exaggerates the deprivation and squalor of his environment, in what he refers to as 'the roughest area there was in London' (9). He claims that he ran around in rags, had no shoes and was 'scrubbed with Dettol, a toilet cleaner solvent we also used for the sinks, to kill off the bugs' (13). If John Healy alludes to Dickensian imagery to portray his childhood in Kentish Town,[13] Lydon wholeheartedly embraces it to describe his family home in Holloway:

> The Victorian slum dwelling on Benwell Road, off Holloway Road, isn't there anymore. They pulled it down. It's now illegal in Britain to rent out buildings like that. It wasn't a house, just two rooms on the ground floor. The whole family shared the same bedroom and a kitchen. [...] There used to be enormous rats that would come up from underneath the sink. Apparently the sewer line broke underneath, and they ate their way up. Great big sewer rats. I remember because I watched them kill a cat. They tore it to pieces. (12–13)

Of course, Lydon may have chosen such lurid images in order to reinforce his public persona as the front-man of punk rock, but he exacts maximum dramatic effect from its specifically London Irish context, describing, for instance, how his relatives in Ireland (who were even poorer than his immediate family in London) used to fight with each other in the backyard when they came to stay (10).

Although Lydon insists that coming from such a deprived background is nothing to be proud of, he regularly expresses his admiration for his parents and the way that they succeeded in instilling self-confidence in him from an early age. Unlike Healy, he clearly admires his father, especially his physical prowess as a crane-driver. He refers to his hands as 'shovels' (10) and insists that it is 'no disgrace' to be the son of a navvy (12). In an environment where second-generation Irish children were aware of their anomalous status in London, such an uncomplicated and heroic role model would have had considerable attraction for a young boy. It is not surprising, therefore, that after leaving school Lydon worked for a while with his father on the buildings. If Lydon is not fully conscious of the mythological antecedents of the navvy as a symbol of Irish masculinity, he is certainly fully versed in the cultural significance of his earliest childhood memory: being given a red-hot poker, at the age of three, to put into a mug of Guinness before drinking it (10). Whether this was true or not, it is revealing that Lydon should choose to begin his memoir by mentioning a family ritual that has such overtly Irish connotations.

As Lydon gets older, accent proves to be a bone of contention even (as was the case for Healy) within his own family. His maternal grandfather 'hated the English', he states, 'and probably hated me and my brother Jimmy. We spoke with thick cockney accents that he could not stand' (12). Unlike Healy, Lydon was not enamoured of the Ireland he encountered during family holidays. While he does discover a taste for storytelling there which even extends to a desire to learn Gaelic, he concludes that this would be no use to a boy growing up in London. This is an attitude which, in adulthood, he takes towards Ireland more generally, considering the country economically stagnant and backward. 'How can you have a sense of belonging to something that never changes?' he asks (28). This antipathy has its origin in the disappointments he experienced as a youth. He complains about how, when he searched for his Irish roots, the experience left him 'isolated and shallow inside.' 'I wanted to go out of my way and find out about my own Irishness,' he recalls, 'but when I did get there, it was never as romantic as books make it out to be' (27). This discrepancy between literary representations of Irishness and the reality he observes leaves a powerful impression on Lydon. Indeed, his recognition of the dichotomies between fact and fiction in literature is perhaps why he eventually takes such an openly contradictory attitude to the composition of his own memoir. Unfortunately, he does not indicate, precisely, which texts he read, although he does mention that 'the Irish invented stream-of-consciousness literature' (9), suggesting that he was at least aware of the significance of James Joyce's work. Clearly, reading Irish literature in whatever form from the perspective of a London Irish upbringing played an important role in early configurations of Lydon's ethnic identity.

Lydon's parents were not especially devout. However, like most Irish Catholics at the time, they ensured that their children attended Mass. This was for social and cultural reasons as much as religious ones. For their son, however, church was a place full of off-putting smells where women wore 'hideous hats' (19). Furthermore, in the Catholic school he attended, Lydon recalls experiencing overt brutality from the nuns, whom he describes as 'particularly vicious and very cruel' (16). As he grows older, a significant gap opens up between his parents' attitude to religion and his own. However, despite his eventual rejection of the faith, Lydon does admit (again, in typically contradictory style) to a Gothic-like fondness for 'the gaudiness of the icons and religious symbols' (19). While Catholicism and Irishness were inextricably linked in Lydon's upbringing, he points to differing degrees of religious devotion among local Irish families in his neighbourhood:

> Looking back, I guess I had a progressive family [...] It was commonsense Irish. I've seen some 'noncommonsense' Irish people who were absolutely vile to their children. You know, the Holy Joes. They open the religious cupboard every time they think you're doing wrong and make you light a candle and kiss all those statues. (53)

Such nuances might not have been apparent to anybody outside the migrant Irish community, but they are typical of the degrees of cultural allegiance a second-generation Irish child was required to negotiate at this time. This is further illustrated by Lydon's description of his confrontation with anti-Irish and anti-Catholic bigotry. He recalls that certain streets and locations in his neighbourhood were ethnically and religiously demarcated and, like Healy, he soon learnt that transgressing such boundaries could have serious consequences:

> When I was very young and going to school I remember bricks thrown at me by English parents. To get to the Catholic school you had to go through a predominantly Protestant area. That was most unpleasant. It would always be done on a quick run. "Those dirty Irish bastards!" That kind of shit. [...] We were the Irish scum. But it's fun being scum, too. (12)

It is notable that Lydon uses the term 'scum' not only to signify but to celebrate the fact that being Irish and Catholic distinguished him and his family from his working-class neighbours. This suggests that he was content to be an outsider from an early age, something which may have been a factor in his eventual leadership of one of the most iconoclastic groups in popular music. Extended analysis of Lydon's role in the Sex Pistols is beyond the parameters of this study, but while it has been seen by some musicologists as connoting Englishness[14] it can alternatively be read (in the light of Lydon's memoir) as part of a rebellious cross-cultural ethnicity. Sean Campbell notes that there was a 'punk-reggae interface'[15] within London working-class culture at the time and Lydon's predilection for Afro-Caribbean music would find full expression when he established the band Public Image Ltd.

Lydon's dissatisfaction with the conformism of his working-class peers is evident when he recalls his experiences of secondary school.

Here, he enjoyed not just challenging the authority of his teachers but chastising his schoolmates for passively accepting the inadequate educa- tion they were being offered. His readiness to make such criticisms was something which led, eventually, to his being ostracized by his peers. Lydon's questioning of such forms of socialization was evident in rela- tion to ethnicity in an interview for American television, when he stated, 'Well, you're brought up in England with people telling you you're Irish. You go to Ireland and they call you English. So, you're very confused as to what your nationality is. And you end up, quite rightly, not believing in any nationality.'[16] While Lydon's attitude has a note of resignation, it is the cultural contradictions of his upbringing and his consequent rejection of all forms of collective allegiance which ulti- mately defined him as an outsider. In other words, rather than attempting to prove his credentials with regard to class, religion or ethnicity (English or Irish), he created a highly individualized and icon- oclastic public persona. While such rebelliousness was, in one respect, precisely what defined the Sex Pistols, it was also what led to Lydon's disagreements with the group and his decision, in time-honoured Irish fashion, to emigrate.[17]

Some Luck (2002) by John Bird

Like Lydon and Healy, John Bird also reveals the paradoxes and dichotomies of a second-generation London Irish upbringing in his memoir. Bird was the youngest son of Irish parents and the memoir charts his life from a deprived childhood in Notting Hill, through crime, vagrancy and homelessness until his redemption through writing and publishing and his eventual success as founder of *The Big Issue* magazine in 1991.[18] The first third of the book, which covers Bird's childhood, includes numerous references to his Irish background and it is clear that a strong sense of Irishness was instilled in him from a young age. One of his first memories is of his uncle Tom, who 'sat at the table in [Bird's] front room' and 'spoke about Ireland and what the English did to his mother country'.[19] This overtly nationalist interpretation of the histor- ical relationship between England and Ireland illustrates one of the ways in which a second-generation child's sense of self is defined by what Marianne Hirsch terms 'postmemory' (i.e. the experience of growing up under the influence of one's parents' or grandparents' testimonies). The fact that Bird chooses to prioritize this particular incident from his early childhood suggests that it must have made a powerful impression on him. Moreover, its occurrence within the context of a London upbringing foregrounds the conflicts of identity with which Bird will wrestle for the rest of his life.

As was the case for Healy and Lydon, just such a conflict is apparent during and after a holiday in Ireland. On the family farm, his grand-mother calls him 'a "little Cockney"' (16) because of his accent. After he returns to London, Bird identifies strongly with his Irishness, but this brings him into conflict not only with his peers but with his siblings as well. Like his older brothers, Pat and Tommy, he is a member of a local gang led by a boy called Sonny, but when Bird discovers that an Irish gang exists in the neighbourhood, a clash of allegiance arises and he finds himself at odds with members of his own family:

> 'We should be in their gang. We're Irish. Sonny's gang isn't Irish.' Tommy told me to shut up. I said that I was going to join the Irish gang: we were Irish, and I loved Ireland and wanted to be with Irish boys. Tommy grabbed me, said if I so much as talked to the Irish gang then I'd be hit. (37)

From an early age, therefore, Bird is forced to make stark choices with regard to his ethnic identity. Being older, his brothers were possibly more aware of the wider ramifications of such decisions (at a time when anti-Irish racism was common) and anxious that their younger brother should not disclose facts about their family background which might make them vulnerable to attack. The incident is a good example of how the ambiguities of second-generation allegiances are exposed in the public domain and how cultural identities are differentially narrativized according to knowledge and experience within the same family. Although Bird eventually complies with his brothers' demands, he retains a stronger association with Ireland than they do, something which plays a crucial role in his later development.

This also raises questions concerning his respective relationships with his Catholic mother and Protestant father. As the youngest, Bird may have felt closer to his mother than to his father, and it is notable that he was brought up in his mother's faith rather than his father's. Religious allegiance is highlighted when he reaches the age of seven and makes his First Holy Communion.[20] After the service, the synonymous rela-tionship between Irishness and Catholicism is impressed on the boy by his mother, who talks to him about the importance of his faith and how she remembers the same day in her own childhood. "'I cried my eyes out,'" she recalls. '"In Ireland everyone makes a big fuss of you. Not like here, in this God-forsaken country"' (48). By drawing attention to the cultural differences between English and Irish Catholicism, Bird's mother implies (with recourse to a narrative of her own childhood) that the latter is a more social and family-oriented form of religious observance than the former. In another example of 'postmemory', these comments appear to have resulted in a conflation of religious and ethnic identity for her son. When Bird describes how he then knew that he 'was going to be the best Catholic ever' (51), it is clear that he had already begun to configure an identity from what Paul John Eakin describes as the 'crucible of family stories and cultural scripts'.[21] So, while in the case of his uncle Tom's story about the Irish suffering at the hands of the English, ethnicity is defined for Bird by one form of narrative (i.e. nationalist), here it is defined by another (i.e. religious). This time, rather than political differences between England and Ireland being juxtaposed, it is differences in the way that Catholicism is practised in the two countries that are placed in opposition. Further nuances of Irish/Catholic identity are revealed in his relationship with his childhood girlfriend, Geraldine, in the following passage:

> Even though I liked having lunch and being in Geraldine's house, I felt better out on the street. There were pictures of Jesus and Our Lady everywhere. Her family were Irish, but they were Holy Irish, as my mother called them. Irish people who took God very seriously. They were different to us. (86–87)

Bird's use of the term 'Holy Irish' echoes John Lydon's term 'Holy Joes'. Both children come from Irish Catholic backgrounds and are aware not just of the ways in which religion ethnically segregated them from the host community, but also of the way that subtle gradations of religious observance segregated families within the migrant community itself. In this respect, the term 'Holy Irish', when voiced, could sound like 'wholly Irish', thus implying that Bird's family (quite apart from his father's Protestantism) were not fully Irish by virtue of their less than whole-hearted embrace of Roman Catholicism.

These experiences illustrate how, in Brah's terms, a 'confluence of narrativity' between nation and religion in diaspora space can take place intra-ethnically, as well as inter-ethnically. As he grows older, Bird becomes aware of further distinctions within Irishness. After the family moves to Fulham, an Irish-born boy called Dominic joins Bird's school and immediately becomes the victim of bullying due to his accent. Although he identifies with the boy because of his nationality and goes so far as to physically defend him on one occasion, Bird is conscious of an important difference between himself and Dominic. He 'wasn't like us boys,' he recalls. 'We had grown up in London and were London-Irish boys' (80). Bird makes an important distinction, therefore, between differing forms of Irishness that were, respectively, the product of an upbringing in Ireland and an upbringing in the diaspora. Similar conflicts arise when he becomes active in republican and socialist politics and meets an Irishman called Matt who recruits him to sell the *United Irishman* newspaper in north London pubs. 'I was a good Irish patriot,' he writes, 'One day I would help Ireland free itself from the English.' He even decides to change his name to Sean, and when he tells Matt about this, the older man exclaims, '"Ah, a little Irish boy."' But Bird corrects him by insisting that he is 'London-Irish' (207). He is anxious to ensure, in other words, that his acquaintances appreciate an important ethnic distinction because, notwithstanding his commitment to Irish nationalism, he retains an equal allegiance to the London part of his hyphenated identity.[22] Precisely what London signifies for Bird, however, is open to conjecture. It may be a metonym for British or English, or his way of asserting one or more other possible positions (e.g. urban; working-class; multicultural), all of which could have been associated at the time with the area of London in which he grew up. What is clear is that Bird is now self-confident enough to assert a culturally nuanced form of identity in an environment in which he would have been under considerable pressure to conform to more essentialized notions of allegiance.

In Bird's relationships with the opposite sex, however, such allegiances are once again put to the test. After falling for Liz, a beautiful English art student, he reverts to using 'John' rather than his newly adopted Irish name. Likewise, with Linda (a softly spoken Scottish woman), he changes his name again, but this time to Jonathan. 'I was pretending to be posh' (230), he says, in the hope that this would impress her. His choice of name on this occasion is clearly driven as much by class-consciousness as by nationality. The ability to 'respond to competing situational demands', identified by Philip Ullah as a characteristic of second-generation subjects, becomes increasingly important for Bird as the issue of class not only challenges Irishness for precedence in his worldview, but becomes an issue of contention with family and friends. When he wins a place at Chelsea College of Art, his mother announces that '"[w]orking-class people don't go to college"' (223), and he gets a similar reaction from his best friend, Brian, who believes he has sold out (223–24).[23] In other words, Bird's hopes of configuring one identity are challenged by another, more established and dominant identity from his past. By changing his name (in the celebrated fashion of his forebears), Bird is able to adopt a new identity, but it lacks credibility due to the absence of a narrative, a fictional back-story. This is graphically illustrated when Linda invites him to meet her family in Edinburgh and the precarious nature of his strategically deployed but inappropriately narrativized identity is revealed. 'I had no family in Edinburgh,' he writes, 'I had working-class Irish-Scottish cousins in the Gorbals in Glasgow. But they wouldn't fit my rich De La Rue image, so I didn't mention them' (231). In other words, Bird realizes that when one aspect of his identity (i.e. sexuality) is in the ascendant, other aspects (i.e. class and ethnicity) are not as easy to disown or uncouple as he might have wished.

As he moves from adolescence to adulthood, Bird's identity continues to ebb and flow between different registers of cultural allegiance. His identification with his working-class background reasserts itself, for instance, when his relationship with his girlfriend Linda breaks down and he becomes active in left-wing politics. By the time he is in his early twenties and meets Tessa, he no longer hides this aspect of his background, even though she is the daughter of a baronet. They move in together and eventually settle down in Acton and have a daughter. It is not until many years later, in 1988, when his brother Pat dies, that Bird's past returns to trouble him. After the funeral he decides to revisit the Notting Hill streets where he grew up. Note how, in the following passage, Bird (like Lydon) employs the term 'scum' to make an ethnic distinction between his upbringing and that of his working-class neighbours:

> I must have been outraged and angry about Pat's death. For the first time in years I found myself wandering drunk around the streets of Notting Hill, almost looking for fights. Walking to where we had lived and lived no more. Every Bird had been removed from Notting Hill and Portobello. The area had become posh; its little streets formed some new privileged zone. Only white liberals and poor blacks in council housing lived there now. None of the Irish, none of the scum I had come from. Notting Hill as I'd known it was a fiction. It had never existed. (324–25)

Pat's untimely death stirs up memories of a past which Bird now realizes has had its signifiers erased by the gentrification of his neighbourhood. By describing it as 'a fiction', Bird alludes to the fact that, when something becomes part of the past, it can only be reconfigured through the partially imaginative process of memory. This is one clear cause of his grief. But it also leads to anger, illustrated by his assertion that his Notting Hill 'had never existed'. This anger is partially directed at the privileged middle classes who are content to see working-class lives airbrushed out of a segment of London history. But it is also provoked by the fact that he knows he has chosen to move away from his family and neighbourhood roots as much as they appear to have been taken away from him. In the light of this, Bird's memoir might be read as his attempt to come to terms with the degree to which he has changed as an individual as much as a project of reclaiming a lost inheritance.

The texts I have looked at in this chapter reveal how three subjects from second-generation London Irish working-class backgrounds narrativize their experiences of growing up through the medium of memoir. A common ethnic background is apparent in their shared experiences of family rituals and holidays, street-life, schooling and religious observance. Each subject, however, responds in different ways to the cultural conflicts of his upbringing, and clear divergences are apparent in the regeneration and reconfiguration of these experiences across the narrative diaspora space of the literature. This is due to the individual personalities of the authors, their differing relationships with their parents and the specific circumstances in which they find themselves. As subjects at the time and as authors in retrospect they clearly struggle to resolve the ambiguities of their cultural identities. But by writing about them from the dual perspective of two cultures, they provide valuable insights into the second-generation condition and go some way towards configuring narrative identities appropriate to their circumstances.

The role of the father is a notable feature of these texts. In Healy's case, the lack of a supportive father figure in his childhood contributes to his descent into alcohol abuse and vagrancy. But despite his dysfunctional family background and the numerous challenges he faces in later life, he survives to produce a unique and moving testimony within which the conflicts of second-generation London Irish identity play a key role. In Lydon's case, his father's supportive approach to his upbringing results in a much more self-confident negotiation of these challenges and disjunctions. This is reflected in a deliberately iconoclastic attitude to his memoir whereby, rather than mulling over how to represent the dilemmas of his split inheritance, he openly celebrates (in a suitably anarchic manner) its inherent contradictions. Even where the father figure is generally absent, as in Bird's case, it is notable how surrogate figures of Irish masculinity (i.e. the characters of Matt, the republican activist and his uncle Tom) play an important role in the development of his identity.

Bird's account is possibly the most nuanced of the three. His avowedly hyphenated identity is something he was probably unable to articulate until adolescence. But it provides him with a means of asserting and defending his dual ethnic identity as he grows older. When factors of class and sexuality come into play, its limitations are exposed, something which Bird does not attempt to disguise. He conveys a stronger sense than Healy and Lydon of the anxieties and indecisions provoked by the cultural disjunctions he encounters. The narrative register he adopts, which more fully replicates the voice of a boy or young man at the time he is describing, reinforces this effect. Although Lydon acknowledges the elisions between fact and fiction, Bird goes somewhat further in exposing the temporal distortions and gaps between events and their recollection and the consequence this has for his sense of self. In this regard, *Some Luck* has some resemblances to the memoir and the novel I address next.

Notes

1 Ien Ang, 'On Not Speaking Chinese: Postmodern Ethnicity and the Politics of Diaspora', *New Formations* 24 (Winter 1994), p. 4.
2 Sidonie Smith, 'Construing Truths in Lying Mouths: Truthtelling in Women's Autobiography', *Studies in Literary Imagination* 23.2 (1990), p. 145.
3 Colin McCabe, 'Introduction' to John Healy, *The Grass Arena: An Autobiography* (London: Faber and Faber, 1988), p. ix. Subsequent references to *The Grass Arena* are cited in parentheses.
4 A series of questions and answers used to test knowledge of the Roman Catholic faith.
5 The Holy Rosary is a devotional prayer cycle which was commonly recited in Irish Catholic families.
6 Benediction is an evening service consisting of the singing of hymns and a blessing of the congregation with the consecrated host (representing the body of Christ). There are overtones here of Stephen Dedalus's experiences while a prefect of the sodality of the Blessed Virgin Mary. See James Joyce, *A Portrait of the Artist as a Young*

Man (London: Penguin, 1992), pp. 111–12.

7   These aspects of second-generation identities are under-researched, but the ubiquitous tropes of 'Mother Ireland' and 'the Virgin Mary' in the development of Irish cultural nationalism could, arguably, be a contributing factor to the narrativization of such identities. For further discussion of this in Irish literature more generally, see David Cairns and Shaun Richards, 'Tropes and Traps: Aspects of "Woman" and Nationality in Twentieth Century Irish Drama', in Toni O'Brien Johnson and David Cairns (eds.), *Gender in Irish Writing* (Milton Keynes: Open University Press, 1991), p. 131.

8   See Liam Greenslade, 'White Skin, White Masks: Psychological Distress Amongst the Irish in Britain', in Patrick O'Sullivan (ed.), *The Irish Worldwide: History, Heritage, Identity, Vol. 2: The Irish in the New Communities* (Leicester: Leicester University Press, 1992), p. 220.

9   Sean Albeiz, '"Know History!": John Lydon, Cultural Capital and the Prog/Punk Dialectic', *Popular Music* 22.3 (2003), p. 360.

10 John Lydon (with Keith and Kent Zimmerman), *Rotten: No Irish, No Blacks, No Dogs* (New York: St. Martin's Press, 1994). Subsequent references to this text are cited in parentheses.

11 Online introduction by the author to Lydon, *Rotten*, at http://www.johnlydon. com/jlbooks.html, accessed 7 June 2008.

12 McCourt's book is widely credited with inaugurating the commercially successful genre of 'misery memoir'. Frank McCourt, *Angela's Ashes: A Memoir of Childhood* (London: Flamingo, 1997).

13 For a discussion of how Dickensiana remained in the popular imagination long after most of its physical and social manifestations had disappeared, see White, *London in the Twentieth Century*, p. 6.

14 Martin Cloonan, 'State of the Nation: "Englishness", Pop, and Politics in the Mid-1990s', *Popular Music and Society* 21.2 (Summer 1997), p. 63.

15 Sean Campbell, 'Sounding Out the Margins: Ethnicity and Popular Music in British Cultural Studies', in Gerry Smyth and Glenda Norquay (eds.), *Across the Margins: Cultural Identities and Change in the Atlantic Archipelago* (Manchester: Manchester University Press, 2002), p. 130.

16 Interview with Tom Snyder on US TV, *The Late Late Show* (CBS Television, 23 May 1997). http://www.johnlydon.com/jlints.html, accessed 17 May 2008.

17 It is notable that Morrissey, the second-generation Irish lead singer with the Smiths, also eventually opted to migrate to the same location, Los Angeles.

18 *The Big Issue*, which is sold on the streets by homeless people, was established as a means of providing its vendors with an income and improving their self-esteem. Over the intervening years, it has generated similar ventures in cities across the world. See http://www.bigissue.com.

19 John Bird, *Some Luck* (London: Hamish Hamilton, 2002), p. 9; pp. 13–14. Subsequent references to this text are cited in parentheses.

20 Holy Communion is a Roman Catholic sacrament which commemorates the Last Supper, the final meal that Jesus Christ shared with his disciples before his crucifixion.

21 Eakin, *How Our Lives Become Stories*, p. 117.

22 This may explain why Bird literally adopts the hyphen in his writing of 'London-

Irish', in contrast to the way in which it is more commonly written elsewhere, i.e. 'London Irish'.

23 Janet Behan, the niece of the playwright Brendan Behan, describes a similar experience growing up in south London of Irish parents who considered her schooling 'a bourgeois affectation'. See Libby Purves, 'Interview with Janet Behan' on *Midweek*, BBC Radio 4 (23 January 2008), http://www.bbc.co.uk/radio4/factual/midweek_20080123.shtml, accessed 14 July 2008.

11

Elastic Paddies

In September 2009, Fintan O'Toole wrote an article in the *Irish Times* in tribute to the late second-generation Irish poet, Michael Donaghy. Born in the Bronx, Donaghy lived most of his life in London and, through his work, epitomized the ambivalent yet undeniable attachment to Ireland experienced by many of the second generation. In the article, for which O'Toole coined the term I have used to title this chapter, he makes the following statement about Irishness:

> Irish culture is nothing if not persistent. It can sometimes seem so elastic, so open to infinite variation and appropriation, as to be virtually meaningless. Yet this elasticity also makes it stretch, not just through space (the many Irelands of the diaspora) but also through time. While cultural nationalists fear that its lack of definition makes the vague idea of Irishness easy prey to the obliterating homogeneity of globalization, it is often this very quality of adaptability that makes it linger.[1]

By inventing the expression 'Elastic Paddy', O'Toole provides a clever lexical counterpoint to the derogatory term 'Plastic Paddy' which had been used since the 1980s (mainly by Irish-born members of the Ryanair generation) to refer to people of Irish descent whom they perceived as having bogus or dubious claims on Irishness.[2] By so doing, he emphasizes the positive characteristics of second-generation Irishness that Philip Ullah identified in the 1980s, i.e. its resilience and adaptability. Crucially, O'Toole also highlights the way that it operates through time as well as space, a feature of identity formation which echoes the narrative dimension developed in Ricoeur's work and which is particularly relevant to migrant memoir.

Second-generation identities have, for many years, been interrogated through the concept of 'hybridity', popularized by Homi Bhabha in the 1990s.[3] When allegiances of class, religion and sexuality are all competing for precedence alongside nationality, one can see why such a concept might be useful in discussing the second-generation condition. However, the extent to which 'hybridity' is an appropriate term to describe the identities of the subjects I cover in this chapter is questionable. While it has been useful as a means of challenging uncritical assumptions of ethnic essentialism, its suggestion of an inexorable fusion of cultural traditions tends to obscure the fact that varying degrees of ethnic distinctiveness and allegiance continue to exist within migrant groups according to specific socio-political contexts. Philip Ullah's research found that the descendents of Irish migrants simultaneously claimed and maintained contrary ethnic positions (sometimes in necessarily essentialized form) according to different circumstances. Memoir and autobiographical fiction, which in their different ways thread the events of a life together, are productive sites for examining how these processes of what Avtar Brah terms 'contingent positionality' are refracted and mediated through narrative.[4]

In the previous chapter I critiqued three autobiographical works. Here I compare a memoir and an autobiographical novel. While their authors have differing class backgrounds (the former middle class, the latter working class), these texts depict very similar experiences of second-generation Irish upbringing in London in the late 1950s. Published within a year of each other, John Walsh's memoir *The Falling Angels: An Irish Romance* (1999) and Gretta Mulrooney's novel *Araby* (1998) are both written in the first person from the perspective of a middle-aged man attending to his dying mother in Ireland. The focus on the relationship between the subject/protagonist and his mother is stronger than in the accounts from the previous chapter and chimes with the theme of return and the maternal tropes of Irishness discussed earlier in the book. There is further evidence here also of how the domestic environment of the home can become an acutely contested space, when issues of nationality, class and religion converge and provoke fundamental questions of cultural allegiance. Likewise, once in Ireland and surrounded by Irish friends and relatives, it is striking how powerfully the London part of these subjects' identities comes to the fore. Furthermore, this allegiance to London and more broadly, Englishness, becomes an intrinsic part of the way identity is narrativized in these texts.

The Falling Angels: An Irish Romance (1999)
by John Walsh

John Walsh is approximately the same age as John Lydon and grew up of Irish parents in Clapham and Battersea in the 1950s and 1960s. At the opening of his memoir, Walsh's parents have returned to live in his father's home town of Athenry some thirteen years previously, when he is summoned to the hospital bed of his mother who is dying of cancer. Suddenly, he has time to reflect at length on the peculiarities of growing up in London and the twin emotional charges of his upbringing: 'I sit here, between Battersea and Galway, two poles I know with two levels of intimacy, one of them my resting place, the other my "true home" [...] While the figure who did most to turn me into this curious hybrid lies dying beside me.'[5] By beginning his memoir at a moment in the near-present and integrating his present thoughts and emotions with memories of his childhood, Walsh creates a narrative which is decidedly more self-reflexive than the texts discussed in the previous chapter. The eventual death of his mother becomes the catalyst for an extended examination of his upbringing. During the course of the memoir, Walsh interrogates his Irish background and what it meant for him as a boy growing up in London. He makes a series of acute observations about the ambiguities of his identity and reflects on the fact that he seems consigned forever to oscillate between the attractions and antipathies of each culture. 'How do you measure where you really belong?' he asks. 'Genetically, I was as Irish as Bertie Ahern and rather more than De Valera. Accent- and behaviour-wise, I was as English as Stilton' (260). This is not simply a personal testament, therefore, but a sophisticated auto-critique by someone embroiled in the tantalizing, yet frustratingly inconclusive, search for his sense of self. Walsh does not emerge from his self-analysis with a fixed conclusion about his nationality/ethnicity. Instead he is more concerned to reflect as fully as possible the many nuances and gradations of cultural allegiance wrought by his dual inheritance.

Growing up in a distinctly Irish family and community in south London, strong ethnic influences were at work on Walsh from an early age:

> They were everywhere. Irish things, Irish people, Irish faces, Irish songs, Irish voices, Irish names, Irish drink, Irish newspapers, Irish gossip, Irish tales, Irish woe, Irish exile – it permeated the life I lived in Battersea, it hung

around like a great green fug. [...] Irishness got in your hair and got under your fingernails. (58)

These tactile signifiers of Irishness suggest that a benign form of cultural contamination has taken place, courtesy of the vernacular customs and habits of a specific experience of diaspora. This is particularly highlighted by the central role of language and music in Walsh's upbringing. He explains how his parents' Hiberno-English lexicon lodged in his mind (in the same way that the words of the Rosary did for John Healy) 'as a signifier, a code or tribal rallying cry', and how, when small, he had 'a Galway accent as thick as turf' (92–93). After attending school 'most traces of shebeen and shamrock', as he terms it, 'had been eliminated' by peer-group pressure (93). At certain times, however, his identification with Ireland remained strong, illustrated by his insistence on wearing the said shamrock on St Patrick's Day. Despite being taunted by his classmates for this overt display of national loyalty, he proudly recalls being 'a one-boy identity protest'. By asserting his Irishness 'in the midst of this Anglo-Saxon throng' (95), Walsh demonstrates that he was prepared, on occasions, to render himself an outsider among his peers for the sake of loyalty to his ethnic background.

This fidelity to nationhood was expressed in another way when, as a young boy, Walsh was expected to sing at parties. He notes, for instance, that Irish songs 'played in the background of your life – the second chamber of your burgeoning sensibility' and 'make you sing yourself into becoming Irish' (77, 82). Through the ritualistic act of singing, Walsh affirms his national identity for family and friends, thereby securing a form of tribal endorsement. His behaviour can be understood, perhaps, in the light of Anne-Marie Fortier's findings in her research on the post-war London-Italian community, where she observes that 'cultural ethnicity may be "incorporated" through repeated performative acts, the result of which is to produce the imaginary effect of an internal ethnic "essence"'.[6] Another signifier of Irishness for Walsh is smell. Like Lydon, who describes the reek of his mother's boiled cabbage and bacon permeating the house,[7] he recalls the aroma of his mother's Irish stew which, emanating from the family kitchen, 'stole up the stairs and wrapped itself around [him] like a cloak' (59). The maternal connotations of this account are unmistakable and are reinforced by a subsequent humorous recollection. One Saturday morning, while walking in the neighbourhood, Walsh mistakes the pungent aroma from the local brewery for something closer to home:

I stood there glowing with delight and the warmth of camaraderie, convinced that everyone in my new home of Battersea, everyone that lunchtime, in every kitchen in every house, was making Irish stew. My heart swelled with a sense of involvement. So this was how it felt when a people shared a culture – they all have the same thing for lunch. Battersea had turned into a vast, Hibernian soup-kitchen, dishing out gallons of boiled mutton and carrots to a grateful giant family. (59–60)

The passage reveals how smell plays a key role in the way Walsh develops a sense of belonging to a discrete familial and cultural constituency. Although, in this instance, it is based upon an entirely erroneous interpretation, fictional determinants of 'narrative identity' (referred to by Ricoeur) prove to have just as acute an influence on the subject concerned as their factual counterparts. Importantly, the passage reveals that home for Walsh is not just the domestic space of the family dwelling. This incident illustrates how it can seep out, in an aspirational sense, into the public space of the neighbourhood and community, becoming, as Avtar Brah observes, 'the lived experience of a locality [...] as mediated by the historically specific everyday of social relations' (192). While Walsh's neighbourhood was indeed inhabited by large numbers of Irish people, his sense of ethnicity remains largely in the realm of the imaginary, or to use Brah's words 'the mythic place of desire'. Nevertheless, as far as the emergence of his personal identity is concerned, this unintentionally fictional configuration has just as powerful an influence on Walsh's sense of belonging as if it had been true.

As he grows older, Walsh learns that cultural identity even within the family home itself can be radically contested. This is vividly illustrated by the following passage, where Walsh describes how he felt when a visit to the house by a local genteel English priest coincides with that of a drunken Irish patient. Because his parents are upstairs taking an afternoon nap at the time, the junior Walsh is left to deal with the situation and diplomatically takes the Irishman (who is singing an Irish rebel song) into the waiting room of his father's surgery, and the priest (who is preoccupied with discussing the finer points of English church music) into the family dining room:

I stood in the hall between two rooms that were far more than rooms. They were two worlds that could never be brought together. One was a correct and formal, well-mannered and tidy sort of place, where people glided about discussing books and floral displays and classical music, and made slightly

obscure little jokes and laughed as if they were coughing. The other was a
shockingly informal, pungent, hairy, large-booted, shouty-voiced class of
establishment where the people never looked right sitting on chairs, their
conversation made no sense and they seemed to come alive only in a crowd.
(106–107)

The respective rooms (and the kind of sounds with which they are
imbued) signify a complex set of identifications with regard to social
class and ethnicity for the boy. Whilst the priest (like Walsh) is middle-
class, he is, nevertheless, archetypally English and, as such, an outsider
in this thoroughly Irish household. On the other hand, while the
Irishman is more of an insider by virtue of his nationality, he is decidedly an outsider by virtue of his class. Walsh, therefore, finds himself
physically and metaphorically astride a form of diaspora space, on the
threshold between adjacent territories of cultural allegiance (represented
by the rooms) and contested narratives of identity (represented by their
occupants and the particular music to which they subscribe).

As he enters adolescence such conundrums multiply and Walsh feels
impelled to choose an identity on one side or other of the ethnic divide.
Discovering that an attachment to Ireland undermines his status with
his teenage peers in London, he learns to downplay his Irishness. 'I was
desperate to be cool,' he recalls, but, 'at the same time, nothing in the
world seemed less cool than Ireland' (134). This statement reminds us
that by the early 1970s, when the activities of the IRA in London were
at their height, Irish identity was subject to highly politicized and polarized discourses. It also reveals, as Patrick Joyce observes, how at certain
times 'narratives choose us rather more than we choose them', rendering
expressions of identity even more fraught with difficulty than usual.[8]
However, there is evidence that Walsh's withdrawal from Irishness had
begun prior to adolescence. Referring to the way in which, even by the
age of eleven, his rather formal way of speaking had begun to distance
him from his parents' Irish peer-group, he admits he had 'turned into a
little Englishman' (61). This was clearly something with which he did
not feel comfortable and he records how, in the presence of Irish family
friends, he 'writhed with Englishness' and sounded 'adenoidal, stuffy
and slow beside their quicksilver, allusive chat' (67). Revealingly,
Walsh's confusion about his identity appears to have been partly the
result of his parents' own differing attitudes to theirs. His father was 'too
Irish to be happy in England', while his mother 'had become too English
to be happy anywhere else' (42). If his father's overtly declared alle-

giance to Ireland had clearly left its mark on the boy, his mother, by
quietly aspiring towards English customs, had unintentionally influenced her son in a more subliminal but perhaps more effective way.
Certainly, when choices are unavoidable, Walsh chooses to prioritize
the latter over the former. Once he reaches middle age and finds himself
at the deathbed of his mother, the performative skills he acquired as a
child have found their expression not so much in a fictional form of
Irishness, but in an equally fictional form of Englishness. 'I lived for her
in photographs and phone-calls,' he states. 'And when I came to see her
in the flesh, and met her friends, I was conscious of playing a role. [...]
I hammed up Englishness for her [...] It was a pretence, a series of courtly
playlets' (240). Ethnic identity for Walsh, therefore, only finds expression through a form of postmodern pastiche, wary of any claims to
authenticity. In effect, he regards his Englishness, like his Irishness, as
partially manufactured and ultimately opts for a peculiarly second-
generation form of cultural identity, referred to by Aidan Arrowsmith
as 'genuinely inauthentic'.[9]

The appeal for Walsh of such ambiguities is immediately apparent
when he begins to spend time with family friends, the Fitzpatricks. He
is attracted to their 'un-English hedonism and un-Irish sophistication'
and 'their neither-one-thing-nor-the-otherness. Their mixed-upness.
Their English-Irishness' (70). Finally, in an attempt to find a suitable
narrative to represent his dual sense of belonging, Walsh calls upon a
myth from the Aran Isles about falling angels suspended between heaven
and earth, the image of which provides him with the title of his book.
During a visit to Inishmaan after his mother's funeral, he discovers, by
way of reading Synge's *The Aran Islands* (1907), that the islands had a
history of intermingled Gaelic and Saxon blood, and wonders if this
place 'beyond England and Ireland' might best represent his sense of
cultural identity (280–82). However, Walsh struggles to convey the
same kind of passion for this hybrid conceit as the respective poles of
his ethnic identity. His desire for an ethnic essence remains, to quote
Richard Kirkland, 'a ghosted presence haunting the hybrid formation,
always at once removed from itself and recognizable by its absence'.[10]
As a term to describe his sense of identity, therefore, 'hybridity' seems
intellectually attractive but emotionally inadequate. Ultimately, it is only
through the mercurial if somewhat treacherous process of formulating
a narrative that Walsh begins to reflect the multiple ambivalences of the
second-generation condition.

Araby (1998) by Gretta Mulrooney

Gretta Mulrooney's novel is, in many ways, a fictional equivalent of Walsh's memoir. Its main protagonist, Rory Keenan, travels to Ireland to attend to his sick mother, ten years after his parents' return to Ireland. The experience of nursing and, subsequently, grieving for his mother stirs up memories of his childhood in Tottenham. Mulrooney grew up of Irish parents in the nearby and socially comparable neighbourhood of Walthamstow, and the storyline of *Araby*, despite the fact that the key protagonist is male, is largely autobiographical.[11] At the opening of the novel, Rory is sitting at his mother's bedside in Ireland, reflecting on her past life in London, her incorrigible personality, her unpredictable mood swings and her hopes and fears while bringing him up in a foreign country. He recalls how his mother's obsessions 'had held our household in thrall', while he, like the rest of the family, was rendered a mere spectator, 'responding to the drama being enacted'.[12]

As in the case of John Walsh, performative customs of London Irish culture are imparted to Rory at an early age. His mother had a love of music and was keen that her son should be educated in Irish traditional song from infancy. 'My mother didn't teach me nursery rhymes,' he reveals, 'she passed on the tunes she'd grown up with. Before I went to school I knew the words of "Skibbereen", "Brian o' Linn" and "The Foggy Dew"' (128). However, when cajoled by family and friends into reciting a prayer or singing an Irish song, Rory feels 'like a tortoise tormented from its shell' (109). Similarly, when his mother insists on playing records of sentimental ballads about Irish emigration, such as 'If We Only Had Old Ireland Over Here',[13] it makes him 'hot with embarrassment' (14). This is especially the case during the summer when the windows of their house are wide open and his mother is singing along 'in her trilling soprano' (14). The image of Irish music wafting out of the windows of the family home and into the surrounding neighbourhood is reminiscent of the aroma of Irish cooking, described by Walsh, and is another vivid example of how expressions of cultural identity can move, physically in this case, from the private to the public domain.

Rory is aware, however, that such demonstrations of cultural difference have the effect of placing him in an invidious position with his London peers. Despite the fact that she has chosen to bring up her family in London, Rory's mother is determined to maintain an avowedly Irish identity. For her son, however, the questions of identity are more conflicted. When his mother's favourite music starts, he retreats upstairs to his bedroom where he immerses himself, instead, in reading about 'swinging London'. However, Rory feels that this particular 'mythic place of desire' is 'mysteriously inaccessible even though it is happening all around' (14). While not wishing to offend his mother or completely reject his ethnic inheritance, Rory is anxious to claim a London identity, which at the time (in the 1960s) was in the cultural ascendant on an international scale. The very house he grows up in, therefore, becomes (as for Walsh) a site of cultural contestation, with downstairs and upstairs representing distinctly different allegiances underpinned by their respective narratives. From Rory's point of view, his London identity is constantly under threat from the all-pervasive influence of his Irish upbringing. So, when a chance arises to explore and express his pride in being a Londoner, he grasps it with both hands. At a family wedding in Southend, for example, he takes the opportunity to act out a 'swinging London' identity for the benefit of his cousin, Danny. 'He seemed to think that I spent all my time on Carnaby Street and the King's Road,' he recalls, 'and I played up to this, fabricating a hectic social life' (64). By seizing the opportunity to perform in this way, Rory appropriates and subverts one of the mechanisms of his cultural conditioning in order to articulate the identity he chooses, rather than one chosen for him by his parents.

When he starts going to school and begins to mix with English children, the dilemmas of ethnic belonging and the central role of language and accent, discussed earlier, are clearly apparent. Anxious to fit in, he suppresses his 'infant brogue' and learns 'to speak in a cockney accent' (129). He describes how his survival strategy in this in-between world was to develop, like Walsh, into 'a hybrid creature' or 'a cultural schizophrenic' (129). In Rory's case, another possible reason for this is revealed by his recollection of family feuds. He divulges how he found his extended family 'bewildering in its silences and feuds', and recalls how easy it was 'to be drawn into the webs they had spun' and 'pulled inexorably into its depths' (169). He is aware, in other words, that it is ultimately impossible not to be entangled in and implicated by the narrative machinations of family history.[14] When he explains that he 'would leave well alone, stay silent', yet know that his silence 'added another strand to the tangled skein' (169), he demonstrates how the identities that emerge from such experiences are products of often unvoiced narratives and discourses beyond an individual's control. This claustrophobic family frame also means that Rory (like John Healy) is denied access to any sense of a wider ethnic network against which to define his sense of self. This is illustrated by the following passage:

> I sensed that certain markers were missing in my life, a wider safety net of
> relations who would have contributed to my identity and of whom I had
> been deprived. It added to my feeling of not quite belonging. […] Perhaps
> being dispersed without points of reference caused a rift that couldn't be
> made whole again and this rift was passed onto children with their generic
> inheritance. (57)

Rory refers, here, to the phenomenon of dispersal that partially defines
the term 'diaspora' and suggests that his familial identity is subject to the
deficit of a ruptured migrant legacy. His family relations, in other words,
are so fragmented or inactive that (to paraphrase Seamus Heaney) his
prospects of configuring an identity adequate to a second-generation
predicament seem remote.[15] One particular larger-than-life figure,
however, features prominently in Rory's imagination. This is his uncle
Jack, who had disappeared during the Blitz and whom he resembles
physically, as he knows from surviving family photographs (59). He
recalls how, in a desperate attempt to connect with the extended family
he never met, he used to search for a resemblance to his uncle in the
faces of local Irish navvies. As in previous accounts, a familiar trope of
Irish migrant masculinity is invoked as a means by which a second-
generation male child positions his identity. When extrapolated into the
wider narrative diaspora space of London Irish literature, therefore, it is
possible to see how the cultural identities that are configured by second-
generation writers can be influenced, through postmemory, by
hegemonic narratives from previous generations. For Rory, as for John
Lydon, this takes place courtesy of migrant narratives from his parents'
generation and shows how second-generation texts partly rely for their
ethnic validity on the regeneration of cultural narratives from a time
prior to the immediate experiences they recount.

While family stories can provide the foundations for a narrative identity, in Rory's case their unreliability is also the source of some concern.
He recalls the numerous maladies, some real, some imagined, from
which his mother suffered when he was growing up. 'Tending to her
health,' he recalls, 'was a career and each new symptom and medication
a promotion. Her illness framed my childhood, trapping and bewildering me. She had taught me to count using her bottles of pills' (13).
Caring in this way for his mother meant that Rory had something of a
reversed maternal relationship with his mother. Moreover, as far as her

health was concerned, the 'line between imagination and reality [...] had always been blurred. She had told herself so many stories that even she found it confusing' (18). These are all possible reasons why Rory finds it difficult to configure a reliable narrative identity. However, after spending extended time with his mother for the first time in years, Rory learns to forgive her faults and better appreciate her half-forgotten qualities: her zest for life; her endearing eccentricities; her ability to fight her corner. More importantly, he begins to learn about himself, in two key respects. Firstly, despite feeling 'cloaked in [his] English persona' (166), he discovers a deep connection with Ireland in the everyday ways of the people who surround and support him during his mother's final hours.[16] Secondly, Rory discovers (like John Walsh) that his mother, despite having returned to live in Ireland, has harboured a marked ambivalence about her own sense of home and has clung to fond memories of 'the bustle of London' (4). Through the experience of return, she appears, ironically, to have developed an affection for London which she did not acknowledge when she lived there. As a result, the definition of 'home' for Rory's mother is called into question and is revealed, through the narrative characteristics of diaspora space, to be determined by personal memory as much as by geographical location. Most revealingly, in a telling reversal of the conceit alluded to in the ballad, 'If We Only Had Old Ireland Over Here', Rory notices how all the family furniture and belongings in his mother's Irish home were placed in the identical positions that they had occupied back in Tottenham. The existence in the west of Ireland of what amounts to a replica London Irish living room illustrates how the binary opposition between home and away in diaspora space can be not only disrupted but inverted as a result of return. When Rory describes how, when he closed his eyes, he imagined hearing 'the throaty hum of a red bus' (15), the metonymic as well as metaphoric resonances of such processes are clearly apparent.

After his mother is diagnosed with cancer and he is confronted with the prospect of her imminent death, Rory is forced to revisit long abandoned dilemmas about the connection between Catholicism and his national/ethnic identity. He recalls that, due to its rigorous and questioning nature, the Jesuit education his parents had been so keen to provide for him ironically turned out to be the reason for his eventual rejection of the faith. 'I used to enjoy baiting my mother and seeing her colour rise,' he recalls. 'I had secretly abandoned the stranglehold of Catholicism by then and thought myself a bit of a sophisticate.' He adds, 'I viewed my mother's fervent, superstitious belief with distaste bordering on loathing' (2). Rory regrets that this distance between himself and his mother during adolescence is now an impediment to his reconnection with her at her death-bed. He discovers, for instance, that his mother's sister-in-law is better positioned than he is to console his dying mother in her last few days because she is able to draw on a mutual religious conviction for support. 'I wished I was still a Catholic,' he declares, 'so that I could genuinely sit with her and say those litanies that brought her comfort' (127). In a heartfelt attempt to reconnect with his mother at the point of her imminent demise, therefore, Rory calls on a deeply embedded religious ritual from his childhood, but discovers that his connection with Catholicism has been severed by his having long since rejected the discourses within which it functions.

Despite this disavowal, Rory discovers that his mother had kept a missal safe for him in case he returned to the faith and, while attending Mass for the first time in years, he feels 'like an actor who hasn't learnt his lines or moves properly' (180). Likewise, the ritual of an Irish wake becomes a highly charged arena in which, in similar circumstances to his childhood experience of being cajoled into reciting a prayer, Rory's identity is exposed to the scrutiny of family and friends. As a consequence, he is forced to re-engage with the narrative antecedents of his cultural identity. He leads a recitation of the Holy Rosary, discovering, to his relief, that he recollects the words without difficulty. This event becomes for Rory a performed allegiance to a faith he no longer shares, yet an acknowledgement, nonetheless, of an Irish Catholic identity that he is loath to disown completely. Similarly, he discovers that the Irish music he had so despised as an adolescent creates 'a comforting backdrop' while he is temporarily suspended in the 'warm hollow by the glowing turf' (174). Like John Walsh, therefore, Rory is surprised to find himself searching for a form of cultural essence and allegiance he had hitherto rejected. He even finds himself imagining what it would have been like to grow up in Ireland rather than London. 'There was a parallel universe that crouched in my imagination,' he says, 'one where I had attended school in Fermoy, maybe gone to university in Cork or Dublin.' By exploring 'those other Rorys' (137), as he terms it, he demonstrates how a personal identity can be defined by the ghostlike selves of past narrative possibilities, as much as by the more concrete selves of present actualities. As his mother is about to die, however, none of these fictional manoeuvres sufficiently satisfies his need to honour the maternal bond he experienced as a child. Finally, he places some sprigs of rosemary in his mother's coat pocket, the scent of which always reminded her of the Arabic locations which inspired the title of the book.[17] This symbolic act, which (like Walsh's reference to the Aran Isles myth) comes in the closing pages of the text, seems to be an attempt by Rory to pay homage not only to his mother's search for an identity but also to his own.

The closely paired texts I have looked at in this chapter reveal how two London Irish second-generation subjects from distinctly different class backgrounds share common experiences of ethnicity. In both cases, this is explored through intimate relationships between the subjects and their mothers, so that their respective narrative identities are configured through the recollections of childhood, subsequently inflected by the phenomenon of parental return. In the course of reflecting on these experiences from the perspective of middle age, both authors begin to appreciate, if not fully understand, the cultural disjunctions of their second-generation condition. What is strikingly different about these accounts when compared to those of the previous chapter, however, is the degree to which their subjects attempt to anchor their sense of personal identity by narrativizing these very disjunctions. Language, and accent in particular, is central to the ways in which such complexities are negotiated in all the second-generation texts I have examined in this book. However, the degree to which Walsh and Rory learn to manipulate a London Irish vernacular, in its broadest sense, is crucial to how well they recognize, or adjust to, the contested nature of their identities. They discover how the performative apprenticeship of their family upbringing helps them configure self-confident identities in later life, but with this comes a distinctly postmodern trepidation about the reliability of memory and memoir (fictionalized or otherwise) to fully represent their experience.

While both subjects employ the term 'hybrid', neither of them, ultimately, seems entirely comfortable with its implications. In the final pages of both texts, their subjects look to narratives 'beyond England and Ireland' to represent a sense of diasporic belonging. In the case of Walsh, this is configured according to a regenerated postmemory of Anglo-Irishness, which, while suitably hyphenated, does not adequately reflect the complex cultural nuances of his upbringing. For Rory, it is configured through the postmemory of his mother's love of Araby, whose striking oriental imagery mirrors Walsh's equally striking occidental valorization of the Aran Isles.[18] Despite their best intentions and what appears to be a genuine attempt to move away from the hegemony of fixed notions of identity either side of the Irish/English binary, both authors are ultimately drawn to rather essentialized, if somewhat unconscious, narratives of cultural belonging. One is left feeling that writing, no matter how resonant with insights into the second-generation experience, can only be a partially satisfactory means of configuring an identity from the kaleidoscopic array of memories, impressions and reflections that comprise a personal past.

Notes

1   Fintan O'Toole, 'The Bronx Poet who was an Elastic Paddy', *Irish Times*, 6 September 2009, p.46.
2   For an examination of this issue, see Sean Campbell, 'Beyond "Plastic Paddy": A Re-examination of the Second-generation Irish in England', *Immigrants and Minorities* 18.2–3 (1999), pp. 266–88; Marc Scully, '"Plastic and Proud"? Discourses of Authenticity among Second-generation Irish in England', *Psychology and Society* 2.2 (2009), pp. 124–35.
3   Homi Bhabha, 'The Third Space', in Jonathan Rutherford (ed.), *Identity: Community, Culture, Difference* (London: Lawrence & Wishart, 1990), p. 211.
4   Brah, *Cartographies of Diaspora*, p. 149.
5   John Walsh, *The Falling Angels: An Irish Romance* (London: Harper Collins, 1999), pp. 30–31. Subsequent references to this text are cited in parentheses.
6   Fortier, *Migrant Belongings*, p. 6.
7   Lydon, *Rotten*, p. 14.
8   Joyce, 'More Secondary Modern than Postmodern', p. 367.
9   Arrowsmith, 'Plastic Paddy', p. 42.
10 Richard Kirkland, 'Questioning the Frame: Hybridity, Ireland and the Institution', in Colin Graham and Richard Kirkland (eds.), *Ireland and Cultural Theory: The Mechanics of Authenticity* (Basingstoke: Macmillan Press, 1999), p. 218.
11 As confirmed by Mulrooney at Irish Writers in London Summer School, 28 July 1999.
12 Gretta Mulrooney, *Araby* (London: Flamingo, 1998), pp. 89–90. Subsequent references to this text are cited in parentheses.
13 This song is about an emigrant who dreams of famous Irish landmarks appearing in the landscape of exile: 'If the Blarney stone stood out on Sydney Harbour', etc. Different versions of the song have been set in New York and Vancouver. The original is attributed to the Dublin tenor Sean Mooney. See Sean Mooney, 'If We Only Had Old Ireland Over Here' (London: HMV, 1956).
14 In this respect, Rory's experiences are remarkably similar to those of the boy narrator in Seamus Deane's novel *Reading in the Dark* (London: Jonathan Cape, 1996).
15 Seamus Heaney, 'Feeling into Words', in *Preoccupations: Selected Prose 1968–78* (London: Faber & Faber, 1980), p. 56.
16 It is notable that while John Walsh used the 'cloak' metaphor to represent protection in the context of Irishness, Rory uses it in a similar way in the context of

Englishness.

17 It may also have been Mulrooney's intention to make an intertextual reference to a famous short story of the same name. See James Joyce, 'Araby', in *Dubliners* (London: Penguin, 1992).

18 For an examination of orientalist tendencies in Irish culture, see Joseph Lennon, *Irish Orientalism: A Literary and Intellectual History* (New York: Syracuse University Press, 2008).

12
Conclusion

The psychological journey of migration always takes far longer than the geographical one.[1]

The novels, short stories and auto/biographical texts I have examined in this book are written and peopled by men and women who, as well as making journeys from one country to another, have embarked upon narrative journeys of the mind. Unlike the geographical journey of migration, however, narrative is not a linear process. Instead, it possesses an inherent temporal elasticity that often enables writers to deploy inventive methods and modes of storytelling and characterization. Rather than simply providing a series of period snapshots, these texts reveal how identities are configured over time as well as space. In other words, they tell us not just how individuals conceive of their identities in a given moment and place, but how those identities evolve according to changing locations, aspirations, and reflections. Narrative, therefore, is the vehicle upon which authors and their characters rely in order to mediate, if not always resolve, the dilemmas and paradoxes of the diasporic condition.

In the literature of the post-war Irish in London, this endeavour is perhaps most apparent in the relationship between exile and escape. The former has a long history in Irish literature and culture and in the texts covered here produces a range of familiar and not so familiar effects, ranging from comic to tragic. Escape, on the other hand, is generally a much less prominent theme in Irish culture. This may be because of the way it is gendered. Certainly, in post-war London Irish literature, it is predominantly (although not exclusively) evident in the experiences of female protagonists. However, what is most striking in this literature is the extent to which exile and escape are mutually dependent. Rather than polar opposites, they might be regarded as constituting the Janus face of diaspora, looking forwards or backwards according to a migrant's perspective on his or her experience at any given moment.

Questions of cultural identity and belonging are universal. But they are undoubtedly brought into sharper relief as a consequence of migration and the experiences of displacement and transformation this so often entails. Almost all of the texts discussed here reveal how finite an individual's control is over this process. While many of their protagonists are highly motivated individuals who exhibit a considerable degree of self-confidence by leaving in the first place, the degree to which they are able to come to terms with what awaits them in London is seriously limited by economic, social and psychological factors. This is also the case in respect to their relationships with the past and their cultural background. Regardless of whether they are members of the 'mail-boat generation', the 'Ryanair generation' or the second generation, finding a sense of self in the context of migration means confronting powerful hegemonic discourses from both sides of the Irish Sea. Perhaps the most obvious difference between the texts set in the immediate post-war period and those set in the later period is the attitude of the protagonists towards such discourses. In the earlier texts there appears to be a stronger association (albeit under challenge) with metanarratives of nation, romance and literary life. In the later texts there is a much more sceptical and at times antagonistic relationship with such notions. When it comes to accounts by second-generation writers, both attitudes are often in play at the same time. However, the result here is not necessarily a hybrid or a fused identity. Instead the ambivalent and contingent sense of ethnic belonging narrativized in these texts suggests something closer to hyphenation. In other words, they demonstrate how opposing cultural allegiances for the second-generation subject can alternate and sometimes be simultaneously affirmed.

As the London-born son of Irish migrants myself, the experiences portrayed by second-generation writers were the most familiar to me personally. In many cases, their memories had uncanny echoes of my own. In other respects, their stories were quite different to mine, something which gave me pause for reflection upon not only how unique each individual's circumstances and experiences are, but also upon how differently each individual chooses to record them. The more familiar I became with such idiosyncrasies in the texts I examined, the more aware I became of the capacity of London Irish literature more generally to challenge my presuppositions and provoke new ways of understanding diasporic identities. Such questions of identity are not, of course, solely a consequence of migration. They are apparent in Irish culture more generally. It is worth remembering that, during the post-war period, notions of what it meant to be Irish did not only change in the diaspora but changed at home as well. In other words, the template in Ireland against which one might compare Irish identity abroad was itself in rapid evolution. This was borne out by the experience of returning migrants who were often surprised and disorientated by what awaited them back in Ireland; a somewhat ironic outcome given that the perceived lack of change in the country was often what motivated them to leave in the first place.

These differences between perceptions and realities often provide the axis upon which migrant literature pivots. Certainly, the marked exchange of fictional and factual registers across the texts I have examined in this book demonstrates that capturing the experience of diaspora through language is anything but a straightforward enterprise. These texts sit on a continuum between fact and fiction and shift back and forth along that continuum according to the deceptively simple practice of telling a story. In order to shed light on the narrative mechanics of migrant identity formation, therefore, I have read all of them (regardless of genre) with close attention to the ways in which these factual and fictional components interlace and sometimes displace each other. The degree to which this is a conscious or unconscious process in any given text varies according to the author concerned and, to some extent, when the text was written. What is clear, however, is that all the novels and short stories reveal some degree of autobiographical foundation and all the autobiographical texts betray varying degrees of fictional intent.

I started out by noting that no single archetypal writer or text of post-war London Irish migration has yet emerged. On reflection, this state of affairs might be a strength rather than a weakness. Instead of attempting to establish a lost canon or genre of London Irish literature, my enquiry has revealed that a range of distinct yet historically interrelated texts provide (in a suitably diasporic manner) a network of representations of migrant experience and consciousness. This study has analysed the ways in which migrant identities are configured within and across what I have termed 'narrative diaspora space'. A synthesis of Paul Ricoeur's notion of narrative identity and Avtar Brah's paradigm of diaspora space, the concept of narrative diaspora space provides a means of interrogating the cognitive role played by narrative in the configuration of migrant identities. Narrative, one could argue, is at the heart of the construction of all identities, individual and collective. In the context of migration, it both reflects and helps to configure the complex web of positionalities and relationalities of diaspora space. As a methodological tool, narrative diaspora space could be applied elsewhere in different contexts. It could, for instance, have applications in the analysis of oral history and life narratives. It might also bear fruit in a comparative context. The texts I have examined in this book may have commonalities with Irish American or London Asian literatures, or, indeed, the new migrant literatures now emerging in Ireland itself. I have not explored these inter-diasporic dimensions here because I have been primarily concerned with analysing one particularly under-researched field, but they undoubtedly warrant future research.

When it comes to the subject of Irish migration, history has a tendency to repeat itself. The most recent generation of Irish migrants began to arrive in London in 2008 when the catastrophic collapse of the Celtic Tiger economy first started to have an impact. It is not clear yet how large or long-lasting the current phase of migration will be. What is evident already, however, is that it is as different from the previous phase as that was from its predecessor.[2] While London continues to be the favoured destination in Britain, the city now competes not so much with Manchester, Birmingham or Glasgow but with Sydney, Montreal and Berlin as the potential destination for a much more globally aware and globally dependent set of migrants. Members of this new 'Facebook generation' of Irish migrants rely on very different methods of connecting with each other compared to their predecessors. For today's migrants, the internet and online communications bring a whole new meaning to the term 'mobility'. Despite this technological revolution, however, individuals' experiences of migration will undoubtedly be similar in many ways to those of their forebears. How this will manifest itself in prose literature remains to be seen. It is possible that the traditional forms of the novel, short story and memoir will themselves be radically altered by such changes, particularly with the onset of electronic publishing; blogs, for instance, are a good example of how autobiographical writing has developed a new dimension in recent years.

What is not likely to change, however, is the basic desire of writers to tell stories about migration and for us to read them. By reading them, we become more aware of the ways in which identities are narrativized between home and away, between the personal and the collective and between facts and fictions. As a consequence, we are better able to appreciate the dynamic interdependence between narrative, diaspora and identity, and how and why migrants and their communities proclaim or disavow various forms of cultural allegiance.

Notes

1   From a talk entitled 'Ireland's New Migrants', given by Fr. Bobby Gilmore at the Irish Studies Centre, Polytechnic of North London, 31 March 1987.

2   According to the Central Statistics Office in Dublin, net outward migration of Irish nationals rose from 14,440 in April 2010 to 23,100 in April 2011, with large numbers of migrants choosing the UK as their preferred destination. See 'Population and Migration Estimates, April 2011' (Dublin: CSO, 15 September 2011). A number of articles have been written about the current phase of Irish migration to London. See, for instance, Colm Walshe, 'Hard Times for the Irish in London', *Irish Times Weekend* magazine, 21 March 2009. http://www.irishtimes.com/newspaper/weekend/2009/0321/1224243190799.html, accessed 21 March 2009; Peter Geoghegan, 'The Great Migration', *Irish Business Post*, 16 January 2011, http://www.sbpost.ie/post/pages/p/wholestory.aspx-qqqt=INSIDE-STORY-qqqs=agenda-qqqsectionid=3-qqqc=10.1.0.0-qqqn=1-qqqx=1.asp, accessed 22 January 2011; Mark Hennessy, 'Generation LDN', *Irish Times Weekend Review*, 9 July 2011, pp. 1–2.

Author Biographies

Berkeley, Sara (1967–) was born in Dublin, graduated from Trinity College in 1989 and now lives in northern California. She published her first collection of poetry at the age of 16 and moved to London in 1990 before publishing her first collection of short stories the following year. Since then she has published a novel, *Shadowing Hannah* (1999), and four further volumes of poetry, the most recent of which is *The View from Here* (2010).

Bird, John (1946–) was born to Irish parents in Notting Hill and became homeless at the age of five. After spending part of his early years in an orphanage and prison, he began to sleep rough on the streets of London. In 1991, he founded *The Big Issue* magazine, which provides an income for homeless people, a venture which has been duplicated worldwide. In 2010, he launched the creative writing website abctales.com.

Cronin, Anthony (1928–) is a poet, novelist and critic who was born in Wexford and was educated at UCD. After co-editing the Irish literary magazine *The Bell*, he moved to London in the mid-1950s where he edited a similar journal called *Time and Tide*. In 1980, he became cultural advisor to the Taoiseach Charles Haughey and helped create Aosdána, the Irish association of artists. He has written biographies of Samuel Beckett and Flann O'Brien and his most recent collection of poetry, *The Fall*, was published in 2010.

Donoghue, Emma (1969–) is a novelist and literary historian. She was born in Dublin and began publishing short stories and novels in the early 1990s. She was awarded a PhD from Cambridge University in 1997 and the following year settled in Ontario, Canada. Her novel *Room* (2010) was shortlisted for the Man Booker Prize and her short story collection, *Astray*, which has a migration theme, was published in 2012.

193

Healy, John (1943–) was born to Irish parents in London and grew up in Kentish Town. As a young man, he had a successful boxing career while serving in the British Army. After many years as a homeless alcoholic, he became a chess tournament champion. He wrote about his life in the award-winning autobiography *The Grass Arena* (1988) and published a novel, *Streets Above Us* (1990), which is also about a down-and-out in London. A film biography of his life, *Barbaric Genius*, was released in 2011.

Keane, John B. (1928–2002) was a playwright, novelist and essayist from Listowel in Co. Kerry. He lived and worked in Northampton in the early 1950s before returning to his home town to manage a public house and devote himself to writing. Two plays, *Many Young Men of Twenty* (1961) and *Hut 42* (1962), dealt directly with the topic of emigration, and his best-known work, *The Field* (1965), which was later made into an Oscar-winning feature film, depicted the conflict between a farmer and a returned migrant over ownership of a plot of land.

Lydon, John (1956–) was born to Irish parents in London and grew up in Finsbury Park. In 1975, he joined punk band the Sex Pistols as their lead singer and changed his name to 'Johnny Rotten'. The group became one of the most influential acts in the history of Western popular music. From 1978 to 1993, Lydon fronted Public Image Limited, who recently reformed. He has lived in Los Angeles for many years.

Mac Amhlaigh, Donall (1926–89) was born in Co. Galway and moved with his family to Kilkenny in 1940. After joining the Gaelic-speaking regiment of the Irish Army in the late 1940s, he emigrated to Northampton in 1951, where he spent the rest of his life writing and working as a labourer. A committed socialist, he contributed regularly to *The Irish Democrat* and *The Irish Post* newspapers. His first book, *Dialann Deorai* (1960), like most of his novels and autobiography, was first published in Gaelic.

McGahern, John (1934–2006) grew up in Cootehill, Co. Cavan and first moved to London in 1954 where he found work in the construction industry. His second spell there came after his first novel, *The Dark* (1965), led to his dismissal from his teaching post in Dublin. In addition to his novels, which all feature the experience of migration, short stories such as 'Wheels' (1970), 'Faith, Hope and Charity' (1978) and

'A Slip-up' (1978) directly portray the experience of Irish migrants in England. McGahern eventually settled in Mohill, Co. Leitrim in 1974 and published his eponymous memoir in 2005.

Mulvihill, Margaret (1954–) is a historian, editor and novelist. She was born in Dublin and emigrated to England in the 1980s, studying Creative Writing at East Anglia University. As well as writing three novels and a number of short stories, she has published history books for children and completed a biography of Charlotte Despard in 1989. She has lived in Kentish Town in London for many years.

Mulrooney, Gretta (1952–) was born in to Irish parents in Walthamstow in north-east London. She studied in Derry at the University of Ulster and lived for some years in Dublin before returning to England where she took up a career in social work. She has published fiction for both adults and children and her most recent novel is *The Apple of Her Eye* (2010).

O'Brien, Edna (1930–) was born in Tuamgraney, Co. Clare and settled to London in 1959. In her first novel, *The Country Girls* (1960), the depiction of young women's coming of age in a puritanical and hypocritical Ireland of the 1950s caused a sensation. Migration has been a constant theme in her work, as evidenced in novels such as *Night* (1972), *Time and Tide* (1992) and *The Light of Evening* (2006) and short stories such as 'Cords' (1968) and 'Shovel Kings' (2011). Her memoir *Country Girl* was published in 2012.

O'Connor, Joseph (1963–) was born and grew up in Dublin. He studied at UCD and Oxford University and lived in London in the late 1980s where he worked as a part-time journalist. As well as writing novels and short stories, he has written for stage and screen. His novel, *Star of the Sea* (2002), was one of the best-selling novels in Britain that year, and *Ghost Light* (2010), which is partly set in London in the inter-war years, is based on the relationship between J. M. Synge and the Irish actress Molly Allgood.

O'Grady, Timothy (1951–) was born into an Irish family in Chicago and has lived in Ireland, London and Spain. While living in London, he worked as an actor at the Sugawn Theatre in Dalston, which was run by the Irish publican and novelist J. M. O'Neill. O'Grady's award-winning first novel, *Motherland*, was published in 1989 and he was co-author (with Kenneth Griffith) of *Ireland's Unfinished Revolution: An Oral History* (1999). His most recent publication is the travelogue and social study, *Divine Magnetic Lands: A Journey in America* (2009), in which the author returns to the land of his birth thirty-five years after he first left.

Pyke, Steve (1957–) was born in Leicester in 1957. He became active in the music scene in London in the late 1970s and after taking up photography in the early 1980s worked for the influential style magazine *The Face*, where his first cover subject was John Lydon. He specializes in portraiture and has worked for many of the world's leading magazines. In 2004 Pyke received the MBE in the Queen's New Years Honours list for his services to the arts.

Walsh, John (1953–) was raised by Irish parents in Battersea. He was educated at Oxford University and UCD and pursued a career in journalism and the media. Four years after publishing *The Falling Angels* (1999), he published a second memoir entitled *Are You Talking to Me?* (2003), which recounts his childhood and adolescence through the films that influenced him most. He is writes regularly for the *Independent* and lives in Dulwich in south London.

Wilson, Robert McLiam (1966–) was born in Belfast and studied English at Cambridge University. He has published three novels and is also the author, with Donovan Wylie, of *The Dispossessed* (1992), a non-fiction book about poverty in 1980s Britain. A TV adaptation of his most recent novel, *Eureka Street* (1996), was broadcast by the BBC in 1999. An extract from his long-awaited new novel was published by Granta in 2003. He currently lives in Paris.

Bibliography

Abbott, H. Porter. *The Cambridge Introduction to Narrative* (Cambridge: Cambridge University Press, 2002)

Ahmed, Sara, Claudia Castañeda, Anne-Marie Fortier and Mimi Sheller (eds.). *Uprootings Regroundings: Questions of Home and Migration* (Oxford: Berg, 2003)

Albeiz, Sean. 'Know History! John Lydon, Cultural Capital and the Prog/Punk Dialectic', *Popular Music* 22.3 (2003), pp. 357–74

Aliago Rodrigo, Esther. 'Glenn Patterson and Robert McLiam Wilson: Two Contemporary Northern Irish Writers and the Question of National Identity', in Marisol Morales Ladrón (ed.), *Postcolonial and Gender Perspectives in Irish Studies* (La Coruña: Netbiblo, 2007), pp. 85–102

Anderson, Linda. *Cuckoo* (London: The Bodley Head, 1986)

Ang, Ien. 'On Not Speaking Chinese: Postmodern Ethnicity and the Politics of Diaspora', *New Formations* 24 (Winter 1994), pp. 1–18

Anon. 'The London Irish', *Blackwood's Edinburgh Magazine* 170 (July 1901), pp. 124–34

Anon. 'Sonny from Galway', in Jim McCool (ed.), *The Bhoys from the Big House*, http://www.aisling.org.uk/pages/frame2.htm

Anon. 'Geaney', in *Face the Facts: Migrant Workers* (London: BBC Radio 4, 28 July 2006)

Anthias, Floya. 'Evaluating "Diaspora": Beyond Ethnicity?', *Sociology* 32.3 (August 1998), pp. 557–80

Arnold, Matthew. *On the Study of Celtic Literature* (London: Smith, Elder & Co., 1867)

Arrowsmith, Aidan. 'Inside-Out: Literature, Cultural Identity and Irish Migration to England', in Ashok Bery and Patricia Murray (eds.), *Comparing Postcolonial Literatures: Dislocations* (Basingstoke: Palgrave, 2000), pp. 59–69

—. 'Plastic Paddy: Negotiating Identity in Second-generation "Irish-English" Writing', *Irish Studies Review* 8.1 (2000), pp. 35–43

—. 'Photographic Memories: Nostalgia and Irish Diaspora Writing', *Textual Practice* 19.2 (2005), pp. 297–322

Ashcroft, Bill, Gareth Griffiths and Helen Tiffin. *The Empire Writes Back: Theory and Practice in Post-Colonial Literatures* (London: Routledge, 1989)

Ball, John Clement. *Imagining London: Postcolonial Fiction and the Transnational Metropolis* (Toronto: University of Toronto Press, 2004)

Barbaric Genius. Directed by Paul Duane (Dublin: Screenworks, 2011)

Bardwell, Leland. *That London Winter* (Dublin: Co-Op Books, 1981)

Barry, Sebastian. *On Canaan's Side* (London: Viking, 2011)

Beckett, Samuel. *Murphy* (London: Picador, 1973)

Behan, Brendan. *Borstal Boy* (London: Hutchinson, 1958)

Behan, Brian. *With Breast Expanded* (London: MacGibbon & Kee, 1964)

Benjamin, Harrington W. 'The London Irish: A Study in Political Activism 1870–1910' (unpublished MA thesis, Princeton University, 1976)

Bennett, Christopher. *The Housing of the Irish in London: A Literature Review* (London: Polytechnic of North London Press, 1991)

Bensyl, Stacia. 'Swings and Roundabouts: An Interview with Emma Donoghue', *Irish Studies Review* 8.1 (2000), pp. 73–81

Berger, John and John Mohr. *A Seventh Man* (New York: Viking Press, 1975)

Berkeley, Sara. 'The Swimmer', in *The Swimmer in the Deep Blue Dream* (Dublin: Raven Arts Press, 1991)

—. *Shadowing Hannah* (Dublin: New Island Books, 1999)

—. *The View from Here* (Oldcastle: Gallery Press, 2010)

Bhabha, Homi. 'The Third Space', in Jonathan Rutherford (ed.), *Identity: Community, Culture, Difference* (London: Lawrence & Wishart, 1990), pp. 207–21

Binchy, Maeve. 'Shepherds Bush', in *Central Line* (London: Quartet Books, 1978)

Bird, John. *Some Luck* (London: Hamish Hamilton, 2002)

Blumenfeld, Simon. *Jew Boy* (London: Jonathan Cape, 1935)

Boland, Bridget. *At My Mother's Knee* (London: Bodley Head, 1978)

Bolger, Dermot. 'Foreword', in Dermot Bolger (ed.), *Ireland in Exile: Irish Writers Abroad* (Dublin: New Island, 1993), pp. 7–10

Bowen, Elizabeth. 'Coming to London', in Hermione Lee (ed.), *The Mulberry Tree: Writings of Elizabeth Bowen* (London: Vintage, 1999)

Boyle, John. *Galloway Street* (London: Doubleday, 2001)

Brah, Avtar. *Cartographies of Diaspora: Contesting Identities* (London: Routledge, 1996)

Braziel, Jana Evans and Anita Mannur (eds.). *Theorizing Diaspora: A Reader* (Oxford: Blackwell, 2003)

Broderick, John. *London Irish* (London: Barrie & Jenkins, 1979)

Brooks, Peter. *Reading for the Plot: Design and Intention in Narrative* (Oxford: Clarendon Press, 1984)

Brown, Terence. *Ireland: A Social and Cultural History 1922–2002* (London: Harper Perennial, 2004)

Buchanan, George. *Rose Forbes* (London: Constable, 1937)

Bullock, Shan. *Robert Thorne: The Story of a London Clerk* (London: T. Werner Laurie, 1907)

Cairns, David and Shaun Richards. 'Tropes and Traps: Aspects of "Woman" and Nationality in Twentieth Century Irish Drama', in Toni O'Brien Johnson and David Cairns (eds.), *Gender in Irish Writing* (Milton Keynes:

Open University Press, 1991), pp. 128–37

Campbell, Michael. *Oh Mary, This London* (London: Heinemann, 1959)

Campbell, Sean. 'Beyond "Plastic Paddy": A Re-examination of the Second-generation Irish in England', *Immigrants and Minorities* 18.2–3 (1999), pp. 266–88

—. 'Sounding Out the Margins: Ethnicity and Popular Music in British Cultural Studies', in Gerry Smyth and Glenda Norquay (eds.), *Across the Margins: Cultural Identities and Change in the Atlantic Archipelago* (Manchester: Manchester University Press, 2002), pp. 117–36

—. *'Irish Blood, English Heart': Second-generation Irish Musicians in England* (Cork: Cork University Press, 2011)

Canavan, Bernard. 'Story-tellers and Writers: Irish Identity in Emigrant Labourers' Autobiographies, 1870–1970', in Patrick O'Sullivan (ed.), *The Irish Worldwide: History, Heritage, Identity: The Creative Migrant* (Leicester: Leicester University Press, 1994), pp. 154–69

Carlson, Julia (ed.). *Banned in Ireland: Censorship and the Irish Writer* (Athens, GA: University of Georgia Press, 1990)

Casey, Maude. *Over the Water* (London: The Women's Press, 1987)

Casey, Philip. *The Water Star* (London: Picador, 1999)

Chambers, Iain. *Migrancy, Culture, Identity* (London: Routledge, 1994)

Cheever, John. 'The Swimmer', in *The Brigadier and the Golf Widow* (London: Gollancz, 1965)

Citron, Lana. *Sucker* (London: Secker & Warburg, 1998)

Clancy Brothers and Tommy Makem. 'Whack Fol the Diddle', on *The Rising of the Moon: Irish Songs of Rebellion* (New York: Tradition Records, 1959)

Cleary, Joe. *Outrageous Fortune: Capital and Culture in Modern Ireland* (Dublin: Field Day, 2007)

Cloonan, Martin. 'State of the Nation: "Englishness", Pop, and Politics in the Mid-1990s', *Popular Music and Society* 21.2 (Summer 1997), pp. 47–71

Coleman, Terry. *The Railway Navvies* (London: Hutchinson, 1965)

Collis, J. S. *An Irishman's England* (London: Cassell & Co., 1937)

Connor, Rearden. *A Plain Tale from the Bogs* (London: John Miles, 1937)

Connor, Tom. *The London Irish* (London: London Strategic Policy Unit, 1987)

Coogan, Tim Pat. *Wherever Green is Worn: The Story of the Irish Diaspora* (London: Hutchinson, 2000)

Corry, John. *A Satirical View of London* (London: Robert Dutton, 1809)

Coverley, Merlin. *Psychogeography* (Harpenden: Pocket Essentials, 2006)

Cowley, Ultan. *The Men Who Built Britain: A History of the Irish Navvy* (Dublin: Wolfhound Press, 2001)

Cronin, Anthony. *Dead as Doornails* (Dublin: Lilliput Press, 1976)

—. *The Life of Riley* (London: Faber & Faber, 1983)

—. *The Fall* (Dublin: New Island, 2010)

Cullen, Fintan and R. F. Foster. *Conquering England: Ireland in Victorian London* (London: National Portrait Gallery, 2005)

Curtis, Liz. *Nothing but the Same Old Story: The Roots of Anti-Irish Racism*

(London: Information on Ireland, 1984)

—. *Ireland: The Propaganda War: The British Media and the 'Battle for Hearts and Minds'* (London: Pluto Press, 1984)

Curtis, Liz, Jack O'Keefe, Claire Keatinge and Joanne O'Brien. *Hearts and Minds/Anam agus Intinn: The Cultural Life of London's Irish Community* (London: London Strategic Policy Unit, 1987)

Curtis, L. P. *Apes and Angels: The Irishman in Victorian Caricature* (Newton Abbot: David & Charles, 1971)

D'Arcy, Ella. *Monochromes* (London: John Lane, 1895)

Davies, W. H. *An Autobiography of a Super-tramp* (New York: Alfred A. Knopf, 1917)

Deane, Seamus. *Reading in the Dark* (London: Jonathan Cape, 1996).

Debord, Guy. 'Theory of the *Dérive*', in Ken Knabb (ed.), *Situationist International Anthology* (Berkeley: Bureau of Public Secrets, 1981), pp. 50–54

De Certeau, Michel. *The Practice of Everyday Life* (Berkeley: University of California Press, 2002)

Delaney, Enda. *Demography, State and Society: Irish Migration to Britain, 1921–1971* (Liverpool: Liverpool University Press, 2000)

—. *The Irish in Post-War Britain* (Oxford: Oxford University Press, 2007)

Denvir, John. *The Irish in Britain from the Earliest Times to the Fall of and Death of Parnell* (London: Kegan Paul, Trench, Trübner & Co., 1894)

De Valera, Eamonn. 'St. Patrick's Day Address', Radio Éireann (17 March 1943). Available at: http://www.rte.ie/laweb/ll/ll_t09b.html

Devlin, Polly. *Dora or the Shifts of the Heart* (London: Chatto & Windus, 1990)

Dickens, Charles. *Barnaby Rudge* (Oxford: Oxford University Press, 2003)

Donleavy, J. P. *The Ginger Man* (Paris: Olympia Press, 1955)

—. *The History of the Ginger Man* (London: Viking, 1994)

Donoghue, Emma. 'Going Back', in Dermot Bolger (ed.), *Ireland in Exile: Irish Writers Abroad* (Dublin: New Island, 1993), pp. 157–70

—. *Room* (London: Little, Brown & Co., 2010)

—. *Astray* (London: Little, Brown & Co., 2012)

Donovan, Katie, Norman A. Jeffares and Brendan Kennelly (eds.). *Ireland's Women: Writings Past and Present* (London: Kyle Cathie Ltd, 1994)

Dowson, Ernest. 'Vitae summa brevis spem nos vetat incohare longam ("How should hopes be long, when life is short")', in *The Poems of Ernest Dowson* (London: John Lane, 1902), p. 2

Doyle, Martin. 'Is this Really the Face of the Irish?', *Irish Post* (11 April 1998), pp. 20, 33

Du Bois, W. E. B. *The Souls of Black Folk* (Oxford: Oxford University Press, 2007)

Dudley Edwards, Owen. 'The Stage Irish', in Patrick O'Sullivan (ed.), *The Irish Worldwide: History, Heritage, Identity: The Creative Migrant* (Leicester, Leicester University Press, 1994), pp. 83–114

Duffy, Patrick. 'Literary Reflections on Irish Migration in the Nineteenth and Twentieth Centuries', in Russell King, John Connell and Paul White (eds.),

Writing across Worlds: Literature and Migration (London: Routledge, 1995), pp. 20–38

Duggan, George. *The Stage Irishman* (London: Longmans, Green & Co., 1937)

Dunne, Catherine. *An Unconsidered People: The Irish in London* (Dublin: New Island, 2003)

Eagleton, Terry. *The Gatekeeper: A Memoir* (London: Allen Lane, 2001)

Eakin, Paul John. *How Our Lives Become Stories* (Ithaca, NY: Cornell University Press, 1999)

Enright, Anne. *What Are You Like* (London: Jonathan Cape, 2000)

Evaristo, Bernardine. *Lara* (Tunbridge Wells: Angela Royal Publishing, 1997)

Fahey, Paddy. *The Irish in London: Photographs and Memories* (London: Centerprise, 1991)

Feldman, David. '"There was an Englishman, an Irishman and a Jew…": Immigrants and Minorities in Britain', *Historical Journal* 26.1 (1983), pp. 185–99

Foley, Donal. 'His London Appearances', in Sean McCann (ed.), *The World of Brendan Behan* (London: Four Square Books, 1965), pp. 151–57

Foley, Michael. *The Road to Notown* (Belfast: Blackstaff Press, 1996)

Fortier, Anne-Marie. *Migrant Belongings: Memory, Space, Identity* (Oxford: Berg, 2000)

Foster, John Wilson. *Fictions of the Irish Literary Revival: A Changeling Art* (Syracuse: Syracuse University Press, 1987)

Foster, R. F. *Paddy and Mr. Punch: Connections in English and Irish History* (London: Allen Lane, 1993)

Foucault, Michel. 'Of Other Spaces', *Diacritics* 16.1 (1967), pp. 22–27

Gage, John. 'The Rise and Fall of the St. Giles Rookery', *Camden History Review* 12 (1984), pp. 17–24

Gébler, Ernest. *Shall I Eat You Now?* (London: Macmillan, 1969)

Geoghegan, Peter, 'The Great Migration', *Irish Business Post*, 16 January 2011. http://www.sbpost.ie/post/pages/p/wholestory.aspx-qqqt=INSIDE-STORY-qqqs=agenda-qqqsectionid=3-qqqc=10.1.0.0-qqqn=1-qqqx=1.asp

Gibbons, Luke. *Transformations in Irish Culture* (Cork: Cork University Press, 1996)

Gilmore, Fr. Bobby. 'Ireland's New Migrants' (talk given at the Irish Studies Centre, Polytechnic of North London, 31 March 1987)

Gilroy, Paul. 'It Ain't Where You're From, It's Where You're At', *Third Text* 13 (1991), pp. 3–16

—. *The Black Atlantic: Modernity and Double Consciousness* (London: Verso, 1993)

—. 'Diaspora and the Detours of Identity', in Kay Woodward (ed.), *Identity and Difference* (London: Sage, 1997), pp. 299–343

Goodheart, Eugene. *Novel Practices: Classic Modern Fiction* (London: Transaction Publishers, 2004)

Graham, Amanda. '"The Lovely Substance of the Mother": Food, Gender and Nation in the Work of Edna O'Brien', *Irish Studies Review* 15 (Summer 1996), pp. 16–20

Graham, Colin and Richard Kirkland (eds.). *Ireland and Cultural Theory: The Mechanics of Authenticity* (Basingstoke: Macmillan, 1999)

Gray, Breda. *Women and the Irish Diaspora* (London: Routledge, 2004)

Green, David R. 'Historical Perspective on the St. Giles Rookery', in Sian Anthony, *Medieval Settlement to 18th-/19th-Century Rookery* (London: Museum of London Archaeology, 2011), pp. 55–57

Green Ink Writers. *Anthology of Short Stories* (London: Green Ink Writers Group, 1982)

Greenslade, Liam. 'White Skin, White Masks: Psychological Distress Amongst the Irish in Britain', in Patrick O'Sullivan (ed.), *The Irish Worldwide: History, Heritage, Identity, Vol. 2: The Irish in the New Communities* (Leicester: Leicester University Press, 1992), pp. 201–25

Griffith, Kenneth and Timothy O'Grady. *Curious Journey: An Oral History of Ireland's Unfinished Revolution* (Cork: Mercier Press, 1998)

Guppy, Shusha. 'Edna O'Brien: The Art of Fiction, No. 82', *Paris Review* 92 (Summer 1984), pp. 22–50

Hall, Reginald Richard. 'Irish Music and Dance in London 1890–1970: A Socio-cultural History' (unpublished PhD thesis, University of Sussex, 1994)

Hall, Stuart. 'Cultural Identity and Diaspora', in Jonathan Rutherford (ed.), *Identity: Community, Culture, Difference* (London: Lawrence & Wishart, 1990), pp. 222–37

Handley, James. *The Navvy in Scotland* (Cork: Cork University Press, 1970)

Hargreaves, Tamsin. 'Women's Consciousness and Identity in Four Irish Women Novelists', in Michael Kenneally (ed.), *Cultural Contexts and Idioms in Contemporary Irish Literature* (Gerrard's Cross: Colin Smythe, 1988), pp. 290–305

Harrison, Gerry. *The Scattering: A History of the London Irish Centre 1954–2004* (London: London Irish Centre, 2004)

Hart, Peter. *Mick: The Real Michael Collins* (London: Macmillan, 2005)

Harte, Liam. '"Somewhere beyond England and Ireland": Narratives of "Home" in Second Generation Irish Autobiography', *Irish Studies Review* 11.3 (2003), pp. 293–305

—. *Modern Irish Autobiography: Self, Nation and Society* (Basingstoke: Palgrave Macmillan, 2007)

—. *The Literature of the Irish in Britain: Autobiography and Memoir, 1725–2001* (Basingstoke: Palgrave Macmillan, 2009)

Hazelkorn, Ellen. *Irish Immigrants Today: A Socio-economic Profile of Contemporary Irish Emigrants and Immigrants in the UK* (London: Polytechnic of North London Press, 1990)

Healy, Dermot. *Sudden Times* (London: Harvill Press, 1999)

Healy, John. *The Grass Arena: An Autobiography* (London: Faber & Faber, 1988)

—, *Streets Above Us* (London: Macmillan, 1990)

Heaney, Marie. *Over Nine Waves: A Book of Irish Legends* (London: Faber & Faber, 1994)

Heaney, Seamus. 'The Sense of Place', in *Preoccupations: Selected Prose 1968–78* (London: Faber & Faber, 1980), pp. 131–49

—. 'Feeling into Words', in *Preoccupations: Selected Prose 1968–78* (London: Faber & Faber, 1980), pp. 41–60

Hennessy, Mark. 'Generation LDN', *Irish Times Weekend Review* (9 July 2011), pp. 1–2

Hickman, Mary J. *Religion, Class and Identity: The State, the Catholic Church and the Education of the Irish in Britain* (Aldershot: Avebury, 1995)

—. 'Reconstructing Deconstructing "Race": British Political Discourses about the Irish in Britain', *Ethnic and Racial Studies* 21.2 (March 1998), pp. 288–307

Hickman, Mary J. and Bronwen Walter. 'Deconstructing Whiteness: Irish Women in Britain', *Feminist Review* 50 (1995), pp. 5–19

—. *Discrimination and the Irish Community in Britain: A Report of Research Undertaken for the Commission for Racial Equality* (London: Commission for Racial Equality, 1997)

Hillyard, Paddy. *Suspect Community: People's Experience of the Prevention of Terrorism Act in Britain* (London: Pluto Press/Liberty, 1993)

Hirsch, Marianne. *Family Frames: Photography, Narrative and Postmemory* (Cambridge, MA: Harvard University Press, 1997)

Hogan, Desmond. *The Children of Lir: Stories from Ireland* (London: Hamish Hamilton, 1981)

Hughes, Eamonn. '"Lancelot's Position": The Fiction of Irish-Britain', in A. Robert Lee (ed.), *Other Britain, Other British: Contemporary Multicultural Fiction* (London: Pluto Press, 1995), pp. 142–60

—. '"Town of Shadows": Representations of Belfast in Recent Fiction', *Religion and Literature* 28.2–3 (Summer–Autumn 1996), pp. 141–60

—. '"All That Surrounds Our Life": Time, Sex, and Death in *That They May Face the Rising Sun*', *Irish University Review* 35.1 (Spring/Summer 2005), pp. 147–63

Hutchinson, John. 'Diaspora Dilemmas and Shifting Allegiances: The Irish in London between Nationalism, Catholicism and Labourism (1900–22)', *Studies in Ethnicity and Nationalism* 10.1 (2010), pp. 107–25

Hutchinson, John and Alan O'Day. 'The Gaelic Revival in London, 1900–22: Limits of Ethnic Identity', in Roger Swift and Sheridan Gilley (eds.), *The Irish in Victorian Britain: The Local Dimension* (Dublin: Four Courts Press, 1999), pp. 254–76

Hutchinson, Ron. *Rat in the Skull* (London: Methuen, 1984)

I Could Read the Sky (The Arts Council of England/Bord Scannán na hÉireann, 2000)

Ingman, Heather. 'Edna O'Brien: Stretching the Nation's Boundaries', *Irish Studies Review* 10.3 (2002), pp. 253–65

I Only Came Over for a Couple of Years…: Interviews with London Irish Elders. Directed by David Kelly (London: David Kelly Productions, 2005)

Jackson, John Archer. 'The Irish in London: A Study of Migration and Settlement in the Last Hundred Years' (unpublished MA thesis, University of London, 1958)

—. *The Irish in Britain* (London: Routledge & Kegan Paul, 1963)

—. 'The Irish', in Ruth Glass et al. (eds.), *London: Aspects of Change* (London: McGibbon and Kee, 1964), pp. 293–308

Joyce, James. 'Araby', in *Dubliners* (London: Penguin, 1992)

—. 'A Little Cloud', in *Dubliners* (London: Penguin, 1992)

— *A Portrait of the Artist as a Young Man* (London: Penguin, 1992)

— *Ulysses* (Oxford: Oxford University Press, 1998)

Joyce, Patrick. 'More Secondary Modern than Postmodern', *Rethinking History* 5.3 (2001), pp. 367–82

Kaplan, David M. *Ricoeur's Critical Theory* (New York: SUNY Press, 2003)

Kavanagh, Patrick. *The Green Fool* (London: Penguin, 1975)

Keane, John B. *Many Young Men of Twenty* (Dublin: Progress House, 1961)

—. *Self Portrait* (Cork: Mercier Press, 1964)

—. *The Contractors* (Cork: Mercier Press, 1993)

—. *The Field* (Cork: Mercier Press, 1991)

—. *Hut 42* (La Vergne: Lightning Source, 2011)

Keaney, Brian. *Family Secrets* (London: Orchard Books, 1997)

Kearney, Richard. *Modern Movements in European Philosophy* (Manchester: Manchester University Press, 1986)

—. *On Stories* (London: Routledge, 2002)

Kells, Mary. *Ethnic Identity Amongst Young Irish Middle Class Migrants in London* (London: University of North London Press, 1995)

Kelly, Maeve. *Florrie's Girls* (London: Michael Joseph, 1989)

Keyes, Marian. *Last Chance Saloon* (London: Michael Joseph, 1999)

Kiberd, Declan. *Inventing Ireland: The Literature of the Modern Nation* (London: Jonathan Cape, 1996)

—. 'The Fall of the Stage Irishman', in Declan Kiberd, *The Irish Writer and the World* (Cambridge: Cambridge University Press, 2005), pp. 21–41

King, Russell. 'Preface', in Russell King, John Connell and Paul White (eds.), *Writing across Worlds: Literature and Migration* (London: Routledge, 1995), pp. ix–xvi

Kinsella, Thomas. *The Táin* (Oxford: Oxford University Press, 1970)

Kirkland, Richard. 'Questioning the Frame: Hybridity, Ireland and the Institution', in Colin Graham and Richard Kirkland (eds.), *Ireland and Cultural Theory: The Mechanics of Authenticity* (Basingstoke: Macmillan, 1999), pp. 210–28

Knott, Kim. 'Towards a History and Politics of Diasporas and Migrations: A Grounded Spatial Approach', paper presented at 'Flows and Spaces', Annual Conference of the Royal Geographical Society/Institute of British Geographers, London (30 August–2 September 2005), http://www.diasporas. ac.uk

—. 'Space and Movement', in Kim Knott and Seán McLoughlin (eds.), *Diasporas: Concepts, Intersections, Identities* (London: Zed Books, 2010), pp. 79–83

Kureishi, Hanif. *The Buddha of Suburbia* (London: Faber and Faber, 1990)

Lamming, George. *The Emigrants* (London: Michael Joseph, 1954)

Leavey, Gerard, Sati Sembhi and Gill Livingston. 'Older Irish Migrants Living in London: Identity, Loss and Return', *Journal of Ethnic and Migration Studies* 30.4 (July 2004), pp. 763–79

Lee, J. J. *Ireland 1912–1985: Politics and Society* (Cambridge: Cambridge University Press, 1989)

Lees, Lynn Hollen. *Exiles of Erin: Irish Migrants in Victorian London* (Manchester: Manchester University Press, 1979)

Leitch, Maurice. *Tell Me About It* (London: Absolute Audio Books, 2007)

Lennon, Joseph. *Irish Orientalism: A Literary and Intellectual History* (New York: Syracuse University Press, 2008)

Lennon, Mary, Marie McAdam and Joanne O'Brien. *Across the Water: Irish Women's Lives in Britain* (London: Virago, 1988)

Lipson, Eden Ross. 'Review of Maureen Mulvihill, *Natural Selection*', *New York Times* (4 May 1986)

Litvinoff, Emanuel. *Journey through a Small Planet* (London: Penguin, 2008)

Lloyd, David. *Ireland After History* (Cork: Cork University Press, 1999)

Lydon, John (with Keith and Kent Zimmerman). *Rotten: No Irish, No Blacks, No Dogs* (New York: St. Martin's Press, 1994)

Mac Amhlaigh, Donall. *Dialann Deorai* (Baile Átha Cliath: An Clóchomhar Tta, 1960)

—. *An Irish Navvy: The Diary of an Exile*, trans. Valentin Iremonger (London: Routledge & Kegan Paul, 1964)

—. *Schnitzer Ó Sé* (Baile Átha Cliath: An Clóchomhar Tta, 1974)

—. *Schnitzer O'Shea* (Dingle: Brandon, 1985)

— 'Irish Emigration', in *Terence MacSwiney Memorial Lectures* (London: Greater London Council, 1986), pp. 19–38

—. 'Documenting the Fifties', *Irish Studies in Britain* 14 (Spring/Summer 1989), pp. 7–13

MacGill, Patrick. *Children of the Dead End: The Autobiography of a Navvy* (London: Herbert Jenkins, 1914)

—. *The Rat Pit* (London: Herbert Jenkins, 1915)

Macken, Walter. *I Am Alone* (London: Macmillan, 1949)

MacMahon, Sean. 'A Sex by Themselves: An Interim Report on the Novels of Edna O'Brien', *Eire-Ireland* 2.1 (1967), pp. 79–87

MacStiofáin, Seán. *Memoirs of a Revolutionary* (London: Gordon Cremonesi, 1975)

Maher, Eamon. *John McGahern: From the Local to the Universal* (Dublin: Liffey Press, 2003)

Mahon, Derek. 'Unflinching Gaze at the Real World', *Irish Times* (19 December 2004)

Malkani, Guatam. *Londonstani* (London: Fourth Estate, 2006)

Mangan, Anna May. *Me and Mine: A Warm-hearted Memoir of a London Irish Family* (London: Virago, 2011)

Mayhew, Henry. *Mayhew's London: Being Selections from 'London Labour and the London Poor'* (London: Spring Books, 1951)

McCabe, Colin. 'Introduction', in John Healy, *The Grass Arena* (London: Faber and Faber, 1988), pp. viii–xiv

McCafferty, Owen. *The Absence of Women* (London: Faber & Faber, 2010)

McCool, Jim and Alex McDonnell. *One Better Day: A Profile of the Irish Tenants of Arlington House* (London: Bridge Housing Association, 1997)

McCourt, Frank. *Angela's Ashes: A Memoir of Childhood* (London: Flamingo, 1997)

McCrory, Moy. *The Water's Edge and Other Stories* (London: Sheba, 1985)

McDonagh, Martin. *The Beauty Queen of Leenane* (London: Methuen, 1996)

McGahern, John. *The Barracks* (London: Faber & Faber, 1983)

—. *The Dark* (London: Faber & Faber, 1983)

—. *Amongst Women* (London: Faber & Faber, 1990)

—. *The Collected Stories* (London: Faber & Faber, 1992)

—. *That They May Face the Rising Sun* (London: Faber & Faber, 2002)

—. *Memoir* (London: Faber & Faber, 2005)

McGreevy, Ronan. 'A Legend Dies', *Irish Post* (31 July 1999)

McLeod, John. *Postcolonial London: Rewriting the Metropolis* (Abingdon: Routledge, 2004)

McNicholas, Anthony. *Politics, Religion and the Press: Irish Journalism in Mid-Victorian Britain* (Oxford: Peter Lang, 2007)

McWilliams, David. 'Life's a Beach for Ireland's Latest "Generation Exodus"', *Irish Independent* (30 Decmeber 2009)

Men of Arlington. Directed by Enda Hughes (Belfast: Hotshot Films, 2010)

Mills, Richard. '"All Stories Are Love Stories": Robert McLiam Wilson Interviewed by Richard Mills', *Irish Studies Review* 7.1 (1999), pp. 73–77

Monaghan, Patricia. *The Encyclopedia of Celtic Mythology and Folklore* (New York: Infobase Publishing, 2004)

Mooney, Sean. *If We Only Had Old Ireland Over Here* (London: HMV, 1956).

Moore, George. 'Homesickness', in *The Untilled Field* (London: T. Fisher Unwin, 1903)

—. *The Lake* (London: William Heinemann, 1905)

Moore, Jonathan, *This Other Eden* in *Three Plays* (Twickenham: Aurora Metro, 2002)

Morgan, Sarah. 'The Contemporary Racialization of the Irish in Britain: An Investigation into Media Representations and the Everyday Experience of Being Irish in Britain' (unpublished PhD thesis, University of North London, 1997)

Morrison, Blake. *Things My Mother Never Told Me* (London: Chatto & Windus, 2002)

Morrison, Toni. 'Nobel Lecture', 7 December 1993, http://nobelprize.org/nobel_prizes/literature/laureates/1993/morrison-lecture.html

Mulrooney, Gretta. *Araby* (London: Flamingo, 1998)

—. *The Apple of Her Eye* (London: Robert Hale, 2010)

Mulvihill, Margaret. *Natural Selection* (London: Pandora, 1985)

—. *Low Overheads* (London: Pandora, 1987)

—. *St. Patrick's Daughter* (London: Hodder & Stoughton, 1993)

Murphy, Darren. *Irish Blood, English Heart* (London: Oberon, 2011)

Murphy, Jimmy. *Kings of the Kilburn High Road*, in *Two Plays* (London: Oberon, 2001)

Murray, Tony. 'Irish Theatre in Britain 1981–91: A Survey' (unpublished undergraduate dissertation, University of North London, 1992)

—. 'Curious Streets: Diaspora, Displacement and Transgression in Desmond Hogan's London Irish Narratives', *Irish Studies Review* 14.2 (2006), pp. 239–53

Nagle, John. '"Everybody is Irish on St. Paddy's": Ambivalence and Alterity at London's St. Patrick's Day 2002', *Identities: Global Studies in Culture and Power* 12.4 (October–December 2005), pp. 563–83

Naipaul, V. S. *The Mimic Men* (London: Penguin, 1967)

Nasta, Susheila. *Home Truths: Fictions of the South Asian Diaspora in Britain* (Basingstoke: Palgrave, 2002)

Newsinger, John. *Fenianism in Mid-Victorian Britain* (London: Pluto Press, 1994)

Nunes, Charlotte. 'Return to the Lonely Self: Autonomy, Desire and the Evolution of Identity in "The Country Girls" Trilogy', *Canadian Journal of Irish Studies* 33.2 (Fall 2007), pp. 39–47

Nyhan, Miriam. *Are You Still Below? The Ford Marina Plant, Cork, 1917–1984* (Cork: Colllins Press, 2007)

O'Brien, Edna. *The Country Girls* (London: Penguin, 1963)

—. *Girl with Green Eyes* (London: Penguin, 1964)

—. *Girls in Their Married Bliss* (London: Penguin, 1967)

—. *August is a Wicked Month* (London: Jonathan Cape, 1965)

—. *Casualties of Peace* (London: Penguin, 1968)

—. 'Cords', in *The Love Object* (London: Jonathan Cape, 1968)

—. *Night* (London: Weidenfeld & Nicolson, 1972)

—. *Mother Ireland* (London: Weidenfeld & Nicolson, 1976)

—. *The Country Girls Trilogy* (London: Penguin, 1987)

—. *The High Road* (London: Weidenfeld & Nicolson, 1988)

—. 'Epitaph', in *Lantern Slides* (London: Weidenfeld & Nicolson, 1990)

—. *Time and Tide* (London: Viking, 1992)

—. *Down By the River* (London: Weidenfeld & Nicolson, 1996)

—. *The Light of Evening* (London: Phoenix, 2007)

—. 'Shovel Kings', in *Saints and Sinners* (London: Faber & Faber, 2011)

—. *Country Girl* (London: Faber & Faber, 2012)

O'Brien, Flann. *At Swim-Two-Birds* (London: Penguin, 1967)

O'Brien, George. 'The Aesthetics of Exile', in Liam Harte and Michael Parker (eds.), *Contemporary Irish Fiction: Themes, Tropes, Theories* (Basingstoke: Macmillan, 2000), pp. 35–55

—. 'Memoirs of an Autobiographer', in Liam Harte (ed.), *Modern Irish Autobiography: Self, Nation and Society* (Basingstoke: Palgrave Macmillan, 2007), pp. 214–38

O'Brien, H. P. 'Irishmen in London (Old Style)' (unpublished article, Archive of the Irish in Britain, London, 1983)

O'Brien, Kate. *Pray for the Wanderer* (London: Heinemann, 1938)

O'Brien, Peggy. 'The Silly and the Serious: An Assessment of Edna O'Brien', *Massachusetts Review: A Quarterly of Literature* 28.3 (Autumn 1987), pp. 474–88

O'Carrol, Ide, *Models for Movers: Irish Women's Emigration to America* (Dublin: Attic Press, 1990)

Ó Conaire, Pádraic. *Deoraíocht* (Baile Átha Cliath: Conradh na Gaeilge, 1910)

O'Connor, Joseph. *Cowboys and Indians* (London: Flamingo, 1992)

—. 'Last of the Mohicans', in *True Believers* (London: Flamingo, 1992)

—. 'The Wizard of Oz', in *True Believers* (London: Flamingo, 1992)

—. 'Introduction', in Dermot Bolger (ed.), *Ireland in Exile: Irish Writers Abroad* (Dublin: New Island, 1993), pp. 11–18

—. 'Four Green Fields', in Dermot Bolger (ed.) *Ireland in Exile: Irish Writers Abroad* (Dublin: New Island, 1993), pp. 115–51

—. 'Getting to Know the English', in Joseph O'Connor, *The Secret World of the Irish Male* (London: Minerva, 1995), pp. 26–65

—. *Star of the Sea* (London: Secker & Warburg, 2002)

—. 'Two Little Clouds', in Oona Frawley (ed.), *New Dubliners: Celebrating 100 Years of Joyce's Dubliners* (London: Pegasus Books, 2006)

—. *Ghost Light* (London: Harvill Secker, 2012)

O'Connor, Kevin. *The Irish in Britain* (London: Sidgwick & Jackson, 1972)

O'Connor, Maureen. 'Edna O'Brien, Irish Dandy', *Irish Studies Review* 13.4 (2005), pp. 469–77

O'Connor, Ulick. *Brendan Behan* (London: Coronet, 1972)

O'Faoláin, Sean. *Come Back to Erin* (London: Jonathan Cape, 1938)

O'Grady, Timothy. *Motherland* (London: Chatto & Windus, 1989)

—. *Divine Magnetic Lands: A Journey in America* (London: Vintage, 2009)

O'Grady, Timothy and Steve Pyke. *I Could Read the Sky* (London: Harvill Press, 1997)

O'Malley, Mary. *Once a Catholic* (London: Amber Press, 1978)

O'Neill, J. M. *Open Cut* (London: Heinemann, 1986)

—. *Duffy is Dead* (London: Heinemann, 1987)

—. *Canon Bang Bang* (London: Hodder & Stoughton, 1989)

Orwell, George. *Down and Out in Paris and London* (London: Penguin, 1989)

O'Sullivan, Patrick. 'Patrick MacGill: The Making of a Writer', in Sean Hutton and Paul Stewart (eds.), *Ireland's Histories: Aspects of State, Society and Ideology* (London: Routledge, 1991), pp. 203–22

O'Toole, Fintan. 'The Bronx Poet who was an Elastic Paddy', *Irish Times* (26 September 2009) http://www.irishtimes.com/newspaper/weekend/2009/0926/1224255262747.html

Owens Blackburne, Elizabeth. *Molly Carew* (London: Tinsley Bros, 1879)

Passarini, Luisa. *Fascism in Popular Memory* (Cambridge: Cambridge University

Press, 1987)

Peach, Linden. *The Contemporary Irish Novel: Critical Readings* (Basingstoke: Palgrave Macmillan, 2004)

Pelan, Rebecca. 'Reflections on a Connemara Dietrich', in Kathryn Laing, Sinéad Mooney and Maureen O'Connor (eds.), *Edna O'Brien: New Critical Perspectives* (Dublin: Carysfort Press, 2006), pp. 12–37

Philips, Lawrence (ed.). *The Swarming Streets: Twentieth-Century Literary Representations of London* (Amsterdam: Rodopi, 2004)

—. *London Narratives: Post-war Fiction and the City* (London: Continuum, 2006)

Policy Report on the Irish Community (London: GLC, 1984)

Popoviciu, Livia, Chris Haywood and Máirtín Mac an Ghaill. 'Migrating Masculinities: The Irish Diaspora in Britain', *Irish Studies Review* 14.2 (2006), pp. 169–87

'Population and Migration Estimates, April 2011' (Dublin: CSO, 15 September 2011)

Power, Richard. *Apple on a Tree Top*, trans. Victor Power (Dublin: Poolbeg, 1980)

Pratt, Mary Louise. *Imperial Eyes: Travel Writing and Transculturation* (London: Routledge, 1992)

Prescott, Lynda. '"Coming to London" in the 1950s', *Wasafiri* 17.35 (2002), pp. 19–23

Prime Time: Ireland's Forgotten Generation (RTÉ 1, 22 December 2003)

Purves, Libby. 'Interview with Janet Behan', on *Midweek*, BBC Radio 4 (23 January 2008) http://www.bbc.co.uk/radio4/factual/midweek_20080123.shtml

Quinn, Antoinette. *Patrick Kavanagh: A Biography* (Dublin: Gill & Macmillan, 2003)

Raban, Jonathan. *Soft City* (London: Fontana, 1975)

Radcliffe, Zane. *London Irish* (London: Black Swan, 2002)

Renan, Ernest. *The Poetry of the Celtic Races*, trans. W. G. Huttchinson (London: Walter Scott, 1897)

Richards, Shaun. '"To Me, Here Is More Like There"', *Irish Studies Review* 15.1 (2007), pp. 1–15

Ricoeur, Paul. *Time and Narrative, Vol. 1*, trans. Kathleen McLaughlin and David Pellauer (Chicago: University of Chicago Press, 1984)

—. *Time and Narrative, Vol. 3*, trans. Kathleen Blamey and David Pellauer (Chicago: University of Chicago Press, 1988)

—. 'Life in Quest of Narrative', in David C. Wood (ed.), *On Paul Ricoeur: Narrative and Interpretation* (London: Routledge, 1991), pp. 20–33

—. *Oneself as Another*, trans. Kathleen Blamey (Chicago: University of Chicago Press, 1992)

Riddel, Charlotte. 'The Banshee's Warning', in *The Banshee's Warning and Other Tales* (London: MacQueen, 1903)

Robb, Nesca A. *An Ulsterwoman in England 1924–1941* (Cambridge: Cambridge University Press, 1942)

Robinson, Mary. 'Cherishing the Irish Diaspora: Address by Uachtarán na hÉireann Mary Robinson to Joint Sitting of the Houses of the Oireachtas', 2 February 1995, http://www.oireachtas.ie/viewdoc.asp?fn=/documents/addresses/2Feb1995.htm

Roche, Anthony. 'John B. Keane: Respectability at Last!', *Theatre Ireland* 18 (April–June 1989), pp. 29–32

Rossiter, Ann. *Ireland's Hidden Diaspora: The 'Abortion Trial' and the Making of a London-Irish Underground, 1980–2000* (London: Iasc Publishing, 2009)

Roth, Philip. 'Edna O'Brien', in *Shop Talk: A Writer and his Colleagues and their Work* (London: Jonathan Cape, 2001), pp. 101–12

Rottman, David B. and Philip O'Connell, 'The Changing Social Structure of Ireland', in F. Litton (ed.), *Unequal Achievement* (Dublin: Institute of Public Administration, 1982), pp. 63–88

Ryan, James. 'Inadmissible Departures: Why Did the Emigrant Experience Feature so Infrequently in the Fiction of the Mid-Twentieth Century?', in Dermot Keogh, Finbarr O'Shea and Carmel Quinn (eds.), *The Lost Decade: Ireland in the 1950s* (Cork: Mercier Press, 2004), pp. 221–32

Ryan, Liam. 'Irish Emigration to Britain since World War II', in Richard Kearney (ed.), *Migration: The Irish at Home and Abroad* (Dublin: Wolfhound, 1990), pp. 45–67

Ryan, Louise. 'Family Matters: (E)migration, Familial Networks and Irish Women in Britain', *Sociological Review* 52.3 (2004), pp. 351–70

Ryle, Martin. 'Place, Time and Perspective in John McGahern's Fiction', Seminar Paper: Institute for Study of European Transformations, London Metropolitan University (28 February 2007)

Said, Edward. *Orientalism* (London: Routledge & Kegan Paul, 1978)

—. 'The Mind of Winter: Reflections on Life in Exile', *Harper's & Queen* 269 (September 1984), pp. 49–55

Salmon, Mary. 'Edna O'Brien', in Rudiger Imhof (ed.), *Contemporary Irish Novelists* (Tübingen: Gunter Narr Verlag, 1990), pp. 143–58

Sandhu, Sukhdev. *London Calling: How Black and Asian Writers Imagined a City* (London: Harper Perennial, 2004)

Schumaker, Jeanette Roberts. 'Sacrificial Women in Short Stories by Mary Lavin and Edna O'Brien', *Studies in Short Fiction* 32.2 (Spring 1995), pp. 185–97

Scully, Marc. '"Plastic and Proud"? Discourses of Authenticity among Second-generation Irish in England', *Psychology and Society* 2.2 (2009), pp. 124–35

Selvon, Samuel. *The Lonely Londoners* (London: Allan Wingate, 1956)

Senior, Hereward. *Orangeism in Ireland and Britain, 1795–1836* (London: Routledge & Kegan Paul, 1966)

Shanahan, Deirdre. 'Dancehall', in *Green Ink Writers: Anthology of Short Stories* (London: Green Ink Writers' Group, 1982), pp. 6–10

Sheridan, Kathy. 'Interview with John B. Keane on his 73rd Birthday', *Irish Times* ('Weekend' magazine, 21 July 2001)

Sinclair, Iain. *Lights Out for the Territory* (London: Granta, 1997)

Smith, Sidonie. 'Construing Truths in Lying Mouths: Truthtelling in Women's Autobiography', *Studies in Literary Imagination* 23.2 (1990), pp. 145–63

Smith, Zadie. *White Teeth* (London: Hamish Hamilton, 2000)

Smithson, Annie M. P. *Myself – and Others: An Autobiography* (Dublin: Talbot Press, 1944)

Smyth, Cherry. *Lesbians Talk Queer Notions* (London: Scarlet Press, 1992)

Smyth, Gerry. *The Novel and the Nation: Studies in the New Irish Fiction* (London: Pluto Press, 1997)

Somers, Margret. 'The Narrative Constitution of Identity', *Theory and Society* 23.5 (October 1994), pp. 605–49

Spalding, Frances. *Stevie Smith: A Critical Biography* (London: Faber & Faber, 1998)

Spinley, B. M. *The Deprived and the Privileged* (London: Routledge & Kegan Paul, 1953)

Stein, Mark. *Black British Literature: Novels of Transformation* (Columbus: Ohio State University Press, 2004)

Strutt, Joseph. *The Sports and Pastimes of the People of England* (London: William Reeves, 1830)

Swift, Jonathan. 'Journal to Stella', in *The Works of Jonathan Swift, D.D.* (London: A. Constable, 1814)

Taylor, Lawrence J. 'Bás In Eirinn: Cultural Constructions of Death in Ireland', *Anthropological Quarterly* 62.4 (October 1989), pp. 175–87

The Late Late Show (CBS Television, 23 May 1997)

Thompson, Bonar. *Hyde Park Orator* (London: Jarrolds, 1935)

Thomson, David. *In Camden Town* (London: Hutchinson, 1983)

Timbs, John. *Curiosities of London* (London: David Bogue, 1855)

Tóibín, Colm. *Brooklyn* (London: Viking, 2009)

Trevor, William. 'Another Christmas', in *The Stories of William Trevor* (Harmondsworth: Penguin, 1983)

Ullah, Philip. 'Second-generation Irish Youth: Identity and Ethnicity', *New Community* 12 (Summer 1985), pp. 310–20

Walsh, John. *The Falling Angels: An Irish Romance* (London: Harper Collins, 1999)

—. *Are You Talking To Me? A Life through the Movies* (London: Harper Collins, 2003)

Walshe, Colm. 'Hard Times for the Irish in London', *Irish Times* (*Weekend* magazine, 21 March 2009), http://www.irishtimes.com/newspaper/weekend/2009/0321/1224243190799.html

Walter, Bronwen. *Outsiders Inside: Whiteness, Place and Irish Women* (London: Routledge, 2001)

—. 'English/Irish Hybridity: Second-generation Diasporic Identities', *International Journal of Diversity in Organisations, Communities and Nations* 5.7 (2005/2006), pp. 17–24

Walter, Bronwen, Sarah Morgan, Mary J. Hickman and Joseph Bradley. 'Family Stories, Public Silence: Irish Identity Construction Amongst the

Second Generation Irish in England', *Scottish Geographical Journal* 118.3 (2002), pp. 201–17

Ward, Brendan. *Builders Remembered* (Cavan: Abbey Printers, 1984)

Ward, Patrick. *Exile, Emigration and Irish Writing* (Dublin: Irish Academic Press, 2002)

Waters, Maureen. *The Comic Irishman* (Albany: State University of New York Press, 1984)

Webb, Timothy. 'Yeats and the English', in Joseph McMinn (ed.), *The Internationalism of Irish Literature and Drama* (Gerrards Cross: Colin Smythe, 1992), pp. 232–52

Wesker, Arnold. 'Chicken Soup with Barley', in Elliot M. Browne (ed.), *New English Dramatists 1* (Harmondsworth: Penguin, 1959)

Whelan, Tony. *The Last Chapter* (Leicester: Matador, 2010)

White, Jerry. *London in the Twentieth Century: A City and its People* (London: Viking, 2001)

—. *London in the Nineteenth Century: A Human Awful Wonder of God* (London: Vintage, 2008)

Whooley, Finbarr. *Irish Londoners: Photographs from the Paddy Fahey Collection* (Stroud: Grange Museum/Sutton Publishing, 1997)

Williams, Rory and Russell Ecob. 'Regional Mortality and the Irish in Britain: Findings of the ONS Longitudinal Study', *Sociology of Health and Illness* 21.3 (May 1999), pp. 344–67

Wills, Clair. *That Neutral Island: A History of Ireland during the Second World War* (London: Faber and Faber, 2007)

Wilson, Elizabeth. *Bohemians: The Glamorous Outcasts* (London: Tauris Parke Paperbacks, 2003)

Wilson, Robert McLiam. *Ripley Bogle* (London: Picador, 1989)

—. *The Dispossessed* (London: Picador, 1992)

—. *Eureka Street: A Novel of Ireland Like No Other* (London: Secker & Warburg, 1996)

Wingfield, Sheila. *Real People* (London: Cresset Press, 1952)

Wolfreys, Julian. *Writing London, Volume 2: Materiality, Memory, Spectrality* (Basingstoke: Palgrave Macmillan, 2004)

Woods, Peter. *Hard Shoulder* (Dublin: New Island, 2003)

Yeats, W. B. 'John Sherman', in *John Sherman and Dhoya* (London: Fisher Unwin, 1891)

Zangwill, Israel. *Children of the Ghetto* (London: Heinemann, 1892)

Index